ASIA

A Selected and Annotated Guide
to Reference Works

ASIA

A Selected and Annotated Guide
to Reference Works

G. Raymond Nunn

The M.I.T. Press

Cambridge, Massachusetts, and London, England

Z
3001
.N79

12/22/71

Contents

Contents

Preface

The writing of this guide has been prompted by the gaps which exist in the present reference bibliography for Asia. Where country reference bibliographies have been developed for China and Japan these ignore significant Western publications. For other countries there has been little or no attempt to compile guides to their reference literature. This guide represents a first attempt to present in an integrated fashion a selection of the whole literature on Asia, without distinction as to place of publication, language of publication or language of materials surveyed.

A total of 975 books and periodicals are cited. Two thirds of these are published in English, but refer in many instances to the bibliographies of materials in Asian languages. The next largest language in terms of works cited is Japanese, with 138 titles, referring mostly to Japan, but with some reference to China and Korea, followed by Chinese referring almost completely to China, and Korean, referring completely to Korea. French, German, Spanish and Dutch works and a wide range of other Asian language works are also cited. Three books are in Russian, representing only a small fraction of the total literature in that language.

The problem of selection has been a difficult one. For most countries an attempt was made to identify a handbook or an encyclopedia with a substantial coverage of information for that country, yearbooks, biographical and other directories, dictionaries, statistical sources, atlases, gazetteers and chronologies. Where there was a choice, a selection was made after examination of contents or on advice of specialists. The criteria for selection included comprehensiveness of the work, avoidance of overlapping with other works cited and the quality of the work itself. In the field of bibliography similar criteria were employed. As comprehensive a coverage of both Western and Asian language material has been attempted, again with as few overlapping works as possible. Subject bibliography has been less emphasized for China and Japan, where for subjects the stress has been laid on Western publications and on the bibliography of Western language material. In the subject fields this guide selectively updates and supplements the excellent bibliographies of Teng Ssu-yu and Knight Biggerstaff *An annotated bibliography of selected Chinese reference works*, Peter Berton and Eugene Wu *Contemporary China, a research guide*, and the *Guide to Japanese Reference books*. A small number of key works were included also for most subject fields. My *South and Southeast Asia, a bibliography of bibliographies*, and *East Asia, a bibliography of bibliographies*, which appeared in the *Occasional Papers* of the East-West Center Library, are both superseded.

There is an obviously modern bias to this guide with its concentration on problems of concern to modern Asia rather than traditional Asia, but materials have not been limited to those with a strictly modern interest. Catalogs of manuscripts have been omitted. Materials published up through the fall of 1970 have been included. With only three exceptions bibliographies which appeared as periodical articles or as parts of books have not been included.

In general the content of the entries attempts to conform to standard library practice, but in some cases the Library of Congress entry has been used purely as a matter of convenience, and not of conviction. This will cause some difficulty for users of the guide who will be looking for particular works which they know under entries other than those used by the Library of Congress.

To simplify transcription on computer tape, the multiplicity of diacritical marks, particularly in Vietnamese, have been ignored. This decision, no doubt, will distress some, but will cause little difficulty for those who know the Asian languages concerned. A list of the Chinese, Japanese and Korean character titles has been appended for works in these languages, but it is hoped that the romanization and translation will be sufficient for most of the works cited in these languages. In all cases the characters have been given in their full unabbreviated forms, although this may not be the form in which they appear in recent Chinese and Japanese imprints.

Arrangement within sections and subsections is chronological by date of publication, except when the works cited are more suitably arranged chronologically by contents. Annotations are as concise as possible, and length of annotation is not necessarily a guide to the importance of a book. In nearly all annotations a quantitative aspect of the work has been estimated, whether this be the number of entries in a bibliography, biographies in a collected biographical work, or words in a dictionary. It is hoped that these figures will be useful, although they constitute no absolute guide to the value of a work.

All items, with the exception of a few not in the United States, and parts of some series or periodicals, have been personally examined. Where the work was not available in the United States, reliance was placed on the evaluation of library specialists in London. Most works are available in the University of Hawaii Library. Unfortunately those which are not will undoubtedly be the unusual, and only one or two copies may exist in the United States.

The index includes in one sequence authors, titles, and translated titles appearing in the work cited. In many cases the title has been abbreviated, but it is believed that this will not detract from its value.

I wish to acknowledge the generous assistance of Dr. Nguyen Dinh-Hoa in the selection of Vietnamese dictionaries, Dr. Philip Jenner for Cambodian dictionaries, Dr. John De Francis for Chinese dictionaries, Mr. John Ward for Filipino dictionaries, and Dr. O. A. Chavarria-Aguilar for Sanskrit and Hindi dictionaries. Dr. Nguyen Dang-Liem checked the Vietnamese romanization, Mr. G. K. De Heer the Indonesian and Dutch, and Dr. Thomas W. Gething the Thai romanization. Mr. William C. C. Hu kindly read through the Chinese entries. The compilation has been greatly aided by the help of Mr. Masato Matsui, Mrs. Lan Hiang Char, Mr. Shiro Saito and Miss Joyce Wright of the University of Hawaii Library, Dr. Elizabeth Huff, the late Dr. Richard Irwin, Mr. Yong-kyu Choo and Mr. Charles Hamilton of the East Asiatic Library of the University of California at Berkeley, Mr. John T. Ma of the Hoover Institution, Stanford University, Dr. Tsuen-hsuin Tsien of the Far Eastern Library, University of Chicago, Mr. Yukihisa Suzuki of the Graduate School of Library Studies, University of Hawaii, Mr. Eugene Wu of the Chinese-Japanese Library, Harvard- Yenching Institute, Miss Miwa Kai of the East Asian Library, Columbia University, Dr. John Echols of Cornell University, and Dr. Edwin G. Beal, Jr., Mr. Key Paik Yang, Dr. Andrew Kuroda, Miss Mayumi Taniguchi, and Miss Hazel Griffin and her staff at the Library of Congress. Mr. James D. Pearson of the School of Oriental and African Studies, and Mr. Kenneth B. Gardner of the British Museum were able to provide information on a number of key reference works not located in the United States. American and Asian students in my seminars in the Summer session of the University of Hawaii Graduate School of Library Studies added their insight to the study of almost all the works cited. Mr. Yam-Wai Choo, of the University of Hawaii Library wrote the Chinese, Japanese, and Korean characters. The Graduate Research Council of the University of Hawaii provided the initial travel grant and the Asian Studies Program at the University gave additional travel support enabling me to survey materials not available in Honolulu. Finally I wish to acknowledge the willing and generous assistance of Dr. W. Wesley Peterson, Acting Director of the University of Hawaii Statistical and Computing Center. In spite of this assistance, advice and correction there are undoubtedly many errors, and indulgence of the reader is requested. The responsibility for these, and for the final selection and arrangement rests with the author.

It is hoped to publish revised editions of this reference guide at regular intervals in the future, and to facilitate this, the text has been transcribed on computer tape. In this way it will be comparatively simple to add, delete and revise entries. I will be most grateful for the comments of readers which will lead to the improvement, and eventually to the perfection of this guide.

Honolulu
September 1970

ASIA

A Selected and Annotated Guide
to Reference Works

A.ASIA

The term Asia is used in a geographical sense to include the whole continent from the Suez Canal to the Bering Straits, and from the Urals to Indonesia. This reference guide deals only with that part of Asia within the arc from Pakistan to Japan and excludes Soviet Asia.

HANDBOOKS AND DIRECTORIES

A 1. London. University. School of Oriental and African Studies. *Handbook of Oriental History*. London, Royal Historical Society, 1963. 265 p.
Written by members of the School's Department of History and intended as an aid to a number of problems in the study of Asia, such as personal and place names, transliteration and pronunciation, glossaries of terms and chronological systems. There are five sections: Near and Middle East, India and Pakistan, Southeast Asia and the Archipelago, China, and Japan. The pre-Islamic Near East is not covered. A reprint of the 1951 edition.

A 2. *Asia Who's Who*. Hong Kong, Pan Asia Newspaper Alliance, 1957-1960. 3 v.
Issues noted for 1957, 1958 and 1960. The 1960 issue contains some 3,500 biographies, about 500 more than that for 1957. All countries of Asia, from Afghanistan to Japan, and including Outer Mongolia, are covered, and the emphasis is on politicians and government officials. The information supplied is brief, but this reference work remains an important source for countries where there is no collective biography.

A 3. Malalasekara,G. P. *Encyclopedia of Buddhism*. Ceylon, Government of Ceylon, 1961-
Projected to be completed in 1971 in 15,000 pages but actually proceeding at a much slower rate of publication. Buddhism in all countries is included, in both Mahayana and Theravada forms. Written by a team of international authorities, including Japanese and Chinese scholars. First fascicule of volume 2, published in 1966,noted.

A 4. Conference of Asian Affairs. *American institutions and organizations interested in Asia,* second edition. New York, Taplinger, 1961. 581 p.
Important but dated directory lists some 1,000 programs related to Asia, including Afghanistan, but excluding Soviet Asia and the Near East. The programs are at American universities, religious and educational organizations, foundations, museums and libraries. Valuable since it can lead to sources of information not otherwise available through bibliographies. Well indexed. A revision of the 1957 edition.

A 5. Wint, Guy. *Asia, a handbook*. New York, Praeger, 1966. 856 p.
Aims to cover events in Asia to March 1965, and in four parts. The first contains basic information for each country in Asia, excluding the Near

East and Afghanistan, but including Soviet Asia. Much of this information relates to the situation in 1962. The second part consists of country surveys written by specialists, and with short bibliographies. The third part is divided into a number of topics as religion, art, literature, political affairs, further subdivided into sections, each written by specialists. The fourth part is a collection of important post-war documents on Asia. Professionally indexed.

ATLAS

A 6. Penkala, Maria. *A correlated history of the Far East, China/Korea, Japan.* Rutland, Tuttle, 1966. 76 p.
18 large black and white maps, with excellent detail illustrate the history of Asia from prehistoric times to the present, with a gap from the Ming dynasty to the thirties. Accompanied by a comparative chronology of Japanese, Chinese and Korean history.

BIBLIOGRAPHY

A 7. Streit, Robert and Johannes Dindinger. *Bibliotheca Missionum.* Aachen, Internationales Institut fur Missionswissenschaftliche Forschung, 1916- Bibliography of books and periodical articles on the Catholic mission movement, with an emphasis on Asia. Each volume is arranged chronologically, with author, person, place, country and peoples, and language indexes. The following volumes are on Asia, and the number of entries is noted in parentheses:
4. Asiatische Missionslitteratur, 1245-1599. 1928. 626 p.(2,052)
5. Asiatische Missionslitteratur, 1600-1699. 1929. 1114 p.(2,811)
6. Missionslitteratur Indiens, der Philippinen, Japans und Indochinas, 1700-1799. 1931. 616 p. (2,005)
7. Chinesische Missionslitteratur, 1700-1799. 1931. 544 p.(4,035)
8. Missionslitteratur, Indiens und Indonesiens, 1800-1899. 1934. 1028 p. (3,201)
9. Missionslitteratur der Philippinen, 1800-1909. 1937. 996 p. (2,408)
10. Missionslitteratur, Japans und Koreas, 1800-1909. 1938. 565 p. (1,475)
11. Missionslitteratur Indochinas, 1800-1909. 1939. 817 p.(2,062)
12. Chinesische Missionslitteratur, 1800-1884. 1958. 745 p.(1,217)
13. Chinesische Missionslitteratur, 1885-1909. 1959. 807 p.(752)
14. Chinesische Missionslitteratur, 1910-1950. 1959-61. 3 v.(3,496)
A 8. Walker, Egbert Hamilton and Elmer D.Merrill. *A bibliography of Eastern Asiatic Botany.* Jamaica Plain, Mass., Arnold Arboretum of Harvard University, 1938. 719 p.
Brought to the end of the fifties by Egbert Hamilton Walker *A bibliography of Eastern Asiatic botany, supplement.* (Washington, American Institute of Biological Sciences, 1960) Eastern Asia includes China, Ja-

pan, Korea, Eastern and Southern Siberia, the Philippines, Thailand, Burma, Indochina and India. The period covered is from 1800, and there are no language limitations. Books and periodical articles are cited, and the arrangement is by author, with subject, geographical and classified indexes.

A 9. Waterman, Richard A. *Bibliography of Asiatic musics.* (n.p.)

3,488 books and periodical articles in Western languages and Russian are cited in 14 instalments, each of which is limited to a region. Over half concerned with the music of the Near East. The installments originally appeared in *Music Library Association notes.* Second series, v.5-8, Dec.1947 to Mar. 1951.

A10. United Nations. E.C.A.F.E. Library. *Asian bibliography,* 1952- Bangkok, 1952- Semi-annual.

Lists selected acquisitions of the Library of the Economic Commission for Asia and the Far East in Bangkok. Its Asian language content is limited, and its emphasis is on the social sciences. Materials are collected from 33 Asian countries, and from Australia and New Zealand. Arranged by the Universal Decimal Classification (UDC) with a country and subject index.

A11. *Bibliography of Asian studies,* 1956- Ann Arbor, Association for Asian Studies, 1957- Annual.

Continues the *Far Eastern bibliography,* 1941-55, itself a continuation of the *Bulletin of Far Eastern bibliography,* 1936-40. With the name change for the 1956 issue, the scope of this bibliography was considerably enlarged to include South Asia, and its size was expanded to cite annually some 13,000 Western language books and periodical articles, published in Asia and the West, and arranged by country and then by an extensive array of subject divisions. Author index. Unevenness in the bibliography reflects the varying qualities of the materials available, and the work of a number of separate voluntary contributors. The singlemost important bibliographical contribution to the field of Asian studies. Author index to this bibliography provided by Association for Asian Studies. *Cumulative bibliography of Asian studies, 1941-1965, author bibliography,* Boston, G.K.Hall, 1969. 4 v.

A12. Garde, P. K. *Directory of reference works published in Asia.* Paris, UNESCO, 1956. 139 p. (UNESCO bibliographical handbooks 5)

1,619 books in Western and Asian languages are arranged by the Universal Decimal Classification (UDC) and subarranged by country of publication. Afghanistan, the Middle East and Soviet Asia are excluded. The value of this pioneering work is limited by the fact that much of the important reference work on Asia has been published in the West, and also by the rapid development of Asian studies since 1956. There are two subject indexes, one in English, the other in French, and an author index.

A13. Hewitt, Arthur R. *Union list of Commonwealth newspapers in London, Oxford and Cambridge.* London, Institute of Commonwealth Studies, 1960. 101 p.

A union list of 2,426 newspapers mostly in English, which have been preserved, in many cases only in the United Kingdom. There are, for example 155 newspapers listed for India. The British Museum collection at Colindale in North London has the strongest representation. The newspapers are arranged first by country, and then by place and title. There is a title index. Holdings and locations are given.

A14. Nunn, G. Raymond. 'Asia.' American Universities Field Staff. *A select bibliography, Asia, Africa, Eastern Europe, Latin America.* New York, 1960. p.1-191.

The Asia section was based on the University of Michigan Undergraduate Library collection on Asia, and was reviewed by two teams of specialists, one at the University of Michigan, and the other with the American Universities Field Staff. The 2,748 books cited are almost entirely in English and have been graded. 'A' and 'B' entries, amounting to 30% of the total have been annotated. The arrangement is by country, with separate author and title indexes. The Asia section includes the Middle East, but excludes Soviet Asia, and the selection is a recommended one for the college library. Three *Supplements* compiled by the American Universities Field Staff were issued in 1961, 1963, and 1965.

A15. Hanayama, Shinsho. *Bibliography on Buddhism.* Tokyo, Hokuseido Press, 1961. 869 p.

Some 15,073 books and periodical articles in English, French, German and Italian on Buddhism are arranged in alphabetical order by author. The entries are not annotated, and include materials published to 1928. Materials published after 1928 will be found in *Bibliographie bouddhique,* 1928- (Paris, P.Geuthner, 1930-) the first volume of which covers Jan. 1928 to May 1934, the second from May 1934 to May 1950, and the third from May 1950 to May 1958. The arrangement of materials in the *Bibliographie bouddhique,* is by subject, with an index in the last number of each volume. The *Bibliography on Buddhism* is supplementary to *Bussho kaisetsu daijiten.*

A16. London. University. School of Oriental and African Studies. Library. *Library catalogue of the School of Oriental and African Studies, University of London.* Boston, G.K. Hall, 1963. 26 v.

554,000 catalogue cards representing some 200,000 titles, have been reproduced in this catalogue. A substantial proportion is concerned with Asia, although the Middle East, Africa and the Pacific Islands are also covered by the Library. The general series section is divided into an author catalog, a title index, and subject catalogs subdivided by major geographical regions. The five-volume Chinese catalog is similarly arranged. There is a single-volume Japanese catalog, and a catalog of manuscripts and microfilms. A key to one of the principal library collections of Asia. ...*first supplement* (1968) in 16 volumes lists another 60,000 titles.

A17. Le Gear, Clara Egli. *A list of geographic atlases in the Library of Congress.* Washington, U.S. Government Printing Office, 1963. 681 p.

This is the second supplement to Phillip's compilation of atlases at the Library of Congress, and is arranged by area. A valuable feature of this list is the section on Asia (9475-10084). Titles are translated and contents described in English. The index lists authors, editors and areas in one sequence.

A18. Gerboth, Walter. *Music of East and Southeast Asia, a selected bibliography of books, pamphlets, articles and recordings.* Albany, University of the State of New York, the State Education Department, 1963. 23 p.
228 books and periodical articles and 75 recordings are arranged by country. Almost entirely in English, and all items located in libraries in New York City. No annotations.

A19. U.S. Department of State. Office of External Research. *Asia, a list of current social science research by private scholars and academic societies,* 1965- Washington, 1965- Annual.
Includes in-progress and unpublished studies, with some annotation provided by authors. In one volume and supersedes *South Asia, Southeast Asia* and *East Asia,* all three compiled by the office of External Research. The Middle East is excluded, but Australia, New Zealand, and the Pacific Islands are included. Arranged by country, with further subject division for China, Japan, India and the Philippines. Approximately 1,000 entries in each issue.

A20. Pearson, James D. *Oriental and Asian bibliography, an introduction with some reference to Africa.* Hamden, Shoestring Press, 1966. 261 p.
The first part consists of an account of the history of Oriental studies, and the second the literature of this field, including over 330 entries for reference books in Oriental and Western languages, which are annotated through the accompanying text. The third part is concerned with library collections and problems.

A21. Morehouse, Cynthia T. *Paperbound books on Asia, sixth revised edition, in print, September 1965.* Ann Arbor, Association for Asian Studies, 1966. 114 p. *(Newsletter of the Association for Asian Studies,* volume xi, supplement no.1)
Arranges some 2,400 paperbound books on Asia in English into one general section and 19 major subject sections, each of which is subdivided by major regions. The Middle East is covered, but Soviet Asia is excluded. There is a useful list of publishers and their addresses. Short bibliographical essays introduce the paperbound books for each region for the purposes of undergraduate teaching. No index.

A22. Texas, University. Population Research Center. *International population census bibliography, Asia.* Austin, Bureau of Business Research, Graduate School of Business, 1966. 1 v. (various paging) (Census bibliography no.5)
Arranged on a country-by-country basis, and covering the whole of Asia, including the Middle East, but not Soviet Asia. Attempts to be a comprehensive guide to population statistics, and includes other sources in addition to those found in the census reports.

A23. Bloomfield, B.C. *Theses on Asia accepted by universities in the United Kingdom and Ireland, 1877-1964.* London, Frank Cass, 1967. 127 p.
2,571 masters' and doctoral dissertations relating to Asia are arranged by

geographical areas and subdivided by major subjects. Oceania, Islam and
the Near and Middle East are included. There is a brief statement on the
availability of theses for photocopying and inter-library lending. Unfortunately most of this material is still not accessible outside the universities
where the dissertations were published.

A24. Asia Society. *Asia, a guide to paperbacks,* revised edition. New York,
1968. 178 p.

Some 900 paperbound books are arranged by region and subdivided by
country. The major countries are further subdivided by major topics. All
entries are annotated. Author and title index.

A25. New York (State)University. Foreign Area Materials Center. *Reprints
and microforms in Asian studies.* Ann Arbor, Association for Asian
Studies, 1968. 145 p. *(Newsletter of the Association for Asian Studies,*
volume xiii, supplement no.1)

Nearly one half lists reprints of books and journals in Western languages,
separating books from journals, and arranging the former by major area.
There are some 700 entries. The second part lists some 1,000 microforms, again dividing these into books and into newspapers and periodicals. Both sections are subdivided regionally. The Near and Middle East is
not included. There is no index. This most useful listing is by no means
complete for microforms, principally since its sources for compilation are
limited.

A26. Stucki, Curtis W. *American doctoral dissertations on Asia* ... Ithaca,
Southeast Asia Program, Department of Asian Studies, Cornell Universi-
ty, 1968. 304 p. (Cornell University, Department of Asian Studies, South
East Asia Program, data paper no. 71)

Doctoral dissertations in the standard bibliographies are usually listed
under major disciplinary categories, and this makes the area approach for
locating dissertations difficult. The important feature of this listing is its
arrangement by region, and subdivision by country and then by subject.
Dissertations are arranged chronologically under subject. Approximately
3,200 doctoral dissertations on Asia, published from 1933 to 1966 are
listed. Author index. Revision of the 1959 and 1963 editions.

JAPANESE PUBLICATIONS

A27. Kyoto daigaku. Jimbun kagaku kenkyujo (Kyoto University. Research
Institute of Humanistic Studies) ... *Toyogaku kenkyu bunken mokuroku*
Annual bibliography of Oriental studies, 1934- Kyoto, Kyoto jimbun
gakkai, Showa 10- (1935-)

This major bibliography includes books, periodicals and periodical articles in Japanese, Chinese, Korean and Western languages, with an area
coverage for the whole of Asia, including the Middle East and Russian
Asia. The bibliography is organized into two sections; the first for materials in Chinese, Japanese and Korea, and the second for materials in Western languages, with the first being generally twice that of the second in

volume. Each section is further subdivided into books and periodical articles, and then arranged by broad subjects. Indexes to Japanese authors by the Japanese syllabary, to Chinese and Korean authors by characters, to Russian authors by the Cyrillic alphabet, and an alphabetical index to Western authors. All areas of knowledge are covered, but that of history is emphasized. This important listing suffers from a lack of cumulation and of an area and country approach, which make it less useful. The 1965 issue was published in 1967. Title varies, from 1935-61 *Toyoshi kenkyu bunken ruimoku.*

A28. Bijutsu kenkyujo(Institute of Art Research) *Toyo kobijitsu bunken mokuroku* (Bibliography on early Oriental art)Tokyo,Zayuho kankokai, Showa 16-29(1941-54) 3 v.

In the first two volumes published in 1941, over 28,000 articles selected from some 250 periodicals are arranged under 28 subjects, too broad a classification for rapid use. There is an author index. The third volume has some 7,500 articles distributed under 56 headings. Volume 4 reported but not seen. Title for first two volumes *Toyo bijutsu bunken mokoroku* (Bibliography on Oriental art)

A29. Tohogakkai, Tokyo (Institute of Eastern Culture) *Books and articles on Oriental subjects published in Japanese during* 1954- Tokyo, 1955- Annual.

The 1964 issue indexes 213 periodicals and 6 festschriften, and contains entries for approximately 1,000 articles. A separate section lists 157 books, most of which are abstracted. The emphasis is on East Asia, excluding Japan, but materials on South and Southeast Asia are included. Arrangement is by country, then by subject, with books in a separate section. Author index from 1958 issue. 1966 issue published in 1968.

A30. Yunesuko Higashi Ajia bunka kenkyu senta, Tokyo (Center for East Asian Cultural Studies) *A survey of Japanese bibliographies concerning Asian studies.* Tokyo, 1963. 300 p.

Some 1,200 bibliographies almost entirely in Japanese are arranged under 34 headings. No annotations. Alphabetical index to titles.

A31. Yunesuko Higashi Ajia bunka kenkyu senta, Tokyo (Center for East Asian Cultural Studies) *Bibliography of bibliographies of East Asian studies in Japan.* Tokyo, 1964. 190 p. (Bibliography no.3)

Compiled as a supplement to *A survey of Japanese bibliographies concerning Asian studies,* but actually there is duplication. 854 bibliographies in book and article form on East Asia and Southeast Asia, excluding Japan, are arranged by area. Nearly all entries are in Japanese. Title index.

A32. Toyoshi kenkyu rombun mokuroku henshu iinkai (Committee for the compilation of a catalogue of articles on Oriental history appearing in Japan) *Nihon ni okeru Toyoshi rombun mokuroku* Japanese studies on Asian history, a catalogue of articles. Tokyo, Showa 39-42(1964-67) 4 v.

In the first three volumes 62,456 articles are compiled from some 550 periodicals and collected works on Asian history, excluding Japan. The bibliography is arranged by name of periodical or collected work, then by

volume and issue, or by its place in the collected works. The fourth
volume is an alphabetical author index. No subject index is provided, a
major disadvantage. Publications surveyed dated from 1880 to 1962.

B.SOUTHERN ASIA

Southern Asia includes the island and mainland areas of Southeast Asia and South Asia, or the Indian sub-continent. Materials on the latter area have been included along with works relating to India.

B1. U.S. Library of Congress. Orientalia Division. *Southern Asia accessions list,1952-60.* Washington, 1952-60.
Issued as a quarterly through volume 5 published in 1956, with title *Southern Asia, publications in Western languages, a quarterly accessions list,* then issued monthly to December 1960. Lists books and periodical articles in Western and in selected Southern Asian languages, books from 1945, Western language articles from January 1951, and from April 1953 for Southern Asian language articles. Materials cited have been acquired by the Library of Congress and some 80 cooperating libraries, and library locations are stated. The list helps to fill the gap in coverage for Southern Asia at a time when national bibliography and the *Far Eastern Bibliography* did not undertake this responsibility. Divided into a Western language section subarranged by country, and minor Southern Asian language section arranged by country and subdivided by language. There are no annotations and no published index.

B2. U.N.E.S.C.O. Science Cooperation Offices for South and South East Asia. *Bibliography of scientific publications of South and South East Asia, 1955-64.* New Delhi, Indian National Science Documentation Centre, National Physical Laboratory, 1955-64. Monthly.
Continues U.N.E.S.C.O. South Asia Science Cooperation Office *Bibliography of scientific publications of South Asia(India, Burma, Ceylon)1949-54* (Delhi,1949-54) which appeared semi-annually in 12 numbers. A bibliography of unannotated English language articles selected from some 400 periodicals, published mostly in India, but with some representation from the Philippines. The items are arranged by subject, and there are annual cumulated subject and author indexes. In 1964 10,253 entries covered a broad range of the sciences, including education, geography and town planning. Partly replaced by the Indian National Science Documentation Centre *Indian Science Abstracts* published from January 1965.

B3. Ajia keizai kenkyujo,Tokyo(Institute of the Developing Economies) *Union catalogue of documentary materials on Southeast Asia.* Tokyo, 1964. 5v.
Lists Western language books, mostly in English, on South and Southeast Asia in 31 Japanese institutions. Textbooks, juveniles, novels and Buddhist materials are excluded. There are sections for Asia as a whole, Southeast Asia, i.e. South Asia, and for individual countries. These are further subdivided into uniform subject divisions. Half of the approxi-

mately 20,000 titles are on India. Volume 5 is an author index. A convenient listing, making no claim to be comprehensive, brings together a great number of important books in a small and handy compass.

B4. Harvard University Library. *Southern Asia.* Cambridge, Harvard University Library, distributed by Harvard University Press, 1968. 543 p. (Widener Library shelflist 19)

Some 10,242 titles are arranged in a classified order, primarily by country and region, with a strong emphasis on South Asia. There is an index by both author and title, and listing of items by date of publication.

C.CEYLON

Ceylon was first occupied by British troops in 1795, and did not gain its independence until 1948.

ENCYCLOPEDIA AND YEARBOOK

C 1. Ceylon. Department of Census and Statistics. *Ceylon yearbook,* 1948- Colombo, 1948-
Official yearbook of the social, economic and general conditions of Ceylon. It does not claim to be exhaustive, but attempts to give the salient information. Ceylon's history, geography, constitution, government and programs of the government in economic and social fields are covered. The issue for 1948 surveys the period from 1939 to 1946. 1966 issue noted.

C 2. *Simhala visvakosaya.* Sinhalese encyclopedia. Kolamba, Samskrtika Departmentuva, Rajaye Mudranalaya, 1963-
A general encyclopedia, with approximately one-fifth of its contents concerned with Ceylon. Articles are not signed and do not have bibliographies, but there is a list of the authorities responsible for the compilation of the encyclopedia. Volume 2, published in 1965 noted.

DIRECTORY

C 3. *Ferguson's Ceylon directory,* 1858- Colombo, Ceylon Observer Press, 1858- annual.
Covers recent legislation, statistics, government developments, lists trades in a classified arrangement and discusses the institutions, agriculture, trade, finance and history of Ceylon. Contains maps and a detailed alphabetical index. 1965 last issue noted.

DICTIONARIES

C 4. Carter, Charles. *A Sinhalese-English dictionary.* Colombo, M.D. Gunasena, 1965. 806 p.
A reprint of the 1924 edition, containing some 56,000 Sinhala words in Sinhala script, with their equivalents in English.

C 5. Carter, Charles. *An English-Sinhalese dictionary,* revised edition, Colombo, M.D. Gunasena, 1965. 535 p.
A reprint of the 1936 revision of the 1891 edition. The 1936 edition added a considerable number of new scientific terms and removed many antiquated expressions, replacing them with modern forms. Some 30,000 English words are given in their Sinhala equivalents in Sinhala script.

BIOGRAPHICAL DICTIONARY

C 6. Ceylon. *Ceylon civil list.* Colombo, Government Press.
A listing of senior civil servants, arranged by departments, with an index
to names. Each entry has date of birth, degrees, salary, and appointments
held. This series commenced in the 19th century.

GAZETTEER

C 7. U.S. Office of Geography. *Ceylon.* Washington, U.S. Government Printing Office, 1960. 359 p. (Gazetteers no.49)
29,600 entries for place and feature names in Ceylon, including variant
forms cross indexed to the standard names approved by the U.S. Board
on Geographic Names. Each name has its longitude and latitude and
indication of its associated administrative unit stated.

CENSUS

C 8. Ceylon. Department of Census and Statistics. *Census of Ceylon,* 1946.
Colombo, Government Press, 1950-52. 4 v.(in 7.)
There have been decennial censuses of Ceylon from 1871 to 1931. There
was no census in 1941. The 1946 census has its first volume in two parts.
The first is a general report and the second a statistical digest. The second
volume classifies the population, the third the female population, and
volume 4, classifies by race, religion and literacy.
C 9. Ceylon. Department of Census and Statistics. *Census of Ceylon,* 1953.
Colombo, Ceylon Government Press, 1957-62. 4 v.(in 10.)
The first volume discusses the census procedures and has a number of
tables concerned with population, race and religion. Volume 2 is in three
parts, and surveys population and growth. Volume 3 is concerned with
race, religion and literacy in two parts, and volume 4, also in two parts,
with one part in three sections, surveys gainfully employed population and income.

STATISTICAL YEARBOOK

C10. Ceylon. Department of Census and Statistics. *Statistical abstract of
Ceylon,*1949-1962. Colombo, Government Publications Bureau, 1949-63.
Statistics collected from government and business sources survey climate,
population, social conditions, education, economy, trade and communication, finance and prices. Nearly all the tables cover a number of years.
The Department's *Quarterly bulletin of statistics* ceased publication from
the first quarter of 1961.

BIBLIOGRAPHY

C11. Wikremasinghe, Martino de Zilva. *Catalogue of the Sinhalese printed books in the Library of the British Museum.* London, British Museum, 1908. 308 cols.
An author catalog of some 2,400 books acquired by purchase or under the Colonial Copyright Acts, and including examples of early Sinhalese printing from the 18th century. Titles are transliterated and translated. There is a title index.

C12. Ceylon. Office of the Registrar of Books and newspapers. *Catalogue of books...* 1960-64? Colombo, Government Press, 1960-64? quarterly.
Continues Part V. Of the *Ceylon Government Gazette* which was first issued in 1885. This list suspended publication during World War II and resumed publication in 1951. Retrospective lists covered the period from 1942 to 1951. Each quarterly issue contained some 1,000 entries, arranged in a classified order, and included government publications. The last issue noted was for Jan- Mar.1964.

C13. Ware, Edith W. *Bibliography of Ceylon.* Coral Gables, University of Miami Press, 1962. 181 p.
Some 10,000 books and periodical articles in 13 languages, but mostly in English, are divided by subjects arranged alphabetically. The bibliography is divided into a large general section and small natural history section. No annotation and no index, making the bibliography difficult to use.

C14. *Ceylon national bibliography,* v.1- 1963- Nugegoda, National Bibliography Branch, Department of the Government Archivist, 1964-
Based on books deposited with the Registrar of Books and Newspapers, and excluding newspapers and periodicals, except for first issues, maps, ephemeral materials, etc. All parts have a classified section arranged by the Dewey system, but modified for Ceylon. Alphabetical index by authors and titles. Number 2 of a preliminary *Ceylon national bibliography,* published in 1962, noted.

C15. U.S. Library of Congress. American Libraries Book Procurement Center, New Delhi. *Accessions list, Ceylon,* 1967- New Delhi, 1967- Quarterly.
1967 issues include some 500 books and periodicals in English and Sinhala.

D.INDIA including South Asia

Britain became the paramount power in India after the Maratha War of 1817-19, and independence did not come to the subcontinent until 1947, when it was divided into two parts, with the largely Muslim areas of the former Indian Empire becoming the new state of Pakistan.

HANDBOOKS AND ENCYCLOPEDIAS

D 1. Balfour,Edward. *The cyclopaedia of India and of Eastern and Southern Asia.* Graz, Akademische Druck- u. Verlaganstalt, 1967-68. 3 v.
A reprint of the third edition published in 1885, and containing 35,000 articles, in most cases short, on the flora and fauna, geography, history, biography, customs, religion and literature of South and Southeast Asia, but with a concentration on South Asia. Articles often have short bibliographical notes. Much of the information is now dated, but there remains a substantial proportion not readily accessible through other reference sources.

D 2. Dowson, John. *A classical dictionary of Hindu mythology and religion, geography, history and literature,* tenth edition. London, Routledge and Kegan Paul, 1961. 411 p.
The major part of this dictionary is concerned with mythological and religious terms, followed by historical names and terms, and the important geographical names referred to in classical Indian literature. There are descriptions of the Sanskrit books mentioned by Western authors. The dictionary is 'derived entirely from the publications of European scholars' and 'not from the original Sanskrit authorities,' and the European literature is frequently cited. Alphabetical arrangement with index.

D 3. Binani, Govarchandas and T.V. Rama Rao. *India, at a glance, a comprehensive reference book on India.* Revised edition. Bombay, Orient Longmans, 1954. 1756 p.
Rather more than a glance, it covers nearly all phases of modern India, including government, economy, foreign policy, defence, the constitution, industry, commerce, and the Indian States. It is arranged by subject with an index. A valuable source, but now largely dated, and of more use as an historical reference.

D 4. *Hindi vishwakosa* (Hindi Encyclopedia) Varanasi(i.e. Benares), Nagari Pracharini Sabha, 1966?-
An excellent and well illustrated encyclopedia in Hindi, which should not be confused with an encyclopedia with the same name published in Calcutta in 1914-31. Nine volumes noted with volume 9 published in 1967. P. K. Garde *Directory of reference works published in Asia* (1956) cites eight encyclopedias and handbooks published in India since 1881. Recently important encyclopedias have been published in Tamil *Kalaikka-*

lanciyam and in Telugu *Vijnana sarvasvamu.*

D 5. Bhattacharya, Sachchidananda. *A dictionary of Indian history.* New York, George Braziller, 1967. 888 p.

A new dictionary with 2,785 entries for persons, places, institutions important in Indian history from earliest times until the present.

YEARBOOKS

D 6. Mitra,H.N. *Indian annual register,* 1919-1947. Calcutta, Annual Register Office, 1919-47.

Each volume commences with a chronicle of events followed by summary accounts of proceedings in central and provincial assemblies. Later issues give fuller accounts of Congress activities and important national affairs. The *Register* appeared annually from 1919-23, and 1930-47, and quarterly with the title *Indian quarterly register,* from 1924-29. Available on microfiche published by the International Documentation Center.

D 7. *Times of India directory and yearbook, including who's who,* 1953/54- Bombay, Times of India, 1953-

In continuation of the *Indian yearbook and who's who,* 1914-47, and the *India and Pakistan yearbook and who's who,* 1948-53, gives short statements on a wide variety of subjects concerned with India, such as meteorology, defence, agriculture, railroads, foreign investment, currency, banking and industry. In addition it has information on the States and cities, with a classified list of trades and professions. There is a short biographical dictionary with some 1,000 biographies. Indexed. 1969 last issue noted.

D 8. *India, a reference annual,* 1953- Delhi, Ministry of Information and Broadcasting, 1953-

Compiled from official sources, and covers political, constitutional, educational, cultural, scientific, financial and other aspects of India. There are a great number of statistics and bibliography is well represented. Succeeding issues duplicate each other considerably. 1967 issue last noted.

DICTIONARIES

D 9. Monier-Williams, Monier. *A dictionary, English and Sanskrit.* Varanasi, Chowkambra Sanskrit Series Office, 1961. 859 p. (Chowkambra Sanskrit Series, studies v.13)

The best one-volume dictionary of the Sanskrit language, with over 25,000 words. The most used and the most usable. Entries are clearly stated. Based on Bohtlingk *Sanskrit-Worterbuch.* Another useful dictionary is Arthur Anthony Macdonnell *A practical Sanskrit dictionary* (London, Oxford University Press, 1924 382 p.) with some 8,000 Sanskrit words, with usage and English equivalents.

D10. Bohtlingk, Otto. *Sanskrit-Worterbuch in kurzerer Fassung.* Graz, Akademische Druck- u. Verlaganstalt, 1959. 7 v.(in 3.)
A reprint of the abridgement of Bohtlingk *Sanskrit - Worterbuch* (1855-77. 7 v.) the definitive dictionary of Sanskrit. The abridgement contains some 120,000 entries and their equivalents in German, and was originally published in St.Petersburg in 1879-89.

D11. Platts, John Thompson. *A dictionary of Urdu, classical Hindi and English.* New York, Oxford University Press, 1930. 1259 p.
Old, but it has been frequently reprinted, and is essential for use with classical and courtly Urdu. It has a tendency to be formal, but is a necessary tool when working with written documents. A reprint of the 1884 edition.

D12. *Bhargava's standard illustrated dictionary of the Hindi language.* (Hindi-English edition) 6th revised and enlarged edition. Banaras, Shree Ganga Pustakalaya, 195- ? 1280 p.
Lists some 35,000 Hindi works and with its companion volume *Bhargava's standard illustrated dictionary of the English language* (Anglo-Hindi edition) 9th edition(Banaras, Shree Ganga Pustakalaya, 1951, 1 v.) with over 30,000 words, is sketchy, simplistic and not reliable since usage is not stated. However it is the only dictionary of its type widely available. For students who cannot read the Devanagari script in which Hindi is normally written, there is *The student's practical dictionary romanized, Hindustani-English, and English-Hindustani.* (Allahabad, Ram Narain Lal, 1952. 363,563 p.)

BIOGRAPHICAL DICTIONARIES

D13. Chitrava, Siddheswarshastri Vishnu *Bharatavarshiya pracina caritrakosa* (Dictionary of ancient Indian biography) Puna (i.e. Poona) Bharatiya Caritra Kosa Mandala, 1964. 1204 p.
The most authoritative and comprehensive biographical dictionary for early India, with some 18,000 names of persons cited in early Hindu, Buddhist and Jain literature. Bibliography of sources. In Hindi.

D14. Beale, Thomas William. *An Oriental biographical dictionary.* New York, Kraus Reprint Corporation, 1965. 431 p.
Contains approximately 6,000 names of historical figures and also some mythical, religious and social terms. The use of the word Oriental in the title is misleading, since the dictionary concerns itself almost exclusively with Muslim and Arabic names gathered from the Muslim histories. The Arabic equivalent is frequently used following the transliterated form of the name. Useful for the Muslim period of Indian history. A reprint of the 1894 edition.

D15. Buckland, Charles E. *Dictionary of Indian biography.* London, Swan Sonnenschein, 1906. 494 p.
Includes some 2,600 biographies, mostly of persons of British descent, for the period of Indian history from about 1750 to the time of publication. A short bibliography and list of works consulted is included.

D16. Hayavadana Rao, Conjeevaram. *The Indian biographical dictionary, 1915.* Madras, Pillar, 1915. 472 p.

Some 2,000 European and Indian living persons are arranged alphabetically with appendices including the warrant of precedence for India, salutes in India, Indian Clubs and Indian titles.

D17. Kabadi, Waman P. *Indian who's who.* Bombay, 1935. 600 p.

Contains some 1,200 biographies of men and women residing in India, and of Indian or British descent. The length of the description depends on the importance of the person. Works are listed for authors.

D18. *Who's who in India, Burma and Ceylon,* 1930-39. Bombay, Modern Press and Publications,1930-39.

The 1937 edition contains some 1,800 biographies divided into three sections, of which the most important is the second, listing Indian princes, chiefs and nobles, and the third, a general section in three parts, each arranged alphabetically. Index to names.

D19. India(Republic). Ministry of Home Affairs. *The Civil list of Indian Administrative Service.* Delhi, Manager of Publications, 1956-

A listing of senior officials, giving their birth date, present position, pay, and arranged by the province on whose administrative cadre they happen to be. Issues noted for 1961-67, and the 1967 issue lists some 4,500 officials. Index to names. Continues the *India Office list,* 1876-1947 recently published on microfiche by the International Documentation Center, Zug, Switzerland. There are also departmental and State Civil lists.

D20. Sahitya Akademi, New Delhi. *Who's who of Indian writers.* Honolulu, East-West Center Press, 1964. 410 p.

Some 6,000 living Indian writers arranged alphabetically. The family name is usually placed first, and personal names have been used in place of the family name only when the latter is not in general use. Date and place of birth, titles, pseudonyms and at the most 6 titles of the author's publications are listed.

DIRECTORIES

D21. *Thacker's Indian directory and the world trade.* 1865- Calcutta, Thacker's Directory, Ltd. 1865-

Divided into an official directory, subdivided by States, and a commercial directory, also subdivided by States, and major urban centers. Separate sections for newspapers, hotels, transport, mining, plantations, foreign trade, and a classified list of firms.

D22. *Trado Indian Directory ...* New Delhi, Trade Builders, 1942-

A directory of commercial firms, educational, medical and scientific organizations. Divided into 21 sections, the first two being for national organizations, and followed by a section each for the 19 regions of India. Each section indexed separately, and there is no index for the whole volume. The information given consists mostly of adresses. Official organizations not included. 1969 issue last examined.

D23. Indian Association of Special Libraries and Information Centres. *Directory of special and research libraries in India.* Calcutta, 1962. 282 p.
Possibly less than half of the 400 special libraries in India are represented, and detailed information for 173 arranged by name, includes size of collections and staff. Another 700 libraries, not all special, are listed by State. Place and subject indexes.

D24. Intra-University Board of India and Ceylon. *Universities' handbook, India and Ceylon,* 1964. New Delhi, 1964. 675 p.
The most exhaustive and authoritative directory of universities, in India and Ceylon. The universities are listed alphabetically, and history, description of facilities, staff and courses are noted. Six smaller universities have been omitted.

D25. Khosla, Raj K. *Men of library science and libraries in India.* New Delhi, Premier Publications, 1967. 1 v. (various paging)
Some 650 biographies of librarians are followed by a listing of some 1,400 libraries arranged by name, with a short note on each, sometimes including size of collection. A third part lists some 3,000 academic libraries, some 360 special libraries, and some 1,100 state and public libraries. No index.

ATLASES

D26. India(Republic). National Atlas Organization. *National atlas of India (preliminary edition)* Calcutta, 1957. 26 maps.
A collection of specialized maps, emphasizing social and economic conditions, with a text in Hindi and English. The maps are colored, and at a scale of 192 miles to the inch.

D27. Davies, Cuthbert Collin. *A historical atlas of the Indian peninsula,* second edition. New York, Oxford University Press, 1963. 94 p. 47 maps.
The first edition was published in 1949, but there is no indication how this volume differs. Each map is accompanied by text, and there are 32 maps for the pre-1900 period and 15 after that period. The maps are concerned with wars and campaigns, economic and social conditions, and only place names mentioned in the text are included. No index.

GEOGRAPHICAL DICTIONARIES AND GAZETTEERS

D28. Dey, Nundo Lal. *A geographical dictionary of ancient and medieval India,* second edition. London, Luzac, 1927. 262 p. (Calcutta Oriental series, no. 21. E13)
Some 2,200 names have been compiled from a number of sources, including inscriptions and classical works. Earlier names are identified with present places.

D29. *Imperial gazetteer of India,* revised edition. Oxford, Clarendon Press, 1907-31. 26 v.

Work commenced on this gazetteer in 1871, and the first four volumes are in a different binding and have title *The Indian Empire*. Volumes 5-25 were published in 1908, and are in the form of an alphabetical gazetteer. Volume 25 is an index to volumes 5-24. Volume 26 is an atlas of 66 maps and plans, and was published in 1931. Although much information is now dated, this is still a principal historical source for India. The *Imperial gazetteer of India, provincial series*, (Calcutta, Superintendent of Government Printing, 1908-9, 25 v.) rearranges the same information by province.

D30. *The gazetteer of India, Indian Union*, v.1- New Delhi, Publications Division, Ministry of Information and Broadcasting, 1965-

Four volumes are projected describing the country and people, history, economy, and administration of India as a whole. The responsibility for the local descriptions now rests with the district gazetteers to be issued by the Indian States. These gazetteers are now being published, but not on a uniform basis.

CHRONOLOGY AND CHRONOLOGICAL TABLES

D31. Sewell,Robert and Sankara Balkrishna Dikshit. *The Indian calendar, with tables for the conversion of Hindu and Muhammedan dates in A.D. dates and vice versa* ... London, Swan Sonnenschein, 1896. 106, cxxxvi, 169 p.

The main text consists of conversion tables for Hindu and Muslim dates, with an explanatory preface. Originally written to help detect forged documents with spurious dating, but now valuable for the historian handling historical materials.

D32. Rickmers,Christian Mabel(Duff) *The chronology of India, from the earliest times to the beginning of the sixteenth century*. Westminster, A. Constable & Co., 1899. 409 p.

A useful, but somewhat dated chronology, listing historical events from the birth of Buddha to the death of Babar in 1530. Sources are cited for almost all entries. The chronology is supported by a full index and a number of chronological and dynastic lists.

D33. Burgess, James. *The chronology of modern India, for four hundred years, from the close of the fifteenth century, A.D.1494-1894*. Edinburgh, 1913. 483 p.

Arranged according to the reign or administration of the head of the state at the time, and emphasizes political events. Index often more full than text, giving ranks for names, and adding districts to placenames.

D34. Andhra Pradesh. Bureau of Economics and Statistics. *Diglott Calendar, volume 1 for the years 1879 to 1930 A.D., Bahman 1288 to Bahman 1340, Fasli Maharram 1296 to Shaban 1349, Hijri*. Fourth edition. Hyderabad, 1961. 624 p.

A comparative Western and Muslim calendar. Volume 2 reported covering the period from 1931 to 2000 A.D.

CENSUS

D35. India (Republic). Census Commissioner. *Census of India, 1951.* Delhi, Manager of Publications, 1952- 447v(projected)

Although censuses were taken by the British administration in different parts of India before 1872, the main national series commenced in that year, and the second census was taken in 1881, and decennially from that year to the present. A full listing of the census volumes may be found in: Texas, University. Population Research Bureau. *International population census bibliography, Asia.* (Austin, 1966) The census was generally divided into a number of provincial volumes, usually subdivided into at least two parts, an administrative part and a part for tables. The number of parts in the 1951 census represented a major advance in the size of the census reporting.

D36. India (Republic) Office of the Registrar-General. *Census of India,* 1961. New Delhi, Manager of Publications, 1962-

The 1961 census publication program was projected to have 1,476 volumes. The general section was to be in 10 parts in 29 volumes. In addition there are 26 States and Union territories, and all of these will have at least two parts, a general report, and a general population table. Others may have as many as 22 parts, and each part may be published in a number of volumes. The most numerous group will be the village surveys, planned to cover 580 villages. For a more complete description refer to: India (Republic). Office of the Registrar-General. *Census of India, guide to the 1961 census publication program,* (1965. 230 p.). In addition to Central publications, there will be series of district census handbooks to be distributed by the States. As part of the 1961 census program a *Census of India* bibliography project will be developed by the National Library.

STATISTICAL YEARBOOKS

D37. India. Department of Commercial Intelligence and Statistics. *Statistical abstract for British India,* 1st-18th issue, 1911-40. New Delhi, Manager of Publications, 1923-43.

Each issue covers the preceding ten years, and includes some 270 tables under approximately 40 headings, as emigration, vital statistics, area and population, pilgrims, railroads, lunatic asylums,etc. There are 4 appendices, for customs tariffs, rates of excise duty on liquor, opium and other drugs, currency, and rates of income tax. Indexed.

D38. India (Republic). Central Statistical Organization. *Statistical abstract of the Indian Union,* 1949- Delhi, Manager of Publications, Government of India, 1950-

The period of coverage is from 5 to 10 years, and the tables under some 39 headings include economic and social development, including area and population, national income, agriculture, livestock, forests, printing presses, publication and education. Brief explanatory notes precede sections of the abstract, which is in itself a useful guide to the Indian central statistical services. Former title: *Statistical abstract, India,* 1966 last issue noted.

BIBLIOGRAPHY

D39. Diehl, Katherine Smith. *Early Indian imprints.* New York, Scarecrow Press, 1964. 533 p.

1,038 annotated titles based on the William Carey Historical Library of Serampore College near Calcutta, and includes all materials dated to 1850, and all titles published at Serampore to 1873. Divided into three major sections: Books in Indian languages; books, other than Bibles, in chronological order; and Bibles arranged by language.

D40. Great Britain. India Office Library. *Catalogue of European printed books.* Boston, G.K. Hall, 1964. 10 v.

Lists some 90,000 volumes in Western languages in the India Office Library, but excludes translations, which are placed with the original languages. Materials acquired to 1936 were cataloged in a sheaf catalog (a loose-leaf catalog of slips on which were pasted entries from printed catalogs and supplementary lists). This comprises v.1-2. V.3-6 reproduce the new author catalog on cards for accessions from 1936, and including about one fifth of the books in the sheaf catalog. V. 7-9 are a subject index to v.3-6. V.10 notes the periodicals held by the Library. Since the India Office Library was a depository library for a substantial period between 1867 and 1947, and has collected after Independence, this catalog is one of the principal reference tools for the study of indian history.

D41. Calcutta. Imperial Library. *Catalogue.* Calcutta, Superintendent of Government Printing, 1904-18. 2 v.(in 4.)

Lists books in Western languages in the Imperial Library, now the National Library of India. The first part, in 2 volumes, is an author-catalog of printed books in European languages and was published in 1904. It also contains a list of newspapers. The second part is a subject index to the author catalog, and is also in 2 volumes. *Supplements 1-2* were published from 1906 to 1939, and include materials received to 1937. Each supplement is in two parts, the first is an author catalog, and the second a subject index.

D42. Calcutta. National Library. *Author catalogue of printed books in European languages.* Calcutta, Manager, Government of India Press, 1941-60. 8 v.

A later and more inclusive listing than the Imperial Library *Catalogue* (1904-18) but lacks the subject index which makes it less valuable. Some 40,000 books are listed, and these are mostly in English, and only one third were published in India. Official publications not included. *Supplement, 1951-1961,* published in 1964, reported.

D43. *Impex reference catalogue of Indian books, the list of all important books (in English) in print...* New Delhi, Indian Book Export and Import Co., 1960. 236, 468 p.

Some 10,000 books published in India and still in print are arranged by 48 subjects, and subarranged by author. Title, publisher, and price are given, but most entries lack pagination. A second section arranges the books by authors. The list lacks professional bibliographical standards with its different forms of titles and author names. *Impex supplement 1960-62* was published in 1962, and has 4,000 titles, over half of those are central and local official publications. Important since it helps to cover the period before the publication of the *Indian national bibliography.* 1957-

D44. *An up-to-date encyclopedia of all Indological publications published in India, and other countries related to ancient India, classified and arranged subjectwise in alphabetical order.* Delhi, Mehar Chand Lachman Das, 1962. 385 p.

A trade catalog listing more than 12,962 titles. The first section includes books in English and Indian languages published in India; the second, books published outside India and the third, books published in Indian languages on Ayurveda, a traditional system of Indian medicine. The first section is arranged under the following subjects: Vedas, philosophy, language and linguistics, history and arts, and the sciences. No index.

D45. Patterson, Maureen L.P. And R.B. Inden. *South Asia, an introductory bibliography.* Chicago, University of Chicago Press, Syllabus Division, 1962. 412 p.

4,369 entries, mostly in English, for books and periodical articles, arranged under eight major headings: general; history; social structure, political and economic structure; political, economic and social change; religion and philosophy; literature, science and the arts. Over 80% of the books are in the library of the University of Chicago. No annotations. Author and title index.

D46. Mahar, J. Michael. *India, a critical bibliography.* Tucson, University of Arizona Press, 1964. 119 p.

A select bibliography of 2,023 entries, mostly in English, and almost entirely books, emphasizing those published after 1940. Arranged by subject, with almost one half on history, and a quarter on religion and philosophy. Entries are annotated, but these are sometimes much less than critical. Author index.

D46.1. Singh, Sher and S.N.Sadhu. *Indian books in print, 1955-67, a select bibliography of English books published in India.* Delhi, Indian Bureau of Bibliographers, 1969. 1116 p.

Claims to include 40,000 books published from 1955 to 1967, but actually there are less than 20,000 titles arranged in order of the Dewey Decimal Classification. There are separate author, title and subject indexes. A list of 1,500 Indian publishers is included with their addresses.

Current bibliography

D47. Calcutta. National Library. *Indian national bibliography,* 1957- Calcutta, 1958-

Originally issued quarterly, with annual cumulations for 1958-1963 now issued monthly. Includes works in English and the major Indian languages, recorded in transliteration, and Central and local official publications. It depends on the deposit of books provided under the Delivery of Books and Newspapers (Public Libraries) Act of 1954, but it has been estimated that 30% of these publications are not deposited, and many have to be purchased by the National Library. Maps, music scores, periodicals and newspapers(except for the first issue under a new title) and ephemeral materials are excluded. Arranged in two parts, the first for general publications, and the second for official materials. Dewey Decimal Classification is used. Author and subject index.

D48. U.S. Library of Congress. American Libraries Book Procurement Center, New Delhi. *Accessions list, India,* 1962- New Delhi, 1962-
A monthly record of the publications acquired by the Center, including both commercial and official publications, newspapers and periodicals. Arranged by language, and within each language section, by author. Cumulative author index is issued annually, and also an annual list of serials. The list records deliveries to some 22 selected libraries in the United States, but unfortunately not all these libraries have the materials under sound bibliographical control and accessible for inter-library loan, a condition of deposit. Since the entry in the *Accessions list* may not always agree with that finally decided upon at the Library of Congress, it may be difficult to locate the book. Also, where the number of copies are short, they are distributed on a priority list, and not all libraries may receive a copy. Finally many libraries are following individual discard policies. In India, the Center attempts some selection, particularly in the field of fiction which is strongly scaled down. In spite of all these limitations, the list is more current and sometimes more complete than the *Indian national bibliography.*

Publications in South Asian languages

BENGALI
D49. Long, James. *A descriptive catalogue of Bengali works, containing a classified list of fourteen hundred Bengali books and pamphlets which have been issued from the press during the last sixty years with occasional notices of the subjects, the price, and where printed.* Calcutta, Sanders, Cones and Co.,1855. 108 p.
488 entries for books in Bengali, with annotations and titles in English. Contains in addition much useful information on the early history of printing in Bengal.

D50. Blumhardt, James Fuller. *Catalogue of Bengali printed books in the library of the British Museum.* London, British Museum, 1886. 150 p.
Some 1,310 books are listed by author and title, and include three types of publication: books in the Bengali language, books translated into other languages, and polyglot publications in which Bengali books appear either in the original or in translation. There is a general index of titles, including variant forms of the author's name found on the title page. There are

two series of catalogs of South Asian language materials issued in London during the late 19th, and early twentieth century. The materials cataloged were frequently the same, and the compilers of the catalogs the same individuals. However the series issued by the British Museum is better organized, more inclusive, and easier for the general reader to understand, than that issued by the India Office Library. For these reasons it has been preferred for entry here.

D51. Blumhardt, James Fuller. *Supplementary catalogue of Bengali books in the library of the British Museum acquired during the years 1886-1910.* London, British Museum, 1910. 470 cols.

2,500 books listed by author and title according to the British Museum cataloging rules. General index of titles, and a subject index providing a subject approach to the original catalog and to this supplement.

D52. Blumhardt, James Fuller. *Second supplementary catalogue of Bengali books in the Library of the British Museum acquired during the years 1911-1934.* London, British Museum, 1939. 678 cols.

Lists some 5,000 books with a similar arrangement to the above catalog.

D53. Calcutta. National Library. *Author catalogue of printed books in Bengali language.* Calcutta, Manager, Government of India Press, 1941-63. 4 v.

Some 15,000 books and periodicals in Bengali, acquired up to the end of 1937, are arranged by author. Titles are transliterated and translated. For a more up-to-date, but selective listing, *The national bibliography of Indian literature 1901-1953* lists some 5,700 entries in Bengali.

HINDI

D54. Blumhardt, James Fuller. *Catalogues of the Hindi, Panjabi, Sindhi, and Pushtu books in the Library of the British Museum.* London, British Museum, 1893. 284,64,24,54 cols.

An author catalog in four parts. The first contains some 1,800 titles in Hindi, the second some 400 in Panjabi, the third some 150 books in Pushtu, and the fourth some 160 in Sindhi. Each part has its own title and subject index.

D55. Blumhardt, James Fuller. *A supplementary catalogue of Hindi books in the Library of the British Museum acquired during the years 1893-1912.* London, British Museum, 1913. 470 cols.

Some 3,000 books arranged by author, or by title for anonymous works. Title and subject index.

D56. Barnett, Lionel David and others. *A second supplementary catalogue of printed books in Hindi, Bihari and Pahri in the Library of the British Museum.* London, British Museum, 1957. 1,678 cols.

Over 6,000 titles are arranged by author, with subject and title indexes. Books on the *Adi granth* have been excluded since this is regarded as part of Panjabi literature.

D57. Singh,Mangalnath. *Hindi mem uccatara sahitya* (The best of Hindi books) Varanasi (i.e. Benares) , Rajnagari Pracharini Sabha, Vikrama 2014(1957) 732 p.

Some 13,000 titles are arranged into 39 subject divisions. For each book, author, title, publication date and price given. Authors are listed by first name under each division. No index.

D58. Tandon, Prem Narayan. *Hindi sevi samsara* (A dictionary of Hindi writers) Lakhanav(i.e. Lucknow), Hindi Sevi Samsara Karyalaya, 1963-65. 2 v.

Lists some 418 bookstores and libraries, 401 publishing houses, 1,806 newspapers and periodicals and 1,077 living writers and their works. Volume 1 covers the situation to 1947, and volume 2 from 1947 to 1963.

D59. Mahajan,Yash Pal and Krishna Mahajan. *Brahad Hindi grantha suchi* (A Hindi bibliography) Delhi, Bharatiya Granth Niketana,1965. 584 p.

Some 24,000 books are arranged by author under family name. The name of the publisher, publishing date, subject and price are given. *Parisishta* (Supplement,1966) published 1967, 141 p., contains an additional 5,000 titles.

HINDUSTANI

D60. Blumhardt, James Fuller. *Catalogue of Hindustani printed books in the Library of the British Museum,* London, British Museum, 1889. 458 cols.

Lists some 2,500 works in Hindustani, and written almost entirely in Perso-Arabic script.

D61. Blumhardt, James Fuller. *Supplementary catalogue of Hindustani books in the Library of the British Museum acquired during the years 1889-1908.* London, British Museum, 1909. 678 cols.

An author catalog of some 7,500 books with a title index and a classified subject index.

KANNADA(KANARESE)

D62. Barnett, Lionel David. *Catalogue of the Kannada, Badaga and Kurg books in the library of the British Museum.* London, British Museum, 1910. 278 cols.

1,600 entries are arranged by author, with a title and subject index. Only 9 books are in Badaga and Kurg. 3,000 titles in Kannada are listed in *the national bibliography of Indian literature, 1901-1953.*

MARATHI

D63. Blumhardt, James Fuller. *Catalogue of the Marathi and Gujarati printed books in the Library of the British Museum.* London, British Museum, 1892. 232, 196 cols.

In two sections, the first listing some 1,200 Marathi books and the second some 1,000 Gujarati books. Both sections are arranged in author order. Subject and title indexes.

D64. Blumhardt, James Fuller. *A supplementary catalogue of Marathi and Gujarati books in the British Museum.* London, British Museum, 1915. 256, 336 cols.

In two sections, the first containing some 2,000 books in Marathi, and the second some 2,300 in Gujarati. Separate subject and title indexes to both sections. 4,500 books in Gujarati are included in *The national bibliography of Indian literature, 1901-1953.*

D65. Date, Shankar Ganesh. *Marathi grantha suchi, 1800-1937* (Bibliography of Marathi publications, 1800-1937) Puna (i.e. Poona), 1943. 1072, 376 p.

A classified catalog arranged by the Dewey Decimal Classification, with some Colon Classification modifications, of 18,768 books in Marathi or on Marathi language, literature and grammar. Manuscripts, periodicals, textbooks, guidebooks, almanacs, reports, liturgical materials and maps are excluded. There is a chronological list of books published from 1805 to 1855. Author and title index. Date's unaided lifetime contribution to Marathi bibliography, with all entries personally inspected by him.

D66. Date, Shankar Ganesh. *Marathi grantha suchi,1938-1950* (Bibliography of Marathi publications, 1938-1950) Puna, 1951. 658 p.

A classified catalog similar to the above bibliography, of 7,839 books, with author and title index. Completed with some assistance from the Sahitya Akademi and the Bombay State Education Department.

PANJABI

D67. Barnett, Lionel David. *Panjabi printed books in the British Museum, a supplementary catalogue* . London, British Museum, 1961. 121 p.

1,300 books arranged in author order, with a subject and title index. Books in Panjabi are in both the Devanagri and the Gurmukhi script. Supplements James Fuller Blumhardt *Catalogues of the Hindi, Panjabi, Sindhi and Pushto books in the Library of the British Museum* (1893)

D68. Ramdev, Jogindar Singh. *Panjabi likhari kosha* (Dictionary of Panjabi authors) Jallandara (i.e. Jullundur), Niu Buk Kampani, 1964. 336 p.

1,700 authors are listed, with a short account of their lives and list of their published works. Based on a questionnaire. 80% of the authors sent materials for this compilation, and the other 20% include some older writers and many no longer living. The first book of its kind.

SANSKRIT, PALI AND PRAKRIT

D69. Haas, Ernst. *Catalogue of Sanskrit and Pali books in the British Museum.* London, Trubner and Co., 1876. 188 p.

An author catalog of some 3,400 works, with a title index. The entries are usually, but not always published in India.

D70. Bendall, Cecil. *Catalogue of Sanskrit, Pali and Prakrit books in the British Museum acquired during the years 1876-92.* London, British Museum, 1893. 624 cols.

Approximately 5,000 books, mostly current. Shows an increase in the number of Jain texts, mostly in Prakrit, over the previous catalog of Ernst Haas. Index of titles and a select subject index.

D71. Barnett, Lionel David. *Supplementary catalogue of Sanskrit, Pali, and Prakrit books in the Library of the British Museum acquired during the years 1892-1906.* London, British Museum, 1908. 1096 cols.

An author catalog of some 8,900 books with a separate title and select subject index. Includes some Burmese titles.

D72. Barnett, Lionel David. *Supplementary catalogue of the Sanskrit, Pali and Prakrit books in the Library of the British Museum acquired during the years 1906-1928.* London, British Museum, 1928. 1694 cols.

Author catalog for some 13,500 books, with separate general index of titles and a select subject index. Contains a few titles in Burmese.

D73. Emeneau,Murray Barnson. *Union list of printed Indic texts and translations in American libraries.* New Haven, American Oriental Society, 1935. 540 p. (American Oriental Series 7)

An excellent guide to resources in the United States and aid for the bibliographer and cataloger. Since it was published there has been a very great expansion of South Asian literature in American libraries, and it is estimated that there are at least twice the number of the 4,491 titles listed in American libraries, with many new locations. Almost all the works were written before 1800, and are in Sanskrit, Pali, Prakrit and Apabhramsa. An appendix lists the serial publication of texts. Holdings of the University of California not included.

TAMIL

D74. Murdoch,John, *classified catalogue of Tamil printed books, with introductory notices.* Madras, 1865. 287 p.

1,755 titles are listed, but some are missionary publications in English. The entries are arranged in subject order, with sections including religion, jurisprudence, philosophy, literature, history, periodicals and newspapers. Index of titles, but not of authors. The extensive introduction surveys Tamil literature and language.

D75. Barnett, Lionel David, and G. U. Pope. *Catalogue of the Tamil books in the library of the British Museum.* London, British Museum, 1909. 590 cols.

An author catalog of over 3,600 books, mostly in Tamil, but some in English or French, with a general index of titles and a select subject index. Includes a short note on Tamil literature.

D76. Barnett, Lionel David. *Supplementary catalogue of the Tamil books in the Library of the British Museum.* London, British Museum, 1931. 696 cols.

Some 3,900 books are in author order, with a general index to titles and a select subject index.

D76.1. Nayagam, Xavier S. Thani. *A reference guide to Tamil studies, books.* Kuala Lumpur, University of Malaya Press, 1966. 122 p.

Lists 1,322 books arranged in a classified order. The first section notes translations and summaries of Tamil literature. Author index. No annotations.

TELUGU

D77. Barnett, Lionel David. *A catalogue of the Telugu books in the Library of the British Museum.* London, British Museum, 1912. 444 cols.

Over 6,000 entries are arranged by author, with a general index to titles
and a select subject index.

Official publications

D78. Campbell,Francis Bunbury Fitzgerald. *Index-catalogue of Indian official
publications in the library, British Museum.* London, Library Supply co.,
1900. 193, 314, 72p.
A subject catalog of approximately 7,500 publications issued mostly subsequent to 1857. Entries are arranged primarily by geographical area and
subdivided by subject.

D79. India. Office of the Superintendent of Government Printing, Calcutta.
*General catalogue of government publications, corrected up to 31st De-
cember,1912. Part I.* Calcutta, 1913. 329 p.
Includes all publications, except acts, regulations and publications not for
sale, and is noted as no.21 in the series. The first part deals with India as
a whole, and is divided into twelve major divisions. The second part is
divided into nine provinces. Subject index. A revised edition, corrected
up to 30th June 1921, in 506 p. was published in 1921.

D80. India (Republic). Publication Branch. *Catalogue of Government of India
civil publications, subjectwise arranged.* Delhi, Manager of Publications,
1926-
Publications are listed by subject, and cover acts and laws, agriculture,
arts and sciences, administration, finance, medical, trade, commerce and
industries. When in Indian languages, the title is given in English only.
Kept up to date with annual supplements. Revised issues for 1948 and
1953 noted. No index.
The 1959 catalog represented a new departure. The contents were completely reorganized according to the Dewey Decimal Classification, and
separate title and author indexes were provided. However the supplements for 1960 and 1963 amend the 1953 issue.

D81. India (Republic). Lok Sabha. Secretariat. *List of publications(periodical
or ad hoc) issued by various ministries of the Government of India,* third
edition. New Delhi, Lok Sabha Secretariat, 1958. 282 p.
Some 3,000 publications are arranged by issuing agency, with information on periodicity, price and source of availability, and whether in print.
Valuable as a supplement to the Publication Branch *Catalogue of civil
publications.* No subject index.

D82. Singh,Mohinder. *Government publications of India, a survey of their
nature, bibliographical control and distribution system.* Delhi, Metropoli-
tan Book Co., 1967. 270 p.
With the government being the largest publisher in India, and issuing so
much of value, it is important that the controls and distribution system
for this material be understood. This work discusses the organization of
the government, and follows this with a detailed statement by 31 divisions, covering publications, distribution and controls. Over 1,500 titles
are cited.

Periodicals and newspapers

D83. Calcutta. National Library. *Catalogue of periodicals, newspapers and gazettes*. Calcutta, Government of India Press, 1956. 285 p.

1697 periodicals, gazettes and newspapers in Western languages only and published from the late 18th century, are arranged in Dewey Decimal Classification order, with a full bibliographical citation including holdings. Title and subject index. Over three-quarters of the titles published outside India.

D84. *Indian press yearbook,* 1949- Madras, Indian Press Publications, 1949-

A journalists' yearbook of which only one third is concerned with a select list of newspapers and periodicals arranged by State. For each entry, editorial staff and circulation stated. No index. The third issue for 1954 latest noted.

D85. India (Republic). National Information Service. *NIFOR guide to Indian periodicals,1955-1956*. Poona, pref. 1955. 385 p.

Lists both newspapers and periodicals, with 2,127 titles. There is also listed another 1,526 concerning which the compiler had little information. Index to titles and subjects.

D86. India (Republic). Office of the Registrar of Newspapers. *Press in India, part II,* 1956- New Delhi, Ministry of Information and Broadcasting, 1957- Annual.

Includes all serials, with frequency ranging from daily to annual. Arranged by State, then by language of publication, together with information on date of establishment, address, publisher and circulation. Title index. The most comprehensive listing of periodicals in India. Title to 1964: *Annual report.*

D87. Sud, Krishna Kanta. *Indian periodicals directory*. Calcutta, Periodicals Indexing Service, Business Forms, 1964. 188 p.

Some 50 newspapers and 1,730 periodicals in English are arranged in broad subject categories. For each item, frequency, date of establishment, publisher, address and circulation are given. Alphabetical index to titles.

D88. *Guide to Indian periodical literature,* v.1, no.1- 1964- Gurgaon, 1964-

Started somewhat unsatisfactorily, but now being issued quarterly, and covering some 150 Indian periodicals. Each issue has some 7,000 entries, and the standard of bibliographical work is high.

Subject bibliography

RELIGION

D89. Renou, Louis. *Bibliographie vedique*. Paris, Adrien Maisonneuve, 1931. 339 p.

6,500 books and articles in Western languages, Hindi and Sanskrit are arranged in 16 subject groups, and then chronologically. Subjects covered include the Vedas, Hindu civilization, the Vedic language, Sanskrit philology, and Indian religion. 68 periodicals are cited, and one third of the entries are briefly annotated. Index to titles and authors.

D90. Dandekar, R.N. *Vedic bibliography.* Bombay, Karnatak Publishing House, 1946. 398 p.
Some 3,500 books and articles in Western and Indian languages are arranged by subject. Some 450 periodicals are cited. The subjects covered include the Indus Valley civilization, the Vedas, Vedic and Indic languages, and Indian religion. There are annotations in English for about one sixth of the entries, but no translation of titles. The standard Indian works tend to be in more modern editions than those cited by Renou. Index to titles and subjects.

D91. Dandekar, R.N. *Vedic bibliography, volume 2.* Poona, University of Poona, 1961. 760 p.
Supplements the previous bibliography with 6,500 books and periodical articles in Western and Indian languages, and arranged into 20 chapters and 93 subsections. One third of the entries are annotated. Title and author index.

D92. Smith, Harry Daniel. *Profile of a library in transition.* Syracuse, (Syracuse University) for the program of South Asia Studies, 1966. 205 p.
The principal part of the text is a bibliography of the history of religion in South Asia based on the holdings of the Syracuse University Library in 1966. Some 3,000 books are arranged in subject order, with library call numbers. No index and no annotation.

Jainism

D93. Guerinot, Armand Albert. *Essai de bibliographie Jaina.* Paris, 1906. 568 p. (Annales du Musee Guimet, Bibliotheque d'etudes 22)
852 books and periodical articles in Western and Indian languages arranged in a classified order, and annotated. Indexes for authors, titles, subjects, places and periodicals surveyed.

D94. Jain, Chhote Lal. *Jaina bibliography.* Calcutta, Bharati Jaina Parisat, 1945. 377 p. (Jaina bibliography series no. 1)
509 books and periodical articles in western languages arranged in seven sections, and chronologically within each section. Annotated. Excludes material listed in Armand Albert Guerinot *Essai de bibliographie Jaina.*

SOCIAL SCIENCES

D95. Gilbert, William Harlen. *Caste in India, a bibliography, part I.* Washington, D.C. 1948. 174 p.
A major introductory statement explains how the bibliography was compiled, and this is followed by a detailed list of contents in which 5,345 entries for materials published to March 1943 were projected. However Part I contains only 1,970 entries nearly all in English. No annotations and no index. No further parts reported.

D96. Mandelbaum, David G. *Materials for a bibliography of the ethnology of India.* Berkeley, Department of Anthropology, University of California, 1949. 220 p.
2,250 unannotated entries in Western languages are arranged by cultural area and subject. Only a few of the entries were personally inspected by

the compiler, and those that are considered important have an asterisk before them. Compiled in 1940-41. Author and subject index.

D97. Dubester, Henry J. *Census and vital statistics of India and Pakistan, contained in official publications and famine documents, an annotated bibliography.* Washington, Library of Congress, Census Library Project, 1950. 118 p.

493 items arranged under six major subjects, and covering census publications from the first available census in 1853 down to 1941, together with official statistical materials with demographic data. References to items in the Library of Congress noted. Geographic index.

D98. U.N.E.S.C.O. Research Centre for the Social Implications of Industrialization in Southern Asia. *Southern Asia social science bibliography.* 1952- Calcutta, 1952- Annual.

Books, articles and reports in English and published in India, Pakistan and Ceylon, are divided into five major subject classes, and further subdivided. Some selected items are annotated. Author and subject index. Volume 14 for 1965 last noted.

D99. Bacon, Elizabeth E., Morris E. Opler and Edward E. LeClair Jr. *Selected and annotated bibliography of the sociology of India.* New Haven, Human Relations Area Files, 1957. 116 p.

559 annotated entries are arranged by subject, and by author within each subject. Table of contents the only key to this bibliography since there is no index.

D100. Furer-Haimendorf, Elizabeth von. *An anthropological bibliography of South Asia, together with a directory of recent anthropological field work.* Paris, Mouton, 1958-64. 2 v.(Le monde d'Outre-mer, passe et present, 4 ser. Bibliographies 3,4)

Based upon and continues David G. Mandelbaum *Materials for a bibliography of the ethnology of India* (Berkeley, 1949). The first volume covers the period 1940-54, with 5,316 books and periodical articles in Western languages, and the second for 1955-59, has 2,761 entries. The main part of both volumes is divided into 19 regional sections and one general section. Author index at the end of each volume. The field research directory entered by researcher is a valuable guide for future research publication.

D101. Damle, Y.B. *Caste, a review of the literature on caste.* Cambridge, Massachusetts Institute of Technology, Center for International Studies, 1961. 125 p.

In three parts. The first is a review of research in the field, and divides publications into 28 categories. The second lists 281 books and articles published between 1950-59 in subject order, and the third contains 116 abstracts of important books on caste arranged by author. No table of contents and no index. No cross references between sections.

D102. Gupta, G.P. *Economic investigations in India, a bibliography of researches in commerce and economics, approved by Indian universities.* Agra, Ramprasad and Sons, 1961-6. 3 v.

Since only 5% of university theses are published, much valuable material is not made accessible. This bibliography attempts to redress this situation. The first part lists dissertations under 18 universities, by date of degree. The second rearranges these materials by topic. Thesis topics which have been approved are listed in the same way. The 1962 supplement includes another 6 universities. 1966 supplement also.

D103. Kirkland, Edwin Capers. *A bibliography of South Asian folklore.* Bloomington, Indiana University Research Center in Anthropology, Folklore and Linguistics, 1966. 292 p. (Indiana University Folklore Institute, Folklore series)

6,852 books and periodical articles cover the whole South Asian region and Tibet, in Western and Asian languages, and are arranged by author. Entries are annotated, with information on the area, linguistic, tribal and ethnic group to which it belongs. This information is brought together in the index. Indian classical literature is included within the term folklore.

D104. De Benko, Eugene and V.N. Krishnan. *Research sources for South Asian studies in economic development, a select bibliography of serial publications.* East Lansing, Asian Studies Center, Michigan State University, 1966. 97 p.

918 entries for official, academic, commercial and private industrial periodicals, with items starred held by Michigan State University, comprising one fifth of the total. The two principal parts, one on economic development, and the other on related social science fields, are arranged by country, and then by author. No annotation. Subject index.

D105. Pareek, Udai. *Behavioural science research in India, a directory, 1925-65.* Delhi, Behavioural Science Centre, 1966. 574 p.

16,729 entries, mostly periodical articles, arranged in a detailed subject order, with 22 main divisions, and over 175 subdivisions. This is a bibliography, not a directory. Author index.

Administration and law

D106. Alexandrowicz, Charles Henry. *A bibliography of Indian law.* New York, Oxford University Press, 1958. 69p.

The first part is a short introduction to Indian law arranged in much the same order as the second part or bibliography, which lists some 700 books and periodicals. Annotation for a limited number of important legal works cited.

D107. Cohn, Bernard S. *Development and impact of British administration in India, a bibliographical essay.* New Delhi, Indian Institute of Public Administration, 1961. 88 p.

Lists some 400 books, mostly in English, in an essay, where they receive the equivalent of an annotation. Bibliography is arranged by author.

D108. Indian Law Institute. *Index to Indian legal periodicals,* 1963- New Delhi, 1963- Semi-annual.

32 periodicals are indexed under subject and author, with the author entries referring to the subject. The scope is not restricted to Indian law, and only a small proportion of the total Indian law literature is covered.

D109. Menge,Paul E. *Government administration in South Asia, a biblio-graphy.* Washington, American Society for Public Administration, Comparative Administrative Group, 1968. 100 p. (Papers in comparative public administration, special series no.9)

Over 1,025 books and articles in English published almost entirely from 1947 to 1967 are arranged by country, with subject divisions for India and Pakistan. The materials listed are available in the United States. Bibliographies and periodicals only are annotated. No index.

Education

D110. Brembeck, Cole S. And Edward W. Weidner. *Education and development in India and Pakistan, a select and annotated bibliography.* East Lansing, Michigan State University College of Education and International Programs, 1963? 221 p. (Michigan State University Education in Asia series 1)

Divided into two sections, one for India and the other for Pakistan. Each of these subdivided into a number of subjects. 241 books and periodical articles, all in English, are given critical and descriptive annotations. No index.

D111. Mukerjee, A.K. *Bibliography of periodicals.* Delhi, Central Institute of Education, 1964. 118 p.

491 periodicals, including those not published in India, located in the National Council on Education Research and Training, and in bound volumes in its different libraries. Arranged by the Dewey Decimal Classification system, with an alphabetical title index.

D112. *Education in India, keyword in context index and bibliography.* Ann Arbor, Comparative Education Program, School of Education, The University of Michigan, 1966. 220 p. (University of Michigan Comparative Education series)

The main body of this bibliography is formed by the keyword in context index (Kwik) and is based on books, periodical articles and Indian unpublished dissertations, mostly in English. Author index, but no statement of sources surveyed.

D113. Greaves, Monica A. *Education in British India, 1698-1947, a bibliographical guide to the sources of information in London.* London, University of London Institute of Education, 1967. 182 p. (Education Libraries Bulletin supplement thirteen)

1,379 books and periodical articles mostly in English, are arranged by author, with a subject index. In addition there is a short section on manuscripts and records. The most complete bibliography of its type.

NATURAL AND APPLIED SCIENCES

D114. Ranganathan,Shiyala Ramamrita. *Union catalogue of learned periodicals in South Asia, v.1, physical and biological sciences.* Delhi, Indian Library Association, 1953. 390 p. (Indian Library Association, English series 7)

Locations and holdings are given for some 6,000 periodicals arranged in subject order, with an alphabetical and subject index. Burma, Indonesia, Malaya and Ceylon were asked to cooperate, but most of the library locations are for India. Pakistan is not covered. The list is dated, and in 1965 it was estimated that there were over 10,000 different periodical titles in India alone.

D115. Guha, Roy K.K. *Bibliography of soil science and fertilizers with reference to India.* Delhi, Manager of Publications, 1954. 131 p. (Indian Council of Agricultural Research, Bulletin no.74)

2,156 periodical articles in Western languages are arranged by subject. Author index. Contains a brief history of soil science in India.

D116. *Index to Indian medical periodicals,* 1959- New Delhi, Central Medical Library, 1959- Semi-annual.

75-100 periodicals are surveyed. The index is divided into two parts, the first arranges the articles by subject, and the second indexes by author. Some 1,200 articles, almost entirely in English, are indexed each year.

D117. India (Republic) Directorate of Economics and Statistics. *Agricultural economics in India, a bibliography.* Second edition. Delhi, Government of India Press, 1960. 342 p.

A substantial revision of the 1953 edition, contains 3,400 annotated entries arranged by subject, and covering agriculture in general, planning, utilization, technology, administration, labor, land problems, legislation, taxation and statistics. No index.

D118. Delhi. National Science Library. *Catalogue of serials in the National Science Library.* New Delhi, Union Catalogue Division, National Science Library, Indian National Science Documentation Centre, 1965. 407 p.

3,447 periodical titles, of which 2,250 are current, and one quarter published in India. The periodicals are arranged alphabetically, with holdings. Classified index, index of issuing organizations, and an index by language.

D119. Wilson, Patrick. *Science in South Asia, past and present, a preliminary bibliography...* New York, Foreign Area Materials Center, University of the State of New York, 1966. 100 p. (Foreign Area Materials Center Occasional Publication no.3)

Over 1,100 printed books and periodical articles in Western languages arranged by subject. The materials are concerned with the history of science and technology in South Asia, and the post-World War II state of scientific research and education. Scientific works,as opposed to books about science, have been excluded. Nearly all entries personally examined by the compiler. Author index.

LANGUAGE,LITERATURE AND DRAMA

D120. Spencer,Dorothy Mary. *Indian fiction in English, an annotated bibliography.* Philadelphia, University of Pennsylvania Press, 1960. 98 p.

The first part consists of an essay on Indian society, culture and fiction, and the second is an annotated list of some 360 works of fiction and autobiography written by Indians in English. Supplemented by Sushil Kumar Jain *Indian literature in English, a bibliography, part III, fiction* (Regina, University of Saskatchewan Regina Campus Library,1965)

D121. *The national bibliography of Indian literature,* 1901-1953. New Delhi, Sahitya Akademi, 1962-
Not restricted strictly to literature, but includes books in other subject fields when these have value as literature. Although selected, it supplements the British Museum series of catalogs of books in South Asian languages. The only English books listed are those published in India, or by Indian writers. The first volume includes works in Assamese (1,500), Bengali(5,700), English(7,200), and Gujarati(4,500). The second, works in Hindi (7,500), Kannada(3,000), Kashmiri(120), and Malayalam(3,900). The approximate number of titles in each language is stated in brackets after each language. Each volume has its own index.

D122. Mehta,Chandravadan Chimanlal. *Bibliography of stageable plays in Indian languages,* vol.1. New Delhi, Published under the joint auspices of the M.S. University of Baroda and Bharatiya Natya Sangha, 1963. 292 p.
5,000 plays in the 14 main languages of India, published between 1901 and 1960. The entries are divided by language, and subarranged by author. For each play the number of acts or scenes, the number of characters and the theme is given.

D123. Pattanayak,D.P. *Indian languages bibliography.* New Delhi, Educational Resources Center, 1967. 84 p.
Over 1,600 selected books and periodical articles arranged under 14 major South Asian languages. The books cited are mostly grammars and dictionaries. No annotations and no index.

HISTORY

D124. *Cambridge history of India.* Cambridge, Cambridge University Press, 1922-37. v. 1,3-6.
The bibliographies for each chapter of the history are placed in a section at the end of each volume. Collectively they form the finest bibliography for South Asian history, with some 3,500 entries for primary and secondary sources in South Asian and Western languages. Reprinted by S. Chand, Delhi, 1958-64. A more up-to-date bibliography may be found at the end of each volume of R.C. Majumdar *The history and culture of the Indian people* (1957-1965) this helps to complete the gap in the coverage of the *Cambridge history of India,* of which v.2 was not published.

D125. Kern Institute, Leiden. *Annual bibliography of Indian archeology,* 1926- Leyden, E.Brill, 1926-
Coverage includes both South Asia and the regions of Southeast Asia under Indian cultural influence. Entries for both historical studies and art in addition to archeology. The 1954-57 issue contains monographs and periodical articles selected from 160 Indian and non-Indian Western language periodicals, with annotations. Author index. Volume 20 for 1962-63 last reported issue.

D126. Fernandes,Braz A. *Annual bibliography of Indian history and Indology,* 1938-42. Bombay,Bombay Historical Society,1938-49. 5 v.
An annotated and classified list of books and articles from some 80 periodicals, with a separate index to authors and subjects, and continuing

the 'Bibliography of Indian history for the years 1927-30' appearing in the *Journal of the Bombay Historical Society,* no.1-4, 1928-32, which selected articles from some 50 periodicals.

D127. Moraes,George Mark. *Bibliography of Indological studies,* 1942-43. Bombay, Examiner Press, 1945-52. 2 v.

The 1942 issue contains 1,974 entries for books and articles in English from 104 periodicals,published mostly in India. Arranged by subject, with a subject and author index. Most entries are annotated.

Modern India

D128. Sharma, Jagdish Saran. *Mahatma Gandhi, a descriptive bibliography.* Delhi, S. Chand, 1955. 565 p. (National bibliographies no.1)

3,671 annotated books and periodical articles in Western and Indian languages, but almost entirely in English, by and about Gandhi, covering the period from 1891 to 1955. Divided into three parts, the first discusses sources of the literature on Gandhi, the second lists biographies of Gandhi in a chronological order, with an alphabetical subject bibliography of books and periodical articles by and about Gandhi, and the third lists books which influenced Gandhi, books for which he wrote forewords, and periodicals he edited. A supplement covers additional writings from April 1954 to April 1955.

D129. Sharma, Jagdish Saran. *Jawaharlal Nehru, a descriptive bibliography.* Delhi, S. Chand, 1955. 421 p. (National bibliographies no.2)

3,710 annotated entries for books and periodical articles by and about Nehru in Western languages, covering the period from 1889 to 1955. Divided into three parts in much the same way as the author's bibliography on Gandhi. The first part lists sources, and biographies arranged chronologically, the second is a subject bibliography of books and articles by and about Nehru, and the third lists books which influenced him and for which he wrote forewords.

D130. Wilson, Patrick. *Government and politics of India and Pakistan, 1885-1955, a bibliography of works in Western languages.* Berkeley, South Asia Studies, University of California, 1956. 365 p. (Modern India Project bibliographical study no.2)

5,294 books, mostly published in India, arranged by broad subjects, with chronological arrangement within each subject. History, political affairs, biographies, constitutional history, and international relations are covered. Locations of books in the United States noted. Author index.

D131. Sharma, Jagdish Saran. *Indian National Congress, a descriptive bibliography of India's struggle for freedom.* Delhi, S.Chand, 1959. 816 p.

The subject covered is broader than the title indicates, being concerned with the cultural, economic, and political development of India, in addition to the major theme of the struggle for freedom. 9,135 books, articles, addresses, reports and resolutions from 1885 to 1958 are included. The materials are in Western languages, and are annotated. Arranged into three parts, the first gives sources, and a subject arranged bibliography, the second has a chronology, and the third lists material for the post-Independence period. Index.

D132. Case, Margaret H. *South Asian history, 1750-1950, a guide to periodicals, dissertations and newspapers.* Princeton, Princeton University Press, 1968. 561 p.

5,400 articles,over half of which are annotated, and selected from 351 periodicals and 650 dissertations, are arranged under some 150 headings. The articles are arranged in the first part, and the dissertations in the second. The third part lists some 341 English language and 251 Indian language newspapers by place of publication and notes holdings in American, British, Canadian and Indian libraries. Author and subject indexes.

D133. Schappert, Linda G. *Sikkim, 1800-1968, an annotated bibliography.* Honolulu, East-West Center Library, East-West Center, 1968. 69 p. (Occasional papers of the East-West Center Library no.10)

342 books, periodical articles and reports are arranged under 16 headings and annotated. Library locations are given in the Boston area. Combined author, title and subject index. Sikkim is a protectorate of the Republic of India.

E.NEPAL

Nepal became a British Protectorate in 1816, and did not become completely independent until 1923.

HANDBOOK

E 1. Elliot, J. H. *Guide to Nepal,* second edition. Calcutta, Newman, 1963. 122 p.
Little more than a short introductory handbook to the culture of Nepal. The 1959 edition was in 130 p.

CENSUS

E 2. Nepal. Department of Statistics. *Census of population, Nepal,* 1952/54 A.D. Kathmandu, 1958. 81 p.
The eastern portion of Nepal was enumerated in 1952 and the western in 1954. This publication abstracts the more important results of the census.

E 3. Nepal. Department of Statistics. *Preliminary report of the national population census,1961,provisional figures.* Kathmandu, 1962. 10 p.
In distinction to the 1952/54 census, the whole population was enumerated at one time. Tables show male and female population by region and district, urban and rural population by region, urban population and housing by towns, and absent population by districts.

BIBLIOGRAPHY

E 4. Fisher, Margaret W. *A selected bibliography of source materials for Nepal.* Berkeley, Institute of International Relations, University of California, 1966. 54 p.
Presents books and periodical articles in a bibliographical essay form, tracing the development of Nepal from earliest times. The table of contents is the only guide to the bibliography, which is a revised, but not updated version of the 1956 edition. Based on the holdings of the University of California and the Library of Congress.

E 5. Wood, Hugh B. *Nepal bibliography.* Eugene, Oregon, American-Nepal Education Foundation, 1959. 108 p.
900 books and periodical articles in Western languages, mostly in English, are arranged in six general categories, and subarranged by author. The first two categories form the major part of the bibliography. References

to mountaineering, Gurkha troop movements outside Nepal and to Hinduism and Buddhism have been excluded.

E 6. U.S. Library of Congress. American Libraries Book Procurement Center, New Delhi. *Accessions list, Nepal,* 1966- Delhi, 1966- quarterly.

Some 450 books and periodicals are recorded for 1967. There is an author index in the last issue for each year. This list will now become our principal bibliographical source for Nepal.

F.PAKISTAN

Pakistan was formed in 1947 from the predominantly Muslim areas of East Bengal and the western part of the Indian subcontinent. These two widely separated areas are known as East Pakistan and West Pakistan. In the one Bengali is the leading language, and in the other Urdu.

REFERENCE BOOKS

F1. Siddiqui, Akhtar H. *A guide to reference books published in Pakistan.* Karachi, Pakistan Reference Publications, 1966. 41 p.
473 English-language reference works published from August 1947 to December 1965 are arranged in an alphabetical subject order. The list has been made as comprehensive as possible. Author index.

YEARBOOKS

F2. *Pakistan,* 1947/48- Karachi, Pakistan Publications, 1948-
Each issue is divided into two parts. The first deals with Pakistan as a whole, and is divided into broad subject headings, further subdivided into minor topics. The second has the same arrangement, but is concerned with the provinces, states and frontier regions of Pakistan. The table of contents serves as an index. 1963/64 issue noted. Title from 1947-53 *1st to 6th year.*

F3. *East Pakistan yearbook,* 1958- Chittagong, The Tempest, 1958-
A series of economic, political, social and literary articles on East Pakistan are included in each issue. No index, and little biographical and directory-type information. Volumes 1-3, for 1958-60 noted.

F4. *East Pakistan annual,* 1961- Chittagong ? n.p., 1961-
In the 1963/64 issue a series of general articles of mainly economic interest is followed by a substantial classified trade directory. Indexed. No directory or index in the fourth volume for 1966/67.

F5. *West Pakistan year book,* 1957- Lahore, Directorate of Publications, Research and Films, Information Department, West Pakistan, 1957-
An official review of political, economic and social activity in West Pakistan, with statistics. No index and no biographical or directory-type information. Issues for 1957 through 1968 noted.

DIRECTORIES

F6. U.N.E.S.C.O. South Asia Science Cooperation Office. *Scientific institutions and scientists in Pakistan.* New Delhi, 1958. 501 p.

Divided into three parts: scientific organizations arranged by subject; scientific associations, societies and technical periodicals of which 46 are listed, and a list of some 2,000 scientists arranged by the Universal Decimal Classification, with their date of birth, position, research interest and publications. Only the natural and applied sciences are included.

F7. Pakistan Bibliographical Working Group. *A guide to Pakistan libraries, learned and scientific societies and education institutions, biographies of librarians,* revised edition. Karachi 1960. 166 p.

The first section lists libraries, giving addresses, size of collections, and their nature, annual additions and other information; the second lists educational institutions, noting their departments; the third lists eight museums and art galleries; the fourth lists learned societies and institutions arranged geographically, and the final section contains 65 biographies of librarians in Pakistan. Indexed. Revision of the 1956 edition.

F8. *Ansari's trade and industrial directory of Pakistan,* 1950/51- Karachi, Ansari Publishing House, 1950-

The first part consists of short and valuable summaries of ten important aspects of Pakistan's economic development, together with a classification of industry, a classification of importers and exporters, and a classification of merchants and agents, separated into East and West Pakistan. The second part is an alphabetical list of merchants and manufacturers, again with a separate listing for East and West Pakistan. Information taken from the most recent government publications. Title varies: *Ansari's trade directory of Pakistan and who's who,* 1950/51, and *Ansari's industrial directory of Pakistan,* 1957-

F9. *Barque's Pakistan trade directory and who's who,* 1963/64- Lahore, Barque and Company, 1965- ?

Noted as the first edition, and in continuation of the first edition of *Barque's All-India trade directory and who's who,* and also containing the biographical material in A. M. Barque *Who's who in Pakistan,* 1962/63(1963), there are four sections: industries, classified; firms arranged under an alphabetical listing of places; a classified trades, professions and commerce section; a listing of importers and exporters by commodity, and the who's who section.

BIOGRAPHICAL DICTIONARIES

F10. Khan, Tahawar Ali. *Biographical encyclopedia of Pakistan,* 1955/56- Lahore, Biographical Research Institute, Pakistan, 1956-

The issue for 1965/66 is noted as the third edition, and in it biographies are arranged into twelve sections, providing a classified approach. For each person there is a list of offices held, and his contribution, including works, when an author. Nearly all of the 2,200 biographies are for living persons. The supplement in the third edition is arranged similarly, and contains materials in revision of the second edition for 1960/61. Indexed.

F11. *Azam's who's who of Pakistan,1962-63.* Lahore, Azam Publications, 196-, 176 p.

Some 300 living persons are arranged alphabetically by surname. More informal than the *Biographical encyclopedia of Pakistan* and useful as a supplement to that work.

F12. Khurshid,M.I. *Who's who in science and research.* Karachi Biographical Information Bureau and Reference Centre, 1961. 157 p.

Lists 789 specialists, with information on their education, positions held, bibliography, membership of societies, and departments where now employed.

F13. Pakistan. Establishment Division. *Civil list of Class I officers serving under Government of Pakistan,* January 1961- Karachi, Manager of Publications, 1961-

Lists officers arranged by department, giving their date of birth, present appointment and emoluments. No index to names. 1964 issue published in 1965 last noted. A *Pakistan civil list,* no. 1- (Lahore, Civil and Military gazette, 1950- also listed higher civil servants. Civil lists and similar directories exist for the governments of East and West Pakistan.

GAZETTEER

F14. U.S. Office of Geography. *Pakistan* ... Washington, U.S. Government Printing Office, 1962. 883 p.

Contains 63,300 entries for places and feature names in Pakistan, together with their classification and longitude and latitude.

CENSUS AND STATISTICS

F15. Pakistan. Office of the Census Commissioner. *Census of Pakistan,* 1951. Karachi, Manager of Publications, Government of Pakistan, 1954-56. 9 v.

The first volume covers the whole of Pakistan, volumes 2-6 regional reports and tables, volume 7 economic conditions of West Pakistan, and volume 8 ecomonic conditions for East Pakistan. Volume 9 is an administrative report issued for official and research scholar use only. Information for the period prior to 1947 will be contained in the census and statistical series noted under India.

F16. Pakistan. Office of the Census Commissioner. *Census of Pakistan,* 1961. Karachi, Manager of Publications, Government of Pakistan, 1962-64. 10 v.(in 13.)

A census of all persons resident in Pakistan for the areas in which they are normally resident. Age, sex, religion, nationality, place of birth, mother tongue, literacy, education, land holding, economic activity, and fertility of women were surveyed. For the first time an attempt was made to survey the number of educated persons in each of the technical and professional fields. The 1961 series includes the Housing Census taken in 1960. Volume 6 is in two parts. Volume 7, in three parts, is for official use only. In addition to the 13 parts of the census, there are 46 district

census reports, and 6 census bulletins.
F17. Pakistan. Commercial Intelligence and Statistics Department. *Statistical digest of Pakistan,* 1950- Karachi, 1950-
A cyclostyled issue of the digest was reported for 1947, but the 1950 issue is noted as the first. Population, production, economy, finance, trade, communications, education, prices and foreign trade are surveyed. The 1950 issue has information for 1947 and 1948.
F18. Pakistan. Central Statistical Office. *Pakistan statistical yearbook,* 1952- Karachi, Manager of Publications, 195 -
Issues have not appeared annually, since the 1963 issue is noted as the sixth, and was published in 1964. Divided into 15 major sections, such as area and population, climate, labor, etc. Each section has introductory information, followed by charts and statistical tables. 1965/66 issue with title *Pakistan statistical annual.*

BIBLIOGRAPHY

For pre-1947 materials on the regions now in Pakistan, bibliographies in the section for India should be consulted.

F19. Ghani,A.R. *Pakistan, a select bibliography.* Lahore, Pakistan Association for the Advancement of Science, 1951. 339 p.
9,000 books and periodical articles in English on the history, description, natural resources and economy of Pakistan, arranged in a detailed subject order, but with no index. Among the subjects omitted are art, architecture, language, education literature and folklore. Compiled to a considerable extent from other bibliographies.
F20. U.S. Library of Congress. American Libraries Book Procurement Center, Karachi. *Accessions list, Pakistan,* 1962- Karachi, 1962-
Records Public Law 480 selections and deliveries to libraries in the United States, but is the only current and substantial bibliographical listing for Pakistan. Commercial, official and serial publications are included, in both English and the languages of Pakistan. Books are arranged by language and there is a monthly and annual cumulated author index.
F21. Pakistan. National Bibliographical Unit. *The Pakistan national bibliography, annual volume,* 1962- Karachi, Manager, Government of Pakistan press, 1966-
Divided into two parts, the first containing publications not issued by the government, and the second official materials. Each part is arranged according to the Dewey Decimal Classification. Index lists authors, titles, and subjects in one sequence. 1962 volume only noted.
F22. National Book Centre of Pakistan. *English language publications from Pakistan, a guide list.* Karachi, 1967. 242 p.
Some 2,000 books arranged by subject. Many of the books were still available in 1967. List of publishers' addresses. No annotations and no index.

Official publications

F23.Moreland, George E., and Akhtar H. Siddiqui. *Publications of the Government of Pakistan, 1947-1957.* Karachi, University of Karachi, 1958. 187 p.

1,578 entries in English concerned with Pakistan, including Government of India Acts which apply to Pakistan. The bibliography is arranged under issuing ministry, and is inclusive of the *Catalogue of the Government of Pakistan publications,* 1956 edition. There is a subject index.

F24. Pakistan. Manager of Publications. *Catalogue of the Government of Pakistan publications.* Karachi, 1962. 168 p.

Lists 1,000 entries in English, arranged by issuing ministry. Includes Acts, including Government of India Acts issued prior to 1947. Materials listed are for sale.

F25. Pakistan. Administrative Staff College, Lahore. *Alphabetico-classed catalogue of government reports, pamphlets, and miscellaneous publications, corrected up to 30th June, 1963.* Lahore, 1963. 122 p.

Approximately 1,200 entries in English, arranged under some 100 general subject sections. There is no alphabetical approach to issuing bodies and titles are abbreviated. A key to the National Administration Library in Lahore, and should be used together with other bibliographies for Pakistan official publications.

Newpapers and periodicals

F26. Moid A., and Akhtar H. Siddiqui. *A guide to periodical publications and newspapers of Pakistan.* Karachi, Pakistan, Bibliographical Working Group, Karachi University, pref. 1953. 60 p. (Publication no. 2)

300 periodicals, with language of publication stated, are arranged under 50 subjects. Also listed are 50 daily newspapers of which 35 are in Urdu; 10 bi-weekly and 144 weekly newspapers.

F26.1. National Book Centre of Pakistan. *English language periodicals from Pakistan, a guidelist.* Karachi, 1967. 55 p.

Some 400 periodicals are arranged under 64 subject headings. Annuals are included. No annotations. Title index.

Social sciences

F27. Keddie, Nikki R., and Elizabeth K. Bauer. *Annotated bibliography for Pakistan sociology, economics and politics.* Berkeley, University of California, Human Relations Area Files South Asia Project, 1956. 64 p.

Over 400 books, periodicals, and periodical articles arranged in subject order, with annotations. No index.

F28. Eberhard, Wolfram. *Studies on Pakistan's social and economic conditions, a bibliographical note.* Berkeley, University of California, Institute of International Studies, Center for South Asia Studies, 1958. 47 p.

Some 450 studies of urban and rural social conditions in Pakistan, mostly unpublished masters' and doctoral dissertations available at the University of the Punjab at Lahore and at the Agricultural College at Lyallpur.

Arranged by author, with subject references in the same alphabetical sequence.

F29. Elahi, Fazal and Akhtar H. Siddiqui. *Union catalogue of periodicals in social sciences held by the libraries in Pakistan.* Karachi, Pakistan Bibliographical Working Group, 1961. 92 p. (Pakistan Bibliographical Working Group publication no. 5)

Lists over 1,000 periodicals of which one quarter are U.S., and one fifth each are Pakistani, Indian and British. Locations and holdings are stated for 55 libraries.

F30. Siddiqui, Akhtar H. *The economy of Pakistan, a select bibliography, 1947-62.* Karachi, Institute of Development Economics, 1963. 162 p.

4,248 books, reports and articles selected from some 190 periodicals are arranged in a detailed subject order with separate author and subject indexes. Materials are in English. The most comprehensive bibliography on the economy of Pakistan.

F31. Bhatti, Allah Ditta. *A bibliography of Pakistan demography.* Karachi, Pakistan Institute of Development Economics, 1965. 59 p.

301 books, reports, periodical articles and papers in progress, with a subject index. No annotation. No author index.

F32. Braibanti, Ralph. *Research on the bureaucracy of Pakistan, a critique of sources, conditions and issues, with appended documents.* Durham, N. C., Duke University Press, 1966. 569 p. (Duke University Commomwealth Studies Center, Publication no.26)

A study of the general conditions under which research may be conducted, together with a major number of references to reports with valuable critical comments.

Literature

F33. Waheed, K. A. *A bibliography of Iqbal.* Karachi, Iqbal Academy, 1965. 224 p.

A comprehensive bibliography of books and articles by or related to Iqbal in Urdu and English.

Geography

F34. Rahman, Mustaqur. *Bibliography of Pakistan geography, 1947-1967.* Karachi, University of Karachi, 1968. 89 p.

Approximately 900 books and periodical articles, mostly in English, are arranged under 25 subject headings. No annotation and no index.

G.SOUTHEAST ASIA

This region, which until recently has often been placed within the Far East, includes the Asia mainland countries of Burma, Thailand, Cambodia, Laos and Vietnam, the island nations of Indonesia and the Philippines, and the peninsular and island kingdom of Malaysia, from which Singapore is now independent.

DIRECTORY

G 1. Association of Southeast Asian Institutions of Higher Learning. *Handbook of Southeast Asian institutions of higher learning.* Bangkok, 1965- annual.
Lists 31 universities in Southeast Asia who are members of the Association. The University of Hong Kong and the Chinese University of Hong Kong are included. The universities are arranged by country, with a background description of each, listing selected staff members and information on publications.

ATLASES

G 2. *Atlas of South East Asia.* New York, St.Martin's Press, 1964. 92 p.
130 colored maps, including eight colored historical maps as endpapers. Each country has been given separate treatment with a group of maps, ranging in number from 10 to 16. Indochina is treated as a unit. A typical section contains maps for physical features, climate, vegetation, and land use, agricultural products, population, including ethnic and linguistic groups, communications, minerals and large scale maps of the major cities. 24 pages of historical introduction by Professor D.G.E. Hall. Index to placenames.

G 3. United Nations. *Atlas of physical, economic and social resources of the Lower Mekong Basin,* prepared under the direction of the United States Agency for International Development ... By the Engineer Agency for Resources Inventories and the Tennessee Valley Authority for the Committee for Coordination of Investigation of the Lower Mekong Basin, United Nations Economic Commission for Asia and the Far East. Washington. 1968. 256 p.
Maps, descriptions and statistical data are arranged under 38 subject headings. The information in the maps includes the Republic of Vietnam, Cambodia, Laos, and Thailand, less its Southernmost provinces, and covers development, transportation, communication, power, tourism, industry, urban areas, health, education, ethnic groups, population, land use, agriculture, minerals, geology and climate. An outstanding atlas and a major contribution to the reference literature of Asia.

BIBLIOGRAPHY

G 4. Cornell University. Library. *Southeast Asia accessions list.* 1959- Ithaca, 1959-
A monthly list of new acquisitions of books and periodicals on Southeast Asia, in all languages, items are arranged by geographical divisions, and then by author. All entries are transliterated, and titles are not usually translated. Approximately 500-1,000 items are listed in each issue. Since there is no indexing and cumulation outside the Cornell University Library catalog, this list is difficult to search. It is, nevertheless, an essential tool for both the researcher and the research library concerned with Southeast Asia. 1959-1966 available on microfilm from Microphoto Division, Bell and Howell, Cleveland.

Western languages
G 5. Cordier, Henri. *Biblioteca Indosinica, dictionnaire bibliographique des ouvrages relatifs a la peninsule indochinoise.* Paris, Imprimerie nationale, E. Leroux, 1912-32, 5 v. (Publication de l'Ecole Francaise d'Extreme Orient, 15-18, 15bis)
The great bibliographical work for mainland Southeast Asia, covering books and periodical articles in Western languages, with an emphasis on French materials published to 1913. There are approximately 60,000 entries, which include 17,600 books and in addition articles from 160 periodicals. The first volume covers Laos, Siam, Assam and Burma; the second, Malaya; the third, French Indochina and Cambodia. There is a detailed table of contents. Four volumes were published from 1912 to 1915, and the author and subject index was published in 1932. Primary arrangement by country, then by subject divisions, including languages, customs, history, geography, government, religion, literature, etc. Some annotations. Continued for Indochina by Paul Boudet and Remy Bourgeois *Bibliographie de l'Indochine francaise.* Reprinted by Burt Franklin, New York.
G 6. Embree, John Fee and Lillian Ota Dotson. *Bibliography of the peoples and cultures of mainland Southeast Asia.* New Haven, Yale University Press, 1950. 821 p.
12,000 books and periodical articles published to 1949, with an emphasis on modern materials. Organized by culture and by political area, and includes Assam, Chittagong, Burma, Thailand, Laos, Cambodia, Vietnam, and the tribes of South China. Each section is further divided into races, social organization and law, religion and folklore, language and writings. Political history, economics and welfare are not included. Only a few short annotations, and no translation of titles. 34 other bibliographies were consulted to compile this bibliography. No author index.
G 7. U.S. Library of Congress. Division of Orientalia. *Southeast Asia, an annotated bibliography of selected reference sources in Western languages,* compiled by Cecil Hobbs. Washington, Library of Congress, 1952, 163 p.
345 annotated entries for books, arranged by country, then by subject.

Author, title and selected subject index. Continued by the same Division *Southeast Asia, an annotated bibliography of selected reference sources in Western languages,* compiled by Cecil Hobbs(Washington, Library of Congress, 1964. 180p.) with 535 entries, mostly published between 1952 and 1962, and with similar arrangement, extensive annotation and indexing.

G 8. U.S. Library of Congress. Division of Orientalia. South Asia Section. *Southeast Asia subject catalog at the Library of Congress.* Washington, 1965. 27 reels.

A microfilm copy of a card file of over 66,000 cards for books and periodical articles, mostly in Western languages, materials are divided first by country, then by subject. The most comprehensive bibliography available for Southeast Asia. Book publication projected.

G 9. Sternstein, Larry and Carl Springer. *An annotated bibliography of material concerning Southeast Asia from Petermanns Geographische Mitteilungen, 1855-1966.* Bangkok, Siam Society, 1967. 389 p.

Some 2,700 reviews of books, 250 maps and illustrative material, 147 articles and 664 notes all in western languages. Included also are a list of 350 periodicals cited, and keys to the entries by area.

G10. The, Lian and Paul W. Van de Veur. *Treasures and trivia, doctoral dissertations on South East Asia, accepted by universities in the United States.* Athens, Ohio University, Center for International Studies, 1968. 141 p.

958 doctoral dissertations are arranged by country and subarranged by major subject. Most comprehensive and up-to-date listing for Southeast Asia. Author index, no annotations. Entries asterisked are to be found in *Dissertation abstracts.*

G11.Tregonning,KennedyG. *Southeast Asia, a critical bibliography.* Tucson, University of Arizona Press. 1969. 103 p.

2,058 annotated entries for books, peridicals and periodical articles, almost entirely in English and published since 1945, the arrangement is by country, subarranged by subject, with introductory paragraphs for the more important. In each subject section entries are arranged with the most authoritative, the most general and the most easily obtainable first.

G12. United Nations. *Selected bibliography, lower Mekong basin.* Washington, Department of the Army, Engineer Agency for Resources Inventories, 1969. 2 v.

3,000 books, periodical articles and reports are arranged by country, and subdivided by subject under agriculture, climate, education. Electricity, fisheries, forestry and vegetation, geology, health, industry, minerals, population, soils, telecommunications, transportation, urban areas, and water resources. Not annotated, but selected on basis of value, currency and availability, all items cited being located in a library. Looseleaf format.

G12.1. Johnson, Donald Clay. *A guide to reference materials on Southeast Asia.* New Haven, Yale University Press, 1970. 176 p. (Yale Southeast Asia studies, 6)

Lists over 2,200 reference works written in the Roman alphabet and located in the Yale and Cornell University libraries. Arrangement is by form and subject and not by country. Index.

Chinese language

G13. Shu, Austin C.W., and William W.L.Wan. *Twentieth century Chinese works on Southeast Asia, a bibliography.* Honolulu, Research Translations, East-West Center, 1968. 201 p. (Annotated bibliography series no.3)

758 entries with romanization in the Wade-Giles system, translation of titles, and characters, with extensive annotations in English. Materials are arranged by country, and 80 percent have library locations. Based to some extent on Hsu Yun-chiao, Preliminary bibliography of the Southeast Asian studies. *Bulletin of the Institute of Southeast Asia, Nanyang University, Singapore. Nan yang yen chiu,* v.1, no.1, 1959, p.1-160, and Li Yih-yuan, Studies on Overseas Chinese in East Asia, a catalog of books and articles in Chinese and Japanese. *Bulletin of the Institute of Ethnology, Academia Sinica.* XVIII, Autumn 1964, p.46-235, but has the advantage of having annotation in English, and employing Wade-Giles romanization. Author and broad subject index.

G14. Nanyang University, Singapore. Institute of Southeast Asia. *Index to Chinese periodical literature on Southeast Asia, 1905-1966* Nan yang yen chiu Chung wen ch'i kan tz'u liao so yin. Singapore, 1968. 363 p.

Indexes nearly 10,000 articles from over 500 periodicals in Chinese published from 1905 to 1966. Entries are arranged first by country, and further subdivided by country. No index or annotations. The most extensive bibliography of Chinese sources on Southeast Asia.

G15. Oey, Giok P. *Survey of Chinese language materials on Southeast Asia in the Hoover Institute and Library.* Ithaca, Department of Far Eastern Studies, Southeast Asia Program, Cornell University, 1953. 73p. (Cornell Southeast Asia Program Data Research, no.8)

287 books in Chinese are arranged by subject, with the largest section on overseas Chinese. Annotations vary from 50 to 150 words in length. One of the most useful sections is a list of overseas Chinese newspapers, giving considerable information concerning each paper. No index.

Japanese language

G16. Irikura, James K. *Southeast Asia, selected annotated bibliography of Japanese publications.* New Haven, Southeast Asia studies, Yale University, in association with Human Relations Area Files, 1956. 544 p. (Behavior science bibliographies)

965 books covering reference materials, geography, history, political affairs, foreign relations, trade, health, education and minorities from the late nineteenth century to 1955. Titles are translated into English, and descriptive annotations are provided. Arranged by geographical areas, then broken down into broad subject groups. Locations in the Library of Congress, Yale, Harvard and Columbia Universities. Author index.

G17. Ichikawa, Kenjiro. *Southeast Asia viewed from Japan, a bibliography of Japanese works on Southeast Asian societies, 1940-1963.* Ithaca, Department of Asian Studies, Southeast Asia Program, Cornell University, 1965. 112 p. (Cornell University Department of Asian Studies, Southeast Asia Program Data Paper no.56)

2,594 entries are divided into five sections: reference works and bibliographies; Southeast Asia as a whole; mainland Southeast Asia, excluding Malaya; island Southeast Asia, including Malaya; and publications based on field research in South China, the Himalayan region and East India when subjects studied are related to Southeast Asia. Appendices include a list of serial publications, and indexes to authors and editors, the emphasis of the bibliography is on social science materials.

Russian language

G18. McVey, Ruth Thomas. *Bibliography of Soviet publications on Southeast Asia as listed in the Library of Congress Monthly Index of Russian acquisitions.* Ithaca, Department of Far Eastern Studies Southeast Asia Program, Cornell University, 1959. 109 p. (Cornell University. Department of Far Eastern Studies, Southeast Asia Program Data Paper no.34)

Approximately 2,000 books and periodicals referring to Southeast Asia and published from 1945 for books, and from 1947 for periodical articles. Entries are divided into thirteen sections, and arranged by author in each section. No index.

G19. Berton, Peter and Alvin Z. Rubinstein. *Soviet works on Southeast Asia, a bibliography of non-periodical literature, 1946-1965.* Los Angeles, University of Southern California Press, 1967. 201 p. (School of Political and International Relations, University of Southern California, Far Eastern and Russian Research Series no. 3)

Over 400 books are arranged by country, and then by broad subject divisions, no annotations. Author index. Contains an extensive introduction to Soviet Southeast Asian studies and translations into Russian from Southeast Asian languages.

Official publications

G20. Horne, Norman P. *A guide to published United States government publications pertaining to Southeast Asia, 1893-1941.* Washington, 1961. 147 p.

A Master of Arts in Library Science dissertation for Catholic University of America, based for the most part on the United States document *catalog* and on the *Monthly catalog of public documents* for 1941. Some 1800 entries cover commerce, foreign relations and the sciences. All of Southeast Asia, except the Philippines, is included. Arrangement by country then by subject. No index.

Periodicals

G21. Yale University. Library, Southeast Asia Collection. *Checklist of Southeast Asia serials.* Boston, G.K.Hall, 1969. 320 p.

Lists 3,800 serials in the Yale University Library system, giving up to August 1966 holdings for those in the Sterling Library. There is an index by country of origin and by subject.

Literature

G21.1. Jenner, Philip N. *A preliminary bibliography of Southeast Asian literatures in translation.* Honolulu, Department of Asian and Pacific Languages, University of Hawaii, 1970. 94 p.

Some 1,600 books and periodical articles compiled from library resources available at the University of Hawaii, represent a major new development in Southeast Asian bibliography. Arranged by country. No index since bibliography is in preliminary form.

History

G22. Hay, Stephen N., and Margaret M. Case. *Southeast Asian history, a bibliographic guide.* New York, Praeger, 1962. 138 p.

632 books, periodical articles and theses, mostly in English, and with no materials in Southeast Asian languages, are arranged by country, with further subdivision into bibliographies, books, articles and dissertations. Selection has been limited to materials most useful for the beginning student or teacher in Southeast Asian history. Separate author and subject indexes. Ceylon is included.

G23. Anderson, Gerald H. *Christianity in Southeast Asia, a bibliographical guide, an annotated bibliography of selected references in Western languages.* New York, Missionary Research Library, 1966. 69 p.

1,200 books, periodicals and periodical articles, not limited to Christianity, but including background history for Southeast Asia. New Guinea, Taiwan and Ceylon are also included. Nearly all entries have short annotations. Author index.

G24. Morrison, Gayle. *A guide to books on Southeast Asian history(1961-1966)* Santa Barbara, ABC-CLIO Press, 1969. 105 p.

556 annotated entries for books, almost entirely in English, are arranged by country, and then by author. The annotations are full and keyed to reviews. Supplements Stephen Hay and Margaret Case *Southeast Asian history, a bibliographic guide* (1962) and includes a few books published before 1961, and not found in this bibliography. Subject and author index.

H.BURMA

Lower Burma was acquired by Britain in 1852, following the Second Anglo-Burmese War, and much of the information concerning Burma from 1852 to 1937, when Burma became independent of India, can be found in Indian official publications. Burma became a sovereign state in 1948.

ENCYCLOPEDIA AND YEARBOOK

H 1. *Myanma svezon kyan* (Burmese encyclopedia) Yangon(i.e. Rangoon), Bathapyan Sabei Athin, 1954- v.1-
A well-produced encyclopedia in an attractive format, but initially giving little space to things Burmese. The proportion of space on Burma has increased as publication proceeds. No bibliographical notes with articles. Volume 10, published in 1966, last volume noted.

H 2. *Burma yearbook and directory,* 1957/58- Rangoon, Student Press, 1957-
Surveys government structure and lists officials, the diplomatic corps, the press, and has materials on Rangoon, and the States, communication, foreign aid, education, health, the economy, and has a short classified trades directory, now primarily of historical interest.

DICTIONARIES

H 3. Judson, Adoniram. *The Judson Burmese-English dictionary...* Rangoon, Baptist Board of Publications, 1953. 1,123 p.
Some 22,000 Burmese words are given with their English equivalents. A reprint of the prewar edition.

H 4. Judson, Adoniram. *English and Burmese dictionary...* Rangoon, Baptist Board of Publications, 1956. 928 p.
A reprint of the 1923 edition, unchanged except for page size, and containing some 27,000 words, with their equivalents in Burmese. Technical terms have been omitted and much of the work on the development of Burmese vocabulary in recent times is not represented. A new dictionary, J.A.S. Stewart and C.W.Dunn. *Burmese-English dictionary* (London, Luzac and Co., 1940-) based on 420,000 slips with words in their context, drawing from Burmese literature from the 15th century, and including colloquial and technical vocabulary, is in progress. The first 4 parts, representing a small fraction of the material, have been published.

BIOGRAPHICAL DICTIONARY

H 5. *Who's who in Burma,* 1961. Rangoon, People's Literature Committee and House, 1961. 220 p.

Not intended to be comprehensive and containing some 500 biographies only. Since the Burmese do not have family names, the last part of the given name of a biographee has been listed alphabetically. Occupation, date of birth, brief information including a list of publications and address is given. Many persons listed are now out of office, and those in office now are often not listed. Of less value today than in 1961.

DIRECTORY

H 6. *Burma trade directory,* 1952- Rangoon, Burma Commerce, 1952-

Arranged alphabetically by subject, with firms under each subject by nationality, 23 trades are listed. Appendices have information on Burmese trade and customs, list commission agents, importers and exporters. There is also a classified list of trades and of individual industrialists. Burmese industry is now nationalized and much of the information in the directory will be of historical value only. Issue for 1963/64 last noted.

GAZETTEER

H 7. U.S. Office of Geography. *Burma* ... Washington, Army Map Service, 1966. 725 p. (U.S. Board of Geographic Names, Gazetteer no.96)

52,600 entries for place and feature names in Burma. Each name is classified, and its longitude and latitude given.

CENSUS AND STATISTICS

H 8. Burma(Union). Census Division. *First stage census, 1953.* Rangoon, Government Printing and Stationery, 1957-58. 4 v.

The published work in four volumes includes the data collected for the first stage in 1953, where 248 cities in Burma and 4 in the Kachin area were surveyed, and for the second stage in 1954, when 2,143 villages in Burma and 1,016 in the Kachin area were covered. The first volume is for population and housing, the second for industry, the third for the Chin special division, and the fourth for agriculture. Since the census does not follow the pattern of previous ones, comparisons are difficult. The fourth volume and a second stage census, 1954, in four volumes are reported in *International population census bibliography, Asia,* but not seen. Previous census information will be found in the one or more Burma volumes of the decennial *Census of India,* from 1881 to 1931. The records of the 1941 census were destroyed during the Japanese occupation.

H 9. Burma(Union). Central Statistical and Economics Department. *Quarterly bulletin of statistics,* 1951- Rangoon, Superintendent, Central Press, Burma, 1951-
Issued quarterly, but often irregular, in Burmese and English text, and arranged under 15 heads, including population, labor, agriculture and forestry, industry, foreign trade, transportation, prices, indices, banking and taxation. Issues for 1963 last noted.

H10. Burma(Union). Central Statistics and Economics Department. *Statistical yearbook.* Rangoon, 19 -
The 1963 issue covers statistics, in some cases going back to the early 1950s, for population, health, education, labor, agriculture, forestry, industry, foreign trade, transportation, prices, and public finance. It has 362 pages, in 1967 a *Statistical pocket book* (104 p.) was issued by the Department.

BIBLIOGRAPHY

H11. New York University. Burma Research Project. *Annotated bibliography of Burma* prepared by F.N.Trager, J.N.Musgrave. New Haven, Human Relations Area Files, 1956. 240 p. (Behavior science bibliographies)
1,018 English language books and periodical articles on Burma divided into six groups, for bibliographies, books, pamphlets, periodical articles, selected Government of Burma publications, and 200 periodicals, all these are annotated, with evaluation for the first four. The sixth group is a topical bibliography with entries arranged in 21 divisions.

H12. Bernot, Denise. *Bibliographie birmane, annees 1950-1960.* Paris, Editions du Centre National de la Recherche Scientifique, 1968. 230 p.
Some 1,700 books and periodical articles are arranged by subject, and then by author. The author arrangement has the full citation together with brief annotations. There is an ethno-linguistic index. This bibliography is valuable since it contains some 230 items in Burmese.

Burmese language

H13. Barnett, Lionel David. *Catalogue of Burmese books in the British Museum.* London, British Museum, 1913. 346 col.
1,800 books published from the early 19th century are listed with an index of titles and an index of subjects including arts and sciences, grammar, lexicography and orthography, law, poetry and religion.

H14. Whitbread, Kenneth. *Catalogue of Burmese printed books in the India Office Library.* London, Her Majesty's Stationery Office, 1969. 231 p.
Lists some 2,800 titles arranged by title and representing the largest collection of Burmese books, and books translated from Burmese outside Burma. Author and subject index.

Official publications

H15. Burma(Union). Government Book Depot. *Catalogue of publications in stock at the Book Depot, Rangoon,* 1960, corrected up to 30th September 1960. Rangoon, 1961. 85 p.

A similar catalog has been issued under various titles since 1919. This issue lists some 2,500 publications, which are mostly acts, ordinances and statutes. Substantial publications account for a very small proportion of the total number of entries.

I. CAMBODIA

In 1863 a French protectorate was proclaimed over the Kingdom of Cambodia, which became part of French Indochina. Cambodia regained its complete independence in 1955.

DICTIONARIES

I 1. Pannetier, Adrien Louis Marie. *Lexique Francaise-Cambodgienne* nouvelle edition. Phnom-Penh, 1922. 505 p.
An enlarged edition of the 1907 Avignon version, which is also suitable. A handy little dictionary for its time, but because of its date, couched in now obsolete orthography and represents a form of Cambodian current before the present Standard Cambodian came into being. There are many typographical errors. The edition contains 11,500 words.

I 2. Guesdon, Joseph. *Dictionnaire Cambodgien-Francais.* Paris, Plon, 1930. 2 v. (Ministere de l'Instruction Publique et des Beaux-arts. Commission Archeologique de l'Indochine)
Far more scholarly than Pannetier, and still the best Khmer-French dictionary. Because of its date, the orthography is obsolete, and very many modern technical terms are not there. Very few errors. Contains some 20,000 words.

BIOGRAPHICAL DICTIONARY

I 3. *Personalites du Cambodge,* edition 1963. Phnom-Penh, Realites cambodgiennes, 1963. 303 p.
Contains approximately 350 biographies, but these are not substantial, since the format of the volume is small, and there are many portraits.

GAZETTEER

I 4. U.S. Office of Geography. *Cambodia...* Washington, U.S. Government Printing Office, 1963. 199 p. (Gazetteer no. 74)
14,000 entries for place and feature names, with their classification and longitude and latitude. A French type of romanization is used which is not suited to the English reader.

CENSUS AND STATISTICS

I 5. Cambodia. Ministere du Plan. *Statistical yearbook of Cambodia, 1937-1957.* Phnom-Penh, 1958. 214 p.

The official statistical yearbook but not published annually. Arranged under broad subject divisions, with the table of contents serving as an index. Population statistics may not be considered as reliable.

I 6. Cambodia. Ministere du Plan. *Annuaire statistique retrospectif du Cambodge, 1958-1961.* Phnom-Penh, 1962? 184 p.

Written in French, with no explanations or introduction, and organized by broad subjects. The table of contents is the only key to the yearbook. According to *International population census bibliography, Asia* a census was conducted in 1962, and published as Institut National de la Statistique et des Recherches economiques. *Resultats finals, recensement de 1962* (1965) in 13 volumes. This census report has not been seen.

BIBLIOGRAPHY

I 7. Dik Keam. *Catalogue des auteurs khmers et etrangers.* Phnom Penh, Association des ecrivains khmers, 1966. 24 p.

304 books mostly in Cambodian and on Buddhism form the first part of this bibliography. The second part contains an additional 380 Cambodian books arranged by author.

I 8. United Nations. E.C.A.F.E. Mekong Documentation Centre. *Cambodia, a select bibliography.* Bangkok, 1967. 101 p.

1,013 books, periodicals and periodical articles, emphasizing the modern period and the social sciences, are arranged in classified order. The bibliography is based on the resources of the E.C.A.F.E. Library in Bangkok. With exception of this and the *Cataloque des auteurs Khmers et etrangers,* there is no substantial bibliography of Cambodia outside the sections in Henri Cordier *Biblioteca Indosinica ...* And John Fee Embree *Bibliography of the peoples and cultures of mainland Southeast Asia.*

J.INDOCHINA including VIETNAM

French influence was first established in Indochina in 1787, but it was not until 1862-67 that Cochin China became a French colony. Cambodia became a French protectorate in 1863. In 1884 a French protectorate was proclaimed over Annam and Tongking, and in 1893 over Laos. Indochina was governed as one political unit from 1887. In 1954 the independent Democratic People's Republic of Vietnam was established in North Vietnam, the Republic of Vietnam in South Vietnam. Cambodia became independent in 1955, and Laos in 1956.

ENCYCLOPEDIA

J 1. *Viet-Nam bach-khoa tu-dien co bo chu chu Han, Phap, va Anh,* do Dao-dang-Vy. Dictionnaire encyclopedique Vietnamien, avec annotations en Chinois, Francais et Anglais. Vietnamese encyclopedic dictionary with annotations in Chinese, French and English. Saigon, 1960-61, v. 1-3, A-Ch.
The greater part of the this encyclopedia, some 60 per cent, is concerned with the anthropology, history, geography, literature and archeology of Vietnam. A remaining fifth is concerned with religion and philosophy, and the final fifth with science, technology and medicine. Articles are not signed, and no bibliography is given.

DICTIONARIES

J 2. Nguyen, Van-Khon. *English-Vietnamese dictionary.* Anh-Viet tu dien. In lan thu hai. Saigon, Khai-tri, 1955. 1741 p.
Over 50,000 English words, with their Vietnamese equivalents, together with examples of usage are given.
J 3. Dao, Duy-Anh. *Phap-Viet tu dien, Chu them chu Han.* Dictionnaire francais-vietnamien... Saigon, Truong-thi xuat ban, 1957. 1958 p.
Some 60,000 French words, with their equivalents in Chinese characters and Vietnamese are given with examples of usage.
J 4. Gouin, Eugene. *Dictionnaire vietnamien chinois francais.* Saigon, Imprimerie d'Extreme Orient(Ideo) 1957, 1,606 p.
Gives some 15,000 key entries, with approximately 150,000 compounds, and their translation into French. Chinese characters for the entries are given where appropriate. Character index.
J 5. Nguyen, Dinh-hoa. *Vietnamese-English dictionary.* Saigon, Binh-Minh, 1959. 568 p.
A compact dictionary with over 30,000 entries in Vietnamese, with their English equivalents. A revision of the author's *Vietnamese-English vocabulary* (Washington,1955).

DIRECTORIES

J 6. Sutter, John Orval. *Scientific and information services of the Republic of Vietnam.* Honolulu, published for the National Science Foundation by the Pacific Science Information Center, 1961. 236 p. (Pacific Science Information no.3)

The first part describes the geographical, political and economic situation in Vietnam in relation to science, and then goes on to discuss scientific manpower and training, research institutions and information activities. The appendices describe science teaching and research at the University of Saigon and the University of Hue. Lists 10 research institutes, 21 scientific publications, and 7 societies.

J 7. *A.E.C. Viet-Nam, annuaire industriel et commercial.* Industrial and commercial directory, 1962-63. Saigon, Trinh-Hung and Co., 1963?1 v. (various paging)

A directory of organizations, firms, importers, exporters, agencies, and some directory-type information for the provinces. Altogether some 28,000 entries.

BIOGRAPHICAL DICTIONARIES

J 8. Nguyen, Huyen-Anh. *Viet-Nam danh nhan tu dien* (Vietnam biographical dictionary) Saigon, Hoi van hoa binh dan, 1960. 380 p.

A dictionary of some 1,000 persons prominent in the history of Vietnam. Dates of birth and death, when known, are given, together with short accounts.

J 9. *Who's who in Vietnam.* Saigon? Vietnam Press, 1967.

Some 150 biographies of prominent South Vietnamese, bound in a loose-leaf format. 1968 issue supplements with another 170 biographies.

GAZETTEERS

J10. U.S. Office of Geography. *Northern Vietnam...* Washington, U.S.Government Printing Office, 1964. 311 p. (Gazetteer no. 79)

22,250 place and feature names are listed with their classification and longitude and latitude.

J11. U.S. Office of Geography. *South Vietnam and South China Sea...* Washington, U.S. Government Printing Office, 1961. 248 p. (Gazetteer no. 58)

17,000 place and features names for South Vietnam and a second list of 400 names for the South China Sea, with classification of the name, and its longitude and latitude.

CENSUS AND STATISTICS

J12. Indo-China, French. Service de la Statistique Generale. ... *Annuaire statistique de l'Indochine, 1913-48.* Hanoi, 1927-48.
Issued irregularly, and presenting departments and aspects of Indochina. Each issue may cover from one to as many as eight years, and was usually published one or two years after the date of the statistics it includes. Alphabetical index.

J13. Vietnam. Vien quoc-gia thong-ke (Institut national de la statistique) *Annuaire statistique du Vietnam,* 1949- Saigon, 1949-
Compiled with the cooperation of government and private agencies, and may cover one or two years, with a delay of one or two years in publication. The statistics are presented in tabular form under 14 main subjects. Published in three languages, Vietnamese, French and English from the 1956 issue. Indexed. Fourteenth issue for 1968-1969 noted.

J14. Vietnam. Vien quoc-gia thong-ke (Institut national de la statistique) *Enquetes demographiques au Vietnam en 1958.* Saigon, 1960. 122 p.
A special study of the population statistics of Vietnam in 1958, based on a census taken in that year. There are 16 headings under which information is given. The data on population is in much greater detail than that in the *Annuaire statistique...*

BIBLIOGRAPHY

J15. Boudet, Paul and Remy Bourgeois. *Bibliographie de l'Indochine francaise...* Hanoi, Imprimerie d'Extreme Orient, 1929-67. 4 v.
Continues the work of Henri Cordier *Biblioteca indosinica* from 1913, and includes books and periodical articles in French, on Indochina only. There are 4,500 entries in the first volume, and more periodical articles than books. Of the 30 most-cited periodicals, 11 are published in Indochina, and the remaining 14 in France. It has an alphabetical subject arrangement, with entries listed by author under each subject. The second part is an alphabetical index to authors, and to titles with anonymous authors. The second volume covering the period 1927 to 1929, was published in 1931 with 2,500 entries, the fourth, 1930 to 1935, contains 5,000 entries, including Vietnamese, and was published in 1967. V.3, for 1930, published in 1933, reported.

J16. Brebion, Antoine. *Dictionnaire de bio-bibliographie general ancienne et moderne de l'Indochine francaise...* Paris, Societe d'Editions geographiques, maritimes et coloniales, 1935. 446 p. (Academie des Sciences coloniales tome VIII)
Summaries of the lives of 1,600 persons prominent in the history of Indochina from 1859 to the 1930's, together with their publications. A subject approach to the persons listed is provided.

J17. U.S. Library of Congress. Reference Department. *Indochina, a bibliography of the land and people.* Washington, 1950. 367 p.

1,850 entries in Western, Vietnamese and Russian languages, published for the most part after 1930. Most entries are annotated to show relationship to other entries and to give additional information. The bibliography is arranged first by language, then by subject. Library locations are given. Indexed.

J18. Hanoi. Thu-vien quoc-gia(National Library) *Muc-luc xuat ban pham.* (Catalog of published works) Hanoi, 1954-

Lists books and other published materials received by the National Library on legal deposit. 2,850 titles of books, and 220 newspapers and periodicals were noted in the 1963 issue. Books are arranged by subject. There are separate sections for music, posters, maps, gramophone records, newspapers and periodicals. Indexes of authors, translators, and titles for books entered under title. The Library of the School of Oriental and African Studies has volumes for 1957 through 1963. 1964 issue published 1965.

J19. Hoc-vien quoc-gia hanh-chanh thu-vien (National Institute of Administration library) Saigon. *Ban thong ke phan-loai sach thu vien* Classified catalog of books in the Library. Saigon, 1960. 606 p.

A classified catalog of books in the library, together with a list of its periodical holdings. There are two subject indexes, one in English and the other in Vietnamese. Approximately 8,000 entries, of which some 60 percent are in English, 20 per cent are in French and 20 per cent are in Vietnamese.

J20. Michigan. State University of Agriculture and Applied Science. East Lansing. Vietnam Advisory Group, Saigon. *What to read on Vietnam, a selected annotated bibliography.* New York, Institute of Pacific Relations, 1960. 73 p.

Lists some 300 books and periodical articles, mostly in English for the period from 1955 to the end of 1959, divided into two parts, the first to November 1958, and a supplement. There is in addition a valuable listing of periodicals, the first part for current publications and the second for periodicals no longer published.

J21. Vietnam. Nha van kho va thu-vien quoc-gia (Directorate of National Archives and Libraries) *Sach moi* Nouvelles acquisitions, 1962-68. Saigon, 1962-68.

A monthly list recording in a subject arrangement approximately 100 books, periodicals and newspapers in Vietnamese and other languages received by the National Library through legal deposit, exchange with other countries, purchases and donations. Author index.

J22. Keyes, Jane Godfrey. *A bibliography of North Vietnamese publications in Cornell University Library.* Ithaca, Southeast Asia Program, Department of Asian Studies, Cornell University, 1962. 116 p. (Cornell University Department of Asian Studies, Southeast Asia Program. Data Paper no.47)

Contains some 800 works in English and French on North Vietnam from 1945 to 1960. The materials are arranged into nine major subjects, and each of these has been divided into a pre-1954 and a post-1954 period.

Materials translated by the Joint Publications Research Service have been annotated. The table of contents has to serve in place of an index, and since there are no cross references, the user will have to check all subjects which appear to be relevant. Supplemented by the author's *A bibliography of Western language publications concerning North Vietnam in the Cornell University Library.* (1966)

J23. Vietnam. Bo thong tin (Ministry of Information) *Tin tuc thu tich, luoc ke cac loai sach moi nhan duoc* (News of bibliography, with listing of new publications received) Saigon, 1964-
A listing of publications received by the Ministry for censorship purposes, and arranged in classified order. In latest issue noted, no.53, published in February 1969, 220 items are listed. Copy in National Library, Saigon.

J24. Auvade, R. *Bibliographie critique des oeuvres parus sur l' Indochine francaise, un siecle d'histoire et d'enseignement.* Paris, Maisonneuve, 1965. 153 p.
Lists 230 works, nearly all in French, of which 150 are arranged under 13 subjects and are fully annotated and cover the period from 1850 to 1950, although the works themselves may be published as late as the 1960s. Has useful indexes by subjects and by author. The first part deals with the history of archives and libraries in Indochina.

J25. Keyes, Jane Godfrey. *A bibliography of Western language publications concerning North Vietnam in the Cornell University Library.* Ithaca, Southeast Asia Program, Department of Asian Studies, Cornell University, 1966. 280 p. (Cornell University, Southeast Asia Program Data Paper no. 63)
2,500 books and serials in Western languages and Russian are arranged in two parts. The first has a subject arrangement covering description, culture, biography, economic conditions, social conditions, politics and government and foreign relations. The second part, over half of the book, consists of J.P.R.S. translations from Vietnamese. Supplements but does not replace the author's *A bibliography of North Vietnamese publications in Cornell University Library.* (1962)

J26. Vietnam. National Commission for U.N.E.S.C.O. *Thu muc chu giai ve van hoa viet-nam* Commented bibliography on Vietnamese culture. Saigon, 1966. 226 p.
229 entries for books, periodicals and periodical articles on anthropology, language and writing, technology, and arts, in French and Vietnamese, with annotations. There is in addition a list of 153 books published in France from 1945-54 on Vietnam. No index.

J27. United Nations. E.C.A.F.E. Mekong Documentation Centre. *Vietnam, a reading list* . Bangkok, 1966. 119 p.
1,251 books and articles, nearly all in French and English, subdivided into a large number of subjects. No index.

J27.1. Vietnam. Nha van kho va thu vien quoc gia(Directorate of National Archives and Libraries) *Thu muc.* Catalogue of books. Saigon, 1965-
Each annual issue notes some 1,500 books, mostly in Vietnamese, and mostly current imprints. Entries are arranged by the Dewey Decimal

Classification. Author index. Last issue noted for 1968.
J28. Vietnam. Nha van kho va thu vien quoc-gia(Directorate of National Archives and Libraries) *Thu tich quoc-gia Viet-Nam* National bibliography of Vietnam, 1967- Saigon, 1968-
Intended to be a quarterly publication, listing new publications arranged by the Dewey Decimal Classification, with author and title indexes. Official publications and serials are excluded. A combined issue no.2 and 3, published September 1968 noted.

Official publications
J28.1. Vietnam. Nha van kho va thu vien quoc gia(Directorate of National Archives and Libraries) *Thu tich ve an pham cong Viet-Nam*. Bibliography on Vietnamese official publications, (1960-1969) Saigon, 1969. 134 p.
717 titles, almost entirely in Vietnamese, are arranged by bureau. Title and author index.

Periodicals and newspapers
J29. Vietnam. Tong-bo van-hoa xa-hoi(Ministry of Cultural and Social Affairs) *Muc-luc bao-chi Viet-ngu, 1865-1965* (Catalog of newspapers and periodicals published in Vietnamese, 1865-1965) Saigon, 1966. (182) p.
1280 newspapers and periodicals are arranged in order of date of first publication, with dates of ceasing publication also noted. There is some annotation of entries. Alphabetical index to titles.
J30. Tran, Thi Kimsa. *Muc-luc phan-tich tap-chi Viet-ngu, 1954-1964*. A guide to Vietnamese periodical literature,1954-1964. Saigon, Hoc-vien quoc-gia hanh-chanh, 1965. 318 p.
1,976 articles in Vietnamese from 7 periodicals, arranged by subject and not limited to materials on Vietnam. Author index.
J31. Tran, Thi Kimsa. *Bibliography on Vietnam,1954-1964*. Thu tich ve Viet--Nam, 1954-1964. Saigon, National Institute of Administration, 1965. 255 p.
Some 3,000 books and articles from over 100 periodicals in French, Vietnamese and in English, but mostly in English, published in Vietnam and elsewhere, arranged by subjects. Author index.
J31.1. Vietnam. Nha van kho va thu vien guoc gia(Directorate of National Archives and Libraries) *An pham dinh ky quoc noi,1968*. (Comprehensive list of Vietnamese serials) Saigon, 1969? 32 p.
Lists 186 newspapers and periodicals published in South Vietnam in 1968, noting publisher, editor and address. Entries are arranged in order of frequency of publication. Title index.
J31.2. Nunn, G.Raymond. *Vietnam, Cambodia and Laos, an international union list of newspapers*. Honolulu, 1970. 57 p.
The preliminary checklist lists 137 newspapers published in Cambodia, 36 newspapers published in Laos, and 550 newspapers published in Vietnam. Titles are arranged by country, and subarranged by place. Holdings are given for the Bibliotheque nationale in Phnom Penh, the National Library of Vietnam in Saigon, the Bibliotheque nationale in Paris, and for major collections in the United States.

Social sciences

J32. Ti, Tang-Ti. *Muc-luc phan-tich tap-chi khoa-hoc xa-hoi Viet-Nam, 1958-62* Index to Vietnamese social science periodicals. Saigon, Hoc-vien quoc-gia hanh-chanh, 1961-63. 2 v.
The first volume covers 1958 to 1960, the second 1961 and 1962. Only four periodicals are indexed, and entries are arranged by subject. Each volume has an author index.

J33. Bui, Quynh and Nguyen Hung-Cuong. *Thu-tich ve khoa-hoc xa-hoi tai Viet-Nam, 1960-1962.* Elenchus bibliographicus scientiarum socialium in Viet-Nam. Saigon, 1962.
313 books and periodical articles arranged in 12 broad subject groups. Author index.

J33.1. U.S. Department of the Army. Engineer Agency for Resources Inventories. *Vietnam, subject index maps.* Washington, 1970. 182 p.
182 black and white copies of maps of Vietnam are arranged in 24 subject groups. A list of sources given. No index.

J33.2. U.S. Department of the Army. Engineer Agency for Resources Inventories. *Vietnam, subject index catalog.* Washington, 1970. 288 p.
Arranges some 4,000 reports and books, a high proportion of which originate from the Agency for International Development, in broad subject groups. Most of the entries are held by the Library of the A.I.D. Vietnam Bureau or the Engineer Agency for Resources Inventories. No index.

J33.3. U.S. Department of the Army. Engineeer Agency for Resources Inventories. *Vietnam, a selected annotated bibliography, agriculture.* Washington, 1970. 58 p.
Some 300 annotated entries, largely reports from U.S. official sources on of agriculture in contemporary Vietnam. The reports are held in the library of the Vietnam Bureau of the Agency for International Development or in the Engineeer Agency for Resources Inventories.

History

J34. Jumper, Roy. *A bibliography on the political and administrative history of Vietnam,1802-1962.* Saigon, Michigan State University, Vietnam Advisory Group, 1962. 179 p.
964 books and periodical articles in French, English and Vietnamese, of which about one-half are on historical subjects. The materials are arranged under broad subjects, some of which are further subdivided. Annotations are brief. Author index.

J35. Nguyen, The-Anh. *Bibliographie critique sur les relations entre le Viet-Nam et l'Occident, ouvrages et articles en langues occidentales.* Paris, Maisonneuve & Larose, 1967. 310 p.
1,635 books and archive sources, almost entirely in French are arranged in a classified order, with an index to authors and personal names.

K.INDONESIA

The Dutch became established in Indonesia in the beginning of the 17th century, and maintained control of the area until 1949, when Indonesia became independent. From 1811 to 1816, and from 1942 to 1945, there were brief interludes of British and Japanese occupation respectively.

ENCYCLOPEDIAS AND YEARBOOKS

K 1. *Encyclopaedie van Nederlandsch-Indie.* 's Gravenhage, M. Nijhoff, 1917-39. 8 v.
The first four volumes were published from 1917 to 1921, and have been abridged in the *Beknopte encylopaedie van Nederlandsch-Indie.* Volumes 5-8 are supplements to the first four volumes, and were published from 1927 to 1939. Scholarly in treatment, but lacking illustration and maps, this encyclopedia remains an excellent source for the Dutch period. In Dutch.
K 2. *Ensiklopedia Indonesia.* Bandung, The Hague, W. Van Hoeve, 1954-57? 3 v.
A general encyclopedia not restricted to Indonesia, but with an emphasis on Asia. The treatment is popular, with short articles, and black and white photographs and drawings. The value of this encyclopedia lies mostly in its information on Southeast Asia. For other areas it is often dated and less reliable. No index. In Indonesian.
K 3. Dutch East Indies. Departement van Landbouw, Nijverheid, en Handel. *Handbook of the Netherlands East Indies.* Buitenzorg, 1916-30. 4 v.
An official survey of the Netherlands East Indies, with some statistics, and covering population, government, finance, farming, industry, commerce and communications. Issued in 1916, 1920, 1924 and 1930. The 1916 and 1920 issues have title: *Yearbook of the Netherlands East Indies.*

DICTIONARIES

K 4. Pino, Elisabeth and Tamme Wittermans. *Kamus Inggeris.* Djakarta, J.B.Wolters, 1955. 2 v.
This dictionary is oriented towards general and school use in Indonesia. The English-Indonesian volume has over 80,000 words, and the Indonesian-English volume some 15,000 words. Examples of usage are given. An unrevised reprint of the 1953 edition.
K 5. Echols, John H., and Hassan Shadily. *An Indonesian-English dictionary,* second edition. Ithaca, Cornell University Press, 1963. 431 p.
A revision of the 1961 edition with some 12,000 words and intended for

the reader of contemporary materials. Among its excellent features are numerous technical terms and examples of usage.

DIRECTORIES

K 6. *Directory of scientific institutions in Indonesia.* Djakarta, Council for Sciences of Indonesia, 1959. 80 p. (Madjelis ilmu pengetahuan Indonesia. Bulletin no. 1)
106 institutions are listed first by geographical area, then alphabetically by name, with information on address, objectives, name of director, publications, the library and a brief history. There is a subject index.

K 7. Sutter, John Orval. *Scientific facilities and information services of the Republic of Indonesia.* Honolulu, published for the National Science Foundation by the Pacific Science Information Center, 1961. 136 p. (Pacific Scientific Information no. 1)
Detailed information on ten institutions of higher education, surveying scientific education and training. Appendix A and B list another 49 institutions, Appendix C lists scientific publications in Indonesia, and Appendix D 18 scientific societies. Address, membership and sometimes a short history is given for the institutions and societies. Since data was collected in early 1959, this directory is more of historical interest. Indexed.

K 8. Thee,Tjoen Giap. *Pedoman sekolah-sekolah di Indonesia* (Guide to Indonesian schools) Djakarta, Penerbit Kinta, 1962. 177 p.
299 schools are arranged geographically, and information is given on courses of instruction, length of schooling and location. Alphabetical index.

ATLAS

K 9. *Atlas van tropisch Nederland.* Amsterdam, Koninklijk Nederlandsch Aardrijkskundig Genootschap, 1938. 79 maps, including historical maps. Since this atlas covers the whole of the tropical Netherlands colonies, Surinam and Curacao are included with the East Indies. Maps show the sea, flora and fauna, rainfall, and administrative divisions. Each map has an explanatory note in German, French, Dutch and English. The second revised edition of this publication originally issued in 1923. Alphabetical index.

GAZETTEER

K10. U.S. Office of Geography. *Indonesia and Portuguese Timor...* Second edition. Washington, U.S. Government Printing Office, 1968. 901 p. (Gazetteer no.13)
60,000 place and feature names in Indonesia and 600 in Portuguese

Timor in a separate list, with classification of the names and their longitude and latitude.

CENSUS AND STATISTICS

K11. Dutch East Indies. Central Kantoor voor de Statistiek in Nederlandsch-Indie. *Statistisch jaaroverzicht van Nederlandsch-Indie.* Batavia, Landsdrukkerij, 1923-40.
A wealth of statistical tables surveying population, health, education, religion, law, economy, agriculture, trade and finance, and communications. From 1930, this yearbook appeared as Part II of the *Indisch verslag.* For earlier statistical information on the Dutch East Indies, the best source is Netherlands. Departement van Kolonien. *Kolonial verslag,* 1849-1930('s Gravenhage,1850-1930). In Dutch and English.

K12. Dutch East Indies. Departement van Economische Zaken. *Volkstelling,* 1930. Batavia, 1933-36. 8 v.
Volumes 1-5 survey population, races, social conditions, literacy, religion and occupations, and are arranged by region. Volume 6 surveys Europeans, volume 7 Chinese and other Orientals and volume 8 is a summary report. In Dutch and English. A census was also undertaken in 1920. There was no census for 1940.

K13. Indonesia. Biro pusat statistik. *Statistical pocketbook of Indonesia,* 1941- Djakarta, 1947-
Issued for 1941 and 1947, and has appeared annually since 1957. Organized under major subjects into some 300 tables, and compiled from data supplied by government bureaus, in particular, the Statistical Bureau. It also contains a description of the statistics collection process in Indonesia. 1963 issue, published in 1963 noted.

K14. Nugroho. *Indonesia, facts and figures.* Djakarta, Terbitan pertjobaan, 1967. 608 p.
A comprehensive compilation of Indonesian statistics, based on official sources, with data ranging from 1950 to 1965. The section for population includes the Census results for 1961. Other sections are for labor, social statistics, agriculture, manufacturing and power, trade and transport, money and banking. An appendix describes statistical procedures in Indonesia.

BIBLIOGRAPHY

Bibliography to 1941
K15. Sudjatmoko. *An introduction to Indonesian historiography.* Ithaca, Cornell University Press, 1965. 427 p.
Soedjatmoko, the editor of this book, has long been concerned with the development of Indonesian history, and while this is primarily a book on historiography, it is also a valuable annotated and select bibliography,

surveying Javanese, Malay, Dutch, Japanese, Chinese, English and Soviet sources. Individual articles are written by some of the outstanding scholars in the field.

Dutch colonial bibliography

K16. Coolhaas, Willem Ph. *A critical survey of studies on Dutch colonial history.* 's Gravenhage, M. Nijhoff, 1960. 144 p. Instituut voor Taal-, Land-, en Volkenkunde. Bibliographical series 4)

Consists of six chapters, covering archives, journals, books of travel, the area covered by the Dutch East India Company (V.O.C.), the Netherlands East Indies after 1795, and the area covered by the charter of the Westindische Companie. Items cited are in Dutch, English, French and Spanish. Since this is in the form of a bibliographical essay, comments on materials will be found in the text. Personal names index.

K17. Hooykaas,J.C. *Repertorium op de koloniale literatuur of systematische inhoudsopgaaf van hetgeen. voorkomt over de kolonien (beoosten de Kaap) in mengelwerken en tijdschriften, van 1595 tot 1865 uitgegeven in Nederland en zijne overzeesche bezittingen.* Amsterdam, p.n. Van Kampen & Zoon, 1877-80, 2 v.

Includes books, periodicals and other printed material published in the Netherlands and its colonies from 1595 to 1865. The first volume is divided into two parts, the first on the country, and the second on the people, and contains 10,500 items. The second volume has its first part on government, and its second on science. It contains 10,873 entries. Each part is further divided into more specific subjects, and many entries are annotated. There is a general index. Continued by, and bound in the same volume in the University of Hawaii copy, A. Hartmann *Repertorium op de litteratuur ...* (1895.)

K18. Hartmann, A., and others. *Repertorium op de litteratuur betreffende de Nederlandsche Kolonien voor zoover zij verspreid is in tijdschriften en mengelwerken.I. Oost Indie, 1866-1893, II. West-Indie, 1840-1893, met een alphabetisch zaak- en plaatsregister* 's Gravenhage, M. Nijhoff, 1895. 454 p.

Some 12,000 books and periodical articles in Dutch, German, French, Latin and Italian, divided into two parts. The first and by far the greatest part on the East Indies is further divided into sections for country and people, history, government and economics. These sections are further subdivided. There is a general index. Continues J. C. Hooykaas *Repertorium op de koloniale litteratuur...* (Amsterdam). 1877-80, 2 v. Supplements 1-8 for 1894 to 1932 were published from 1901 to 1934, with some 54,000 books and periodical articles, almost entirely on the East Indies, and arranged in subject order, with indexes.

K19. Hague. Koloniale Bibliotheek. *Catalogus der Koloniale bibliotheek van het Kon. Instituut voor de Taal-, Land-, en Volkenkunde van Ned. Indie en het Indische Genootschap.* 's Gravenhage, M.Nijhoff, 1908. 1053 p.

Approximately 26,000 books, periodicals and newspapers are arranged geographically, subdivided into 78 broad subjects, and further divided chronologically. The books are in Dutch, French, German, Spanish, Indonesian and English. There is a subject and title index. Supplements were issued in 1915, 1927, 1937 and 1966, and are similarly arranged as the main work. The 1966 supplement includes acquisitions received through 1959.

Indonesian bibliography

K20. Chijs, Jacobus Anne van der. *Proeve eener Nederlandsche-Indische bibliographie(1659-1870)* Batavia, Bruining, 1875. 325 p. (Bataviaasch Genootschap van Kunsten en Wettenschappen, Verhandelingen v.37.)
Approximately 3,000 books, mostly in Dutch, but with some in Javanese and Malay, are arranged chronologically by date of publication, with separate author-title and subject indexes. Lists of printers and publishers and of newspapers and periodicals are appended. Supplement I, published in 1880, appeared in *Verhandelingen...* v. 39 and supplement II, published in 1903, in *Verhandelingen...* v. 55

K21. Ockeloen, G. *Catalogus van boeken en tijdschriften uitgeven in Nederlandsch Oost-Indie van 1870-1937.* Batavia, Kolff, 1940. 2 v.
Approximately 10,000 books published in the Netherlands East Indies from 1870 to 1937, and continuing Jacobus Anne van der Chijs *Proeve...* (1875) entries in volume 1 are mostly in Dutch, but with some English, French and German titles. Volume 2 contains titles in Indonesian. The bibliography is arranged by author and the lack of an index makes it difficult to locate material on a subject, unless the reader happens to know the authors in the field. An appendix to volume I lists some 500 Indonesian publishing houses and printing firms, arranged by location. Continued by G. Ockeloen *Catalogus...* (1942)

K22. Ockeloen, G. *Catalogus van in Nederlandsch-Indie verschenen boeken in de jaren 1938-1941 en enkele aanvullingen op de gestencilde catalogus verschenen in 1939.* Batavia, Kolff, 1942. 322 p.
An author catalog of some 4,500 books, written almost entirely in Dutch. A second volume for Indonesian language materials lost. No index.

Regional bibliography

BALI AND LOMBOK
K23. Lekkerkerker, Cornelius. *Bali en Lombok, overzicht der litteratuur omtrent deze eilanden tot einde 1919.* Rijswijk, Blankwaardt & Schoonhoven, 1920. 456 p.
Over 800 books and periodical articles listed mostly in Dutch; divided into five parts, the first consisting of books, the second of periodical articles, the third of books and articles not exclusively concerned with Bali and Lombok, the fourth on government publications and the fifth on maps. Each part is divided by subject. Author and subject index. Continued by G. Goris *Overzicht over de belangrijkste litteratuur betreffende Bali over het tijdvak, 1920-1935.* 31 p., with 247 entries for Bali.

MOLUCCAS

K24. Molukken Instituut, Amsterdam. *Overzicht van de literatuur betreffende de Molukken.* Amsterdam, 1928-

Over 4,000 books and periodical articles have been compiled by W.Ruinen, the archivist of the Molukken Instituut. Divided into three parts, the first containing materials exclusively about the Moluccas, the second periodical articles, and the third books not exclusively dealing with the Moluccas. Each part is arranged chronologically, and the materials listed are in the Koloniale Bibliotheek, the Library of the Ministry of Colonial Affairs, or, if not in these two, the location will be stated. Entries are almost entirely in Dutch and annotated. Subject and title index.

SUMATRA

K25. Joustra, M. *Litteratuur overzicht de Bataklanden.* Leiden, L. H. Becherer, 1907. 180 p.

Divided into six major geographical sections, then subarranged by a uniform subject division. Some 2,000 books and periodical articles, mostly in Dutch, are listed with some entries going back as far as 1826.

K26. Wellan,J. W. J., and H. L. Helfrich. *Zuid Sumatra, overzicht van de litteratuur der gewesten Bengkoelen, Djambi, de Lampongsche districten en Palembang*. 's Gravenhage, H. L. Smits, 1923-38.

Lists some 5,000 books, maps, periodicals and periodical articles, almost entirely in Dutch, and arranged by kind of publication, then by author. Volume 1 covers the period to the end of 1915, volume 2 from 1916-25. Annotated. Subject and author index.

NEW GUINEA

K27. Galis, Klaas Wilhelm. *Bibliographie van Nederlands-Nieuw Guinea,* 3e verbeterde en vemeerderde uitg. Den Haag, 1962. 275 p.

Some 6,300 books and periodical articles in Dutch, English, French, German and Indonesian, are arranged by alphabetical author order. The entries have been largely compiled from the collections of the Volkenkundig Instituut te Utrecht, the Koninklijke Instituut de Tropen te Amsterdam in Hollandia, and other bibliographies.

Bibliography after 1941

K28. U. S. Library of Congress. General Reference and Bibliography Division. *Netherlands East Indies, a bibliography of books published after 1930, and periodical articles published after 1932, available in U. S. Libraries.* Washington,1945. 208 p.

Some 2,700 books and periodical articles in Dutch and English are arranged in a detailed subject arrangement including geography, history, economics, social conditions, language and literature, the arts, religion, government and administration, law and individual islands. Indexes for authors, anonymous works and titles. Supplements A. Hartmann *Repertorium op de litteratuur* ... (1895) and supplements for 1894-1932, for periodical articles.

Indonesian language

K29. Echols, John M. *Preliminary checklist of Indonesian imprints during the Japanese period, March 1942-August 1945, with annotations.* Ithaca, Modern Indonesian Project, Southeast Asia Program, Department of Asian Studies, Cornell University, 1963. 56 p. (Cornell University, Modern Indonesia Project, Bibliography series)

Lists 252 entries, of which 216 are monographs, 6 almanacs, 16 newspapers and 13 periodicals, mostly published in Java and Sumatra. Arranged first by form of material, then alphabetically by author or title. To compile the list, American libraries and the library of the Lembaga Kebudajaan Nasional were searched. Only 139 of the entries cited are in Cornell University Library. Estimated that only one-half of the books published in this period are represented. Annotated. Author and title indexes.

K30. Echols, John M. *Preliminary checklist of Indonesian imprints, 1945-1949, with Cornell University holdings.* Ithaca, Southeast Asia Program, Department of Asian Studies, Cornell University, 1965. 186 p. (Modern Indonesia Program. Bibliography series)

1,782 books in an author/title arrangement, with an index to subjects, and to co-authors, editors, preface writers, and variant spellings. Some 750 of the entries represented in the Cornell University Library.

K31. Stanford University. Hoover Institution for War, Revolution and Peace. *Indonesian language publications in the Hoover Library.* Stanford, California, 1953. 21 l.

Approximately 450 entries published from the 1940s to the early 1950s arranged alphabetically by author. No annotations. Important for locating Indonesian materials in the united States.

K32. Ockeloen, G. *Catalogus dari buku-buku jang diterbitkan di Indonesia, 1945-54.* (Catalog of books published in Indonesia, 1945-54) Bandung, Gedung Buku Nasional, 1950-55. 4 v.

Dictionary-type arrangement, compiled by Mr. Ockeloen, who resigned as director of the Office of National Bibliography in 1954, and returned to the Netherlands in 1958. Later volumes may include books with earlier imprints which have not been previously reported. The bibliography depended on the voluntary cooperation of the publishers, and is not complete. Since not all books were personally inspected by the compiler, some of the descriptions are bibliographically deficient. There are some 1,700 books noted in each volume. The first volume is partly superseded for 1945-49 imprints by John M. Echols *Preliminary checklist of Indonesian imprints, 1945-49, with Cornell University holdings* (1965), but contains 1937-41 imprints also.

K33. Indonesia. Kantor bibliografi nasional (Office of National Bibliography) *Berita bulanan dari Kantor bibliografi nasional,* 1953-62. (Monthly report of the Office of National Bibliography) Djakarta, 1953-62. 10 v.

The Office of National Bibliography was established in January 1953, and was given the responsibility of compiling a listing of books, periodicals and government reports, and eventually a cumulated national bibliography. In 1956 it was transferred to the Jajasan Lektur, where it remained for two years. It is now under the Ministry of Education. Although monthly publication was intended, it has appeared irregularly. Arrangement is according to the Dewey Decimal Classification. New periodicals and some non-confidential government reports are noted. No index. Since there is no legal deposit law in force in Indonesia, bibliographical reporting depends of the voluntary cooperation of the publishers. Less coverage than the *Berita bibliografi*. Continued by *Bibliografi nasional Indonesia*, 1963-65.

K34. *Berita bibliografi*, 1955- (Bibliographical report, 1955-) Djakarta, Gunung Agung, 1955-
Lists publications in Indonesian, published in Indonesia and elsewhere, together with some Malayan books. It was compiled and issued as a monthly, with annual cumulations, and later as a quarterly. Dewey Decimal Classification is used, with author and title indexes. The 1961 cumulative index lists some 3,700 entries. On manuscript and not published in 1967 and 1968. March-April 1969 last issue noted.

K35. *Bibliografi nasional Indonesia, kumulasi, 1945-1963*. Djakarta, P. N. Balai Pustaka, 1965. 2 v.
Some 15,000 publications are arranged by author, with subject and author indexes. The 1964-65 supplement contains 796 entries arranged by the Universal Decimal Classification. No annotation. Goverment publications are not included since these are to be found in Rusina Sjahrial-Pamuntjak *Daftar penerbitan pemerintah Republik Indonesia*.

K36. U.S. Library of Congress. American Libraries Book Procurement Center, Djakarta. *Accessions list, Indonesia*, v.1, no.1- July 1964- Djakarta, 1964-
This monthly listing of Indonesian publications sent to selected U.S. Research libraries is arranged alphabetically by author or title. Serials are noted with an S and there is a cumulated list of these issued each year. A cumulated index to authors is issued with each volume. Short annotations are usually little more than a translation of the title. Now the most comprehensive bibliographical listing for Indonesia.

K37. Ikatan Penerbit Indonesia(Ikapi) O.P.S. Penerbitan *Daftar buku 20 tahun penerbitan Indonesia, 1945-1965*. Djakarta, 1965. 416 p.
Some 12,000 entries in a classified arrangement, with official publications listed on p.373-416. Since this cumulated list was published before the coup in 1965, there are many omissions of important writers and their works. No annotations and no index.

Official publications
K38. Lev, Daniel S. *Bibliography of Indonesian government documents and selected Indonesian writings on government in the Cornell University Library*. Ithaca, Southeast Asia Program, Cornell University, 1958. 58 p. (Cornell University. Southeast Asia Program, Data Paper no. 31)
424 items, mostly in Indonesian, but some in English. No Dutch materials are included. The entries are arranged by subject, and subarranged by issuing agencies. Holdings of periodicals are noted. No annotation

other than translation of titles. No index.

K39. Sjahrial-Pamuntjak, Rusina. *Daftar penerbitan pemerintah Republik Indonesia* (List of government publications of the Republic of Indonesia) Djakarta, Perpustakaan Sedjarah Politik dan Sosial, 1964. 56 p.

1,159 books and periodicals, almost entirely in Indonesian are arranged by department. Author index.

Periodicals and newspapers

K40. Indonesia. Biro Perpustakaan (Bureau of Libraries) *Checklist of serials in Indonesian Libraries* Katalogus induk sementara madjalah pada perpustakaan di Indonesia. Djakarta, Biro Perpustakaan de.P.D.Da K., 1962. 3 v.

A union list of periodicals published from 1956 held by Indonesian libraries. The first and second volumes note some 5,000 foreign serials and the third lists some 2,000 Indonesian serials. The entries are arranged alphabetically by title, except for those issued by corporate bodies, which are issued under the latest form of the name.

K41. Echols, John M., and Yvonne Thung. *A guide to Indonesian serials, 1945-1965, in the Cornell University Library.* Ithaca, Modern Indonesia Project, Southeast Asia Program, Department of Asian Studies, Cornell University, 1966. 151 p. (Bibliographical series)

1,102 serials listed alphabetically by title, showing holdings. Government publications, reports, annual reports of commercial firms and institutions are also included. This guide updates, except for newspapers, Benedict F. Anderson *Bibliography of Indonesian publications, newspapers, non-government periodicals and bulletins, 1945-1958, at Cornell University* (Ithaca, 1959)

K41.1. Nunn,G.Raymond. *Indonesian newspapers, an international union list.* Honolulu, 1970. 96 p.

A preliminary checklist noting holdings for 970 newspapers published in Indonesia, and located in the Pusat Museen Perpustakaan in Djakarta, in the Koninklijk Bibliotheek in the Hague, in the Koninklijk Instituut voor de Tropen library in Amsterdam, and in major libraries in the United States.

PERIODICAL INDEXES AND ABSTRACTS

K42. *Indonesian abstracts, containing abstracts of scientific articles appearing in Indonesia,* 1959- Djakarta, Madjelis Ilmu Pengetahuan Indonesia, Council for Sciences of Indonesia, 1959-

Each issue contains about 60 abstracts from about 20 Indonesian periodicals, covering all fields of science. The abstracts are in English, and are arranged according to the Universal Decimal Classification. No index. Science is widely interpreted and covers the whole field of knowledge. January-April 1968 last issue noted.

K43. *Index of Indonesian learned periodicals,* 1960- Djakarta, Madjelis Ilmu Pengetahuan Indonesia, Council for Sciences of Indonesia, 1961-

The 1967 issue listed 150 periodicals, and indexed over 454 articles with an emphasis on natural and applied science and the social sciences. The arrangement is by the Universal Decimal Classification. Title index to the periodicals, and author index to the articles. No annotation. First issued with title *Indeks madjalah ilmiah.* Indonesian periodicals index.

Subject bibliography

SOCIAL SCIENCES

K44. Sjahrial-Pamuntjak, Rusina. *Regional bibliography of social science publications, Indonesia.* Djakarta, Ministry of Education and Culture, National Bibliographical Centre, 1955? 65 p.

Lists 594 books and periodical articles in Dutch, English and Indonesian, with an emphasis on the latter, and published from 1945 through 1954. There is an index to authors and subjects, and a list of the 14 principal periodicals indexed. Arranged into 4 major sections.

K45. Suzuki, Peter. *Critical survey of studies on the anthropology of Nias, Mentawei and Enggano.* 's Gravenhage, M. Nijhoff, 1959. 87 p. (Instituut voor Taal-, Land-, en Volkenkunde. Bibliographical series 3)

Some 365 books and periodical articles in Indonesian, English and German. Arranged according to the three cultures, with a section for each. Items inspected by the compiler are annotated.

K46. Jaspan, M. A. *Social stratification and social mobility in Indonesia, a trend report and annotated bibliography.* Djakarta, Seri Ilmu dan Masjarakat, Gunung Agung, 1959. 76 p.

139 articles, of which over half are in Indonesian, are arranged under 6 major categories showing aspects of social structure. 100 entries are annotated fully. The trend report describes the pre- and post-revolutionary periods.

K47. Kennedy, Raymond. *Bibliography of Indonesian peoples and cultures* revised and edited by Thomas W. Maretzki and H. Th. Fischer. New Haven, Southeast Asia Studies, Yale University, by arrangement with Human Relations Area Files, 1962. 207 p. (Behavior Science bibliographies)

Over 11,600 books and periodical articles, over half in Dutch, arranged by islands and island groups, then by peoples, tribes or tribal groups and entries are subdivided within these into Dutch and other languages. The emphasis is on anthropology and sociology, but administration, education, economics, history and geography, with some references to botany, zoology and geology are included. An alphabetical key to islands, peoples, tribal groups and tribes assists in the use of the table of contents. At first books and articles in Yale University Library were marked with an asterisk, but in the revised edition only important items were so marked, leading to confusion.

K48. Hicks, George L., and Geoffrey McNicoll. *The Indonesian economy, 1950-1965, a bibliography.* Detroit, Cellar Bookshop, 1967. 248 p. (Bibliography series no. 9, Southeast Asia studies, Yale University)

1,270 books and periodical articles in Indonesian and English, with

Australian and Indian imprints strongly represented, arranged under 27 subjects. The emphasis is on the post-war situation, but there is some background material. Most entries are annotated. Author and subject indexes.

K49. Hicks, George L., and Geoffrey McNicoll. *The Indonesian economy, 1950-1967, bibliographic supplement.* Detroit, Cellar Bookshop, 1967. 211 p. (Bibliography series no. 10, Southeast Asia studies, Yale University)

807 books and periodical articles in English and Indonesian supplement and update the authors' *Indonesian economy, 1950-1965, a bibliography.* Two thirds of the materials was published before 1965, and fills out the earlier bibliography. The remaining one third was published in 1966 and 1967. Author and subject indexes.

K51. Jankovec, Miloslav. *Zahranicni politika Indoneske republiky, 1945-1967, svazek III, bibliografie vyrbranych documentu.* Praha, Ustav pro mezinarodni politiku a ekonomii, 1968? 103 p.

952 entries in English and Indonesian for books, newpapers and periodical articles, arranged in classified order. No index and no annotations.

LANGUAGE

K52. Voorhoeve, Petrus. *Critical survey of studies on the languages of Sumatra.* 's Gravenhage, M. Nijhoff, 1955. 55 p. (Instituut voor Taal-, Land-, en Volkenkunde, Bibliographical series 1)

205 books and periodical articles are noted in the introduction to the linguistics and history of the languages of Sumatra, and at the end of the survey.

K53. Cense, Ant.Abr., and E.M. Uhlenbeck. *Critical survey of studies on the languages of Borneo.* 's Gravenhage M. Nijhoff, 1958. 82 p. (Instituut voor Taal-, Land-, en Volkenkunde, Bibliographical series 2)

323 books and periodical articles are listed in the survey essay.

K54. Teeuw, A. *Critical survey of studies on Malay and Bahasa Indonesia.* 's Gravenhage, M. Nijhoff, 1961. 82 p. (Instituut voor Taal-, Land-, en Volkenkunde, Bibliographical series 5)

Some 1,000 books and periodical articles are listed by alphabetical author order. They serve as notes to the survey essay on the history, linguistics, and literature of the two languages and on the influence of the West.

L.LAOS

The Kingdom of Laos became a French protectorate in 1899, and formed part of French Indochina. It became independent in 1956.

HANDBOOK

L 1. Berval, Rene de. *Kingdom of Laos.* Saigon, France-Asie, 1959. 506 p.
An encyclopedic survey of the geography, history, arts, ethnography, religion, language and literature, folklore, education, economy and external relations of Laos, with many illustrations and a bibliography of some 500 books and articles, almost entirely in French. No index.

DICTIONARIES

L 2. Guignard, Theodore. *Dictionnaire laotien-francais.* Hongkong, Imprimerie de Nazareth, 1912. 959 p.
16,000 words in Laotian script, followed by romanization and translation into French with no examples of usage. There is a seventy-page introduction to Laotian.
L 3. Boonyavong, Boon Thom. *English-Lao dictionary.* Vientiane, Lao-American Association, 1962. 367 p.
Nearly 6,000 words with Lao equivalents. No examples of usage.

GAZETTEER

L 4. U.S. Office of Geography. *Laos* ... Washington, U.S. Government Printing Office, 1962. 214 p. (Gazetteer no.69)
15,300 place and feature names, together with their classification and longitude and latitude.

STATISTICS

L 5. Laos(Kingdom). Ministere du Plan et de la Cooperation. Service national de la statistique. *Bulletin de statistiques.* Vientiane, 1951-
Statistical tables for trade, transport, finance, industry and population. Quarterly issues noted for 1958, 1961 and 1968. Former title *Bulletin de statistiques du Laos. Annuaire statistique du Laos 1953/57* published in 1961, and noted as fourth in series which commenced in 1951.
L 6. Halpern, Joel Martin. *Population statistics and associated data.* Los Angeles. University of California. Laos project, 1961. 59 p.

76 tables on population, rate of population growth, death rates, distribution of ethnic groups, compiled from 34 periodicals and books, mostly in English, and published from 1900 to 1960. Each table is footnoted and annotated with comments by the author on its reliability. Useful since there has been no modern census in Laos.

BIBLIOGRAPHY

L 7. Lafont, Pierre Bernard. *Bibliographie du Laos.* Paris, Ecole francaise d'Extreme Orient, 1964. 269 p. (Publications de l'Ecole francaise d'Extreme Orient. v. 50)
Includes 1867 books and periodical articles published from 1800 to 1962, mostly in French. There are, however, a few English and German titles, and a short section with Laotian, Vietnamese, Thai and Russian entries. 39 periodicals were surveyed. The bibliography is arranged by broad subjects, and one sixth of the entries are annotated. This bibliography is much more comprehensive than Thao Kene *Bibliographie du Laos* (Vientiane, 1958. 68 p.) and John Mckinstry *Bibliography of Laos and ethnically related areas* (Berkeley, 1962. 89 p.) both of which are arranged alphabetically by author and title and have a much smaller number of entries.

L 8. Laos(Kingdom). Bibliotheque nationale. *Bibliographie nationale, 1968.* Vientiane, 1969? 97 p.
The first volume published by the National Library, but the third sponsored by the Asia Foundation. Separate sections for subject, author and title. Dewey Decimal Classification numbers given. 360 titles are noted. In Lao.

M.MALAYSIA and SINGAPORE

Britain established a foothold in Malaya at Penang in 1786, in Malacca in 1795, and in Singapore in 1819. These three areas became the Straits Settlements, severing their connection with India in 1867. In 1895 the four States of Negri Sembilan, Pahang, Perak and Selangor became the Federated Malay States with their capital at Kuala Lumpur. In 1909 the States of Kedah, Kelantan, Perlis and Trengganu were associated with the other Malay States. Johore did not have its status defined until 1914. The Malayan Union was established in 1946, but was replaced by the Federation of Malaya in 1948, which became independent in 1957. Singapore maintained a separate status as a Crown colony. In 1963 Malaysia was established, and included the former Federation of Malaya, Singapore, Sabah and Sarawak. Brunei remained independent. Singapore became an independent State in 1965.

YEARBOOKS

M 1. *Straits Times directory of Malaysia* 1949- Singapore, Straits Times, 1949-
This directory emphasizes industry and business, but schools, churches, and professional societies are also covered, divided into nine regions, including Singapore, Sabah, Sarawak, Brunei and Bangkok, and under each region entries are arranged alphabetically by firm. There is a subject directory and an alphabetical index to companies, agencies and individuals. Title to 1964 *Straits Times directory of Singapore and Malaya.* 1970 last issue noted.

M 2. *Malaysia year book,* 1956- Kuala Lumpur, Malaya Mail Publishers, 1956-
A reference book similar to the *World Almanac,* but covering Malaysia only. Almost all subjects, except science and literature, are included. Arranged in topical order, with the table of contents arranged alphabetically to serve as an index. Among the special features are maps of the States of Malaysia, a who's who of government officials, and a directory of national organizations. Title to 1963 *Federation of Malaya yearbook.*

M 3. Malaysia. *Official yearbook,* 1961 - Kuala Lumpur, Government Printer, 1961-
In contrast to the *Malaysia year book,* this annual stresses economic and political affairs, with less materials on religion and customs. Divided into 22 chapters, with a detailed table of contents. Appendices contain valuable information on the government, statistics and the constitution. 1964 issue, the last noted, has an index.

BIOGRAPHICAL DICTIONARY

M 4. *Who's who in Malaysia,* 1956- Kuala Lumpur, 1956-
The main part consists of some 2,500 biographies. Other parts list honors
and decorations, rulers of the Malay States, who's who in the Malaysian
government, in the Singapore government and in the Sabah government.
Selection criteria not stated. Biographical information is short, includes
addresses, but no publications. Edited and published by J. Victor Morais.
Title to 1962 *The leaders of Malaya and who's who.* 1969 issue last noted.

DIRECTORIES

M 5. Sutter, John Orval. *Scientific facilities and information services of the
Federation of Malaya and the State of Singapore.* Honolulu, published
for the National Science Foundation, by the Pacific Science Information
Center, 1961. 43 p.
The first section deals with the history, culture and economy of the two
countries. The second consists of a number of appendices, giving information on the facilities of the University of Malaya, listing museums, research institutions and laboratories. The third appendix lists 44 scientific
journals published in Malaya and Singapore to 1959. There is an excellent
subject, author and title index.
M 6. Keeth, Kent H. *A directory of libraries in Malaysia.* Kuala Lumpur,
University of Malaya Library, 1965. 163 p.
Information is based on 66 replies to a questionnaire sent to 93 libraries
in Malaysia and Singapore. Library collections, administration, staff, facilities, and publications are noted. Subject index to library collections.

GAZETTEER

M 7. U.S. Office on Geography. *British Borneo, Singapore and Malaya...*
Washington, U.S. Government Printing Office, 1955. 463 p. (U.S. Board
on Geographic Names Gazetteer no.10)
17,000 names for places and features, with 600 for Brunei, 3,100 for
North Borneo, 3,900 for Sarawak, 800 for Singapore and 8,700 for the
Federation of Malaya. Longitude and latitude given for each name.

CENSUS

M 8. Straits Settlements. *A report on the 1931 census...* London, Crown
Agents for the Colonies, 1932. 389 p.
One of a series of decennial census reports noted from 1901. This issue
covers the Straits Settlements, the Federated and Unfederated Malay
States, including Brunei. Arranged by subjects with the table of contents

serving as an index to both the main body of the report and the tables.

M 9. Malaya (Federation). *A report on the 1947 census of population...* London, Crown Agents for the Colonies, 1949. 597 p.

The first part of the report discusses the census, while the second part consists of 127 tables. The distribution of population is also shown on maps. Among the appendices are population by community as recorded in past censuses, results of Japanese census taking, classification of population, classification of industries, and Malayan migration statistics for the period 1931-41.

M10. Malaya (Federation). Department of Statistics. *Population census, 1957.* Kuala Lumpur, 1957-60. 14 v.

The first volume gives the distribution of the population of the Federation by race and sex for the States, districts, etc. The last two volumes also cover the Federation as a whole, with comments on the characteristics of the population and the changes that have taken place since 1947. The remaining volumes are each concerned with a single state, and give distribution of population by race and sex, and show age, place of birth, literacy, occupation, industry, etc.

STATISTICAL YEARBOOKS

M11. Malaya (Federation). Department of Statistics. *Malayan yearbook,* 1935- Singapore, 1935-

Arranged by subjects and divided by chapters, with an index giving subject, chapter and page. A comprehensive one-volume guide on Malaya up to the end of the year prior to publication. Superseded the *Statistical summary* issued by the same department. 1939 issue last noted.

M12. *Malayan statistics, digest of economic and social statistics (State of Singapore and Federation of Malaya)* Singapore, 1954-61.

Statistical tables on manpower and population, trade, transport, production and prices. Annual figures are given, with some quarterly and monthly figures for more recent statistics. Supersedes *Malayan statistics monthly digest* published to January 1954.

BIBLIOGRAPHY

M13. Tregonning, Kennedy G. *Malaysian historical sources* ... Singapore, University of Singapore, 1962. 130 p.

A series of bibliographical essays on historical materials mainly in Malaysia and on Malaysia, with particular emphasis on early sources, archives and newspapers. There is no index.

M14. Cheeseman, Harold R. *Bibliography of Malaya, being a classified list of books wholly or partly relating to the Federation of Malaya and Singapore.* New York, Longmans, 1959. 234 p.

A largely unannotated list of some 1,000 books and periodical articles in

English arranged by subjects, including history, law, economics, peoples of Malaya, lists of newspapers and periodicals, religion, etc. There is an author index.

M15. Lim, Beda. "Malaya, a background bibliography." *Journal of the Malayan Branch of the Royal Asiatic Society.* v. 35, parts 2-3, 1962. p.1-199.

Some 3,400 books and periodical articles with little annotation and mostly in English, on the Federation of Malaya, the States of Singapore and Brunei, and the Colonies of Sarawak and North Borneo, and covering the period from the earliest Western accounts through 1956. Items are arranged alphabetically by author under eight main subject divisions, including bibliographies, description, history, government, economic conditions. Materials on technical and scientific subjects are excluded, and also materials in Malay and other languages not using a romanized script. This bibliography is based on the resources of the National Library of Australia. Published as a separate.

M16. Cotter, Conrad Patrick. *Bibliography of English language sources on human ecology, Eastern Malaysia and Brunei.* Honolulu, University of Hawaii, Department of Asian Studies, 1965. 2 v.

Over 7,300 periodical articles and books in English cover Sarawak, Sabah, Labuan and Brunei from the first Western accounts to 1964. In spite of its size it is still not claimed to be comprehensive, but it is easily the fullest bibliography of its kind, entries are arranged in alphabetical order by author, and numbered. These numbers are given under a series of broad subjects in an index, but the size of the subjects makes the arrangement unwieldy. Much of the material listed is very difficult to secure. There is some annotation and library locations are also stated. Items not examined are indicated. The appendix contains a list of 1,114 papers of the British North Borneo Chartered Company. The much more limited University of Chicago *Bibliography of North Borneo* (New Haven, Human Relations Area Files, 1956) which lists only 125 items is still useful since it is introductory and its entries are annotated.

M17. Malaysia. Arkib Negara Malaysia. *Bibliografi negara Malaysia,* 1967- Malaysian national bibliography, 1967- Kuala Lumpur, 1969-

The first issue includes some 700 books and pamphlets whether published for sale or not, official publications, maps and music. A classified section, arranged by the Dewey Decimal Classification is followed by an author and title index.

M18. Singapore(City) National Library. *Singapore national bibliography,* 1967- Singapore, 1969-

Lists some 900 commercial and official publications and publications not for sale, and arranges these by a modified Dewey Decimal Classification, author, title and subject index.

M19. Singapore(City). University. Library. *Catalogue of the Singapore/Malaysia collection.* Boston, G.K. Hall, 1968, 757 p.

Lists some 7,500 titles, mostly in English, referring to Singapore and Malaysia arranged in two sequences, the first according to a modified Library of Congress classification, and the second by author and title.

Periodicals and newspapers

M20. Roff, William R. *Guide to Malay periodicals, 1876-1941, with details of known holdings in Malaya.* Singapore, Eastern Universities Press, 1961. 46 p. (Papers on Southeast Asia subjects no. 4)

Lists 14 Malay language newspapers published outside Malaya, but circulated in Malay, with holdings in Malaya, and 147 periodicals also published in Malay, and issued in Malaya. This is arranged chronologically by the date of first issue. Another 6 periodicals published in English, but concerned with Malay interests are also noted. Nearly all items are in Jawi script. Title index.

M21. Hazra, Niranjan K., and Edwin Lee Siew Cheng. *Malayasian serials, a checklist of current official serials of the Malayasian governments.* Singapore, Department of History, Center for South East Asian Studies in the Social Sciences, University of Singapore, 1965. 18 p.

Lists some 300 serials presumably held by the University Library. Since some of these date from the late 1940's, the use of the term current is a broad one nor is the list restricted entirely to official publications, since 28 non-official serials and 11 English language newspapers are listed. The entries are open and there is no indication whether the serial has ceased publication. The arrangement is by political division, and then by title, not by issuing body. No index and no annotation.

M22. Harris, L. J. *Guide to current Malaysian serials.* Kuala Lumpur, University of Malaya Library, 1967. 73 p.

435 periodicals, mostly in English, are arranged in Dewey Decimal Classification order, with date of first publication, frequency, circulation, publisher and brief note often on contents. Annuals, church and house organs are included, but annual reports of companies, newspapers, official government publications and library accessions lists are excluded. A thorough professional bibliography.

M22.1. Lim,Patricia Pui Huen(Wang) *Newspapers published in the Malaysian area, with a union list of local holdings.* Singapore, Institute of Southeast Asian Studies, 1970. p. 157-198. (Institute of Southeast Asian Studies, Singapore. Occasional Paper no.2)

Divided into two sections, with 375 newspapers listed for Western Malaysia and Singapore and 70 for Eastern Malaysia and Brunei. In each section newspapers are subdivided by language, and arranged alphabetically. Lists all newspapers known to have been published in the area, with holdings for major libraries, and for the British Museum, when local holdings cannot be located.

Subject bibliography

SOCIAL SCIENCES

M23. Great Britain. Colonial Office. *An annotated bibliography on land tenure in the British and British protected territories in South East Asia and the Pacific.* London, Her Majesty's Stationery Office, 1952. 164 p.

Includes only material available in the United Kingdom and in English.

Compiled from 1947 to 1950, and arranged geographically, further subdivided into legal sources, legislative proceedings, official statements and reports and special studies.

M24. Tilman, Robert O., and Peter L. Burns. *A guide to British library holdings of government publications relating to Malaysia in the field of the social sciences.* (n.p., n.d.) 67 l.
A preliminary working draft for limited circulation, listing some 469 items in nine libraries in London. It is arranged geographically, then subarranged by subject. Includes annual reports and laws. All items are in English. No annotations.

M25. Singapore(City) University of Malaya. Reference Department. *Education in Malaysia, a bibliography,* compiled by Wang Chen Hsiu Chin. Singapore, 1964. 35 p.
Some 500 books and periodical articles arranged by four geographical areas and subdivided by broad educational topics. No index.

M26. Challis, Joyce. *Annotated bibliography of economic and social material in Singapore, part I. Government publications.* Singapore, University of Singapore Economic Research Centre, 1967. 78 p. (Research bibliography series no.1)
Approximately 150 series and reports relating primarily to Singapore and published from 1946, located in the University of Singapore Library, the Economic Research Center special collection, the National Library, and libraries of government departments. Extensive annotations.

GEOGRAPHY

M27. Pelzer, Karl J. *Selected bibliography of the geography of Southeast Asia, Part III, Malaya.* New Haven, Human Relations Area Files, 1956. 162 p. (Behavior Science bibliographies)
2,520 books and periodical articles, mostly in English, on the geography of Malaya, with some attention being given to anthropology. It is divided into 14 parts. The first lists 276 periodicals and conference proceedings cited, the second is concerned with Malaya, the third with a list of bibliographies, the fourth with government reports, the fifth with description. Parts 6-13 are divided into broad subject headings, and subdivided into smaller headings. The last part is on Singapore. Locations in the Yale University Library System are given. No index and no annotation.

N.PHILIPPINES

The conquest of the Philippines archipelago commenced in 1564 with the Spanish expedition under Legazpi. Spanish rule continued until the 1898 cession of the islands to the United States. In 1946 the Philippines became independent.

ENCYCLOPEDIA

N 1. *Encyclopedia of the Philippines*, third edition. Manila, E. Floro, 1950-58. 20 v.
Arranged by broad subjects, with separate volumes for literature, biography, commerce and industry, art, education, religion, government and politics, science, history and general information. The last volume lists contents for the whole series. The encyclopedia aims at providing the essentials of Philippine culture, and is written to appeal to businessmen, those in the professions, students and teachers. Actually it is more introductory, and primarily suitable for school use. The contributors cannot be considered as authoritative. A first edition in ten volumes was published in 1935-36. The materials for a second edition were destroyed by fire in 1949, and much of the material in the third edition was copied directly from the first.
A dated, but valuable encyclopedic survey, *El archipielago Filipino, coleccion de datos geograficos, estadisticos, cronologicos, y cientificos...* (1900. 2 v.), has its most important parts translated and included in Senate document 138, 56th Congress, 1st session, United States *Serial set* no.3885 v.2 and 3. The subject matter is arranged in a classified order, with an index to each volume.

DICTIONARIES

N 2. Panganiban, Jose V. *Talahulaganang Pilipino-Ingles.* Manila, Surian ng Wikang Pambansa, 1966. 362 p.
A current edition of the *National language-English vocabulary.* (Manila, Insitute of National Language, 1950) compiled by the director of the institute. This and *An English-Tagalog dictionary* are far more complete than any other dictionary available at present. Over 10,000 entries.
N 3. *An English-Tagalog dictionary.* Manila, Institute of National Language, 1960. 412 p.
Has some 10,000 entries, and is now being reissued with Jose V. Panganiban as compiler, and with the title *Tesaurong Ingles-Pilipino* (1965-) in mimeograph form.

BIOGRAPHICAL DICTIONARIES

N 4. *Who's who in the Philippines, a biographical dictionary of notable living men of the Philippine islands, volume 1.* Manila, McCullough Printing Company, 1937. 175 p.
Some 1,350 persons, including officials, professors, doctors, accountants, and Americans in the Philippines. There appears to be no criteria for the selection. Brief information is given on each, such as place and date of birth, education, experience and present position. A considerable part of the dictionary is taken up with non-biographical material such as the Constitution of the Philippines.

N 5. Manuel, E. Arsenio. *Dictionary of Philippine biography, volume one.* Quezon City, Filipiniana Publications, 1955. 512 p.
This first volume contains a complete alphabetical sequence, and the proposed additional two volumes supplementing and indexing the first volume have apparently not been published. Includes some 110 biographies of varying length, and each refers to a person of some prominence in Philippine history. Articles list works of authors and composers.

N 6. *Tableau, encyclopedia of distinguished personalities in the Philippines.* Manila, National Souvenir Publications, 1957. 658 p.
565 biographies of contemporary personalities are written in a popular style that sometimes lacks important information. Length of article depends on the prominence of the personality.

N 7. Retizos, Isidro and Soriano D.H. *Philippine who's who.* Quezon City, Capital Publishing House, 1957. 327 p.
Lists some 400 living residents of the Philippines, mostly Filipinos, compiled from interviews and other sources. Each biography is short, and gives information of place and date of birth, positions held, wife and children and address. Intended to be issued annually, but the first is believed to be the only issue. Since over half of the dictionary is concerned with biographies of politicans and government officials, it lacks balance.

DIRECTORIES

N 8. Philippines (Republic). Office of Public Information. *Republic of the Philippines official directory,* 1949- Manila, 1949-
Lists Philippine elected and appointed officials, arranging them by departments, and subdividing these by office or bureau. A selective, not a comprehensive listing of officials. No index. 1967 issue last noted.

N 9. *Commercial and trade directory of the Philippines,* 1947- Manila, Islanders Publishing Company, 1947-
Gives information on Philippine business, industry, trade, population, and the Constitution. It is divided into four parts; the first lists officials of the Republic, has a street directory of Manila, lists of official holidays, labor unions, etc.; the second lists business organizations and professional

persons; the third is a classified list of firms; the fourth lists residents arranged alphabetically, including their occupation and address. The 1961 edition included 15,000 firms. There have been a number of changes of title. It was first known as the *Commercial and trade directory*, in 1949 it became the *Commercial directory of the Philippines* , and in 1961 it was finally entitled the *A B Commercial directory of the Philippines*, 1963/64 issue latest noted.

N10. Philippines (Republic). National Institute of Science and Technology. Division of Documentation. *Philippine libraries.* Manila, 1961-62. 2 v.
The first volume lists 935 libraries arranged by provinces and then by city, with indexes by place, type of library, and name. The second volume lists the main and branch libraries of 25 Philippine universities.

ATLAS

N11. Hendry, Robert S. *Atlas of the Philippines.* Manila, Phil-Asian Publishers, inc. 1959. 228 p.
Some 56 subject and provincial maps. For each provincial map there is a brief description and history, and a short list of places. In spite of the large format, the amount of information given is disappointing. The lack of an index is a major defect. Although very much older, P. Jose Algue *Atlas of the Philippine Islands* (Washington, Government Printing Office, 1900) a reprint of the 1899 *Atlas de Filipinas* is still useful. It has 30 maps, and over 5,000 placenames in its index.

GEOGRAPHICAL DICTIONARY AND GAZETTEERS

N12. U.S. Bureau of Insular Affairs. *Pronouncing gazetteer and geographical dictionary of the Philippine Islands.* Washington, Government Printing Office, 1902. 933 p.
10,300 entries for islands, provinces, cities, districts and towns, arranged alphabetically, with information on their location, size, boundaries, population, products and government. The first third of this work consists of the Law of the Civil Government of the Philippine Islands, passed by Congress in 1902.

N13. U. S. Coast and Geodetic survey. *Gazetteer of the Philippine Islands.* Washington, 1945. 350 p.
Contains 47,355 original entries and cross references, including variant names. Obsolete and historical names have been omited. For each name the island or area, longitude and latitude are given.

CENSUS

N14. Philippines (Commonwealth). Commision of the Census. ... *Census of the Philippines,1939.* Manila, Bureau of Printing, 1940-43. 4 v.(in 7)

The first volume consists of four parts, and gives the distribution of the population by municipalities and barrios, and the classification of inhabitants by sex, age and race, civil status, literacy, occupation, religion and employment. Each province section commences with a map of the province. The second volume is a summary for the Philippines of the statistics in the first volume, with a general report on the census. V.3 has a similar arrangement to v.1, but is exclusively concerned with agriculture. V.4 reports the result of an economic census for forestry, transport, fisheries, mining and electricity. Earlier censuses have been reported for 1818, 1876 and 1887, under Spanish rule. Censuses for 1903 in 4 volumes, and for 1918 in 4 volumes in 6, have been noted.

N15. Philippines (Republic). Bureau of the Census and Statistics. *Census of the Philippines, 1948*. Manila, Bureau of Printing, 1951-54. 4 v.(in 12.)
The Census appeared in 4 volumes, three of which appeared in parts. The first volume, in six parts, covers the population and is classified by city, municipality and barrio. The second, in three parts, is an agricultural census with information on area, land use, acreage, production and value of different crops and livestock by province and municipality. The third volume is a summary report in two parts, the first on agriculture, the second on population. The fourth volume is an economic census. The census was compiled principally through the help of school teachers, and its accuracy has been questioned since this was the first to be undertaken by the Republic and also since much of Central Luzon was unsettled politically.

N16. Philippines (Republic). Bureau of the Census and Statistics. *Census of the Phillippines,1960. Population and housing*. Manila, Department of Commerce and Industry, 1962. 2 v.
A great advance on the accuracy of the 1948 Census. Questionnaires were pre-tested, and houses were enumerated before the census count. The first volume has 51 sections, one for each province. Information is given for sex, age, citizenship, literacy, school attendance, and language. Each provincial section is in two parts, the first on population, the second on housing.

STATISTICS

N17. Philippines Islands. Bureau of Commerce and Industry. *Statistical bulletin of the Philippine Islands*, no.1-12, 1918-29. Manila, Bureau of Printing, 1918-29.
Each volume has approximately 100-140 tables arranged by subject, and the information is compiled from official returns. There is no index except in the 1920 issue, and the detailed table of contents for each volume is an excellent guide.

N18. Philippines (Republic). Bureau of the Census and Statistics. *Yearbook of Philippines statistics*, 1940-46. Manila, Bureau of Printing, 1941-1947. 2 v.
Valuable since it gives statistical information for the last pre-World War

II year, the period of the Japanese occupation, and the first two years of liberation. Arranged by major subject divisions, as geography, population, education, vital statistics, agriculture, labor, industry, business, banking and finance, domestic and foreign trade.

N19. Philippines(Republic). Bureau of the Census and Statistics. *Journal of Philippine statistics,* 1941- Manila, Bureau of Printing

Issued quarterly to give statistical information on social and economic conditions in the Philippines, and in each issue there are some 50 to 60 tables grouped by subject, and covering prices, labor, education, immigration, business, agriculture, transportation and trade. Lack of uniformity in treatment makes this publication of less value. Issues for 1964 last noted.

N20. Philippines(Republic). Bureau of Census and Statistics. *Yearbook of Philippine statistics,* 1958- Manila, 1958-

The 1966 issue, the second, gives information for the latter part of 1966. Data is collected from government and private sources, including census materials. Chapters on vital statistics, education, law enforcement, labor force, prices, finance, transportation and communication, agriculture, fisheries, mining, manufacture and trade.

BIBLIOGRAPHY

Bibliography to 1900

N21. Medina, Jose Toribio. *La imprenta en Manila desde sus origenes hasta 1810.* Amsterdam, N. Israel, 1964, 280,203 p.

In two parts, the main work and a supplement. Each has a separate index. 565 books are arranged chronologically by date of publication and have full bibliographical descriptions and notes. A reprint of the 1896 Santiago de Chile edition.

N22. Medina, Jose Toribio. *Bibliografia espanola de las Islas Filipinas, 1523-1810.* Santiago de Chile, Imprenta Cervantes, 1897. 556 p.

667 books in Spanish, Latin and other Western languages on the Philippines arranged chronologically. Each entry is annotated in Spanish, and its origins and relation to other works is explained. Author index.

N23. Pardo de Tavera, Trinidad H. *Biblioteca filipina...* Washington, Government Printing Office, 1903. 439 p.

2,850 books on the Philippines, including Jolo and the Marianas are arranged alphabetically by author for the most part, although some are arranged by subject. Most of the material is in Spanish, but English and French works are also included. It is almost complete for books published in the latter half of the 19th century. May be bound with A. P. C. Griffin *A list of books with references to periodicals on the Philippines in the Library of Congress.* Reprinted by Gale, Detroit.

N24. Griffin,A. P. C. *A list of books with references to periodicals on the Philippines in the Library of Congress.* Washington, Government Printing Office, 1903. 397 p.

A classified list of some 2,700 books and 1,000 periodical articles and government reports. The entries are organized first by subject, and then chronologically. There is a separate author and subject index. In addition to the 265-page listing of books and articles, there is a 130-page section noting 860 maps on the Philippines in the Library of Congress. Particularly valuable for the early period of Philippine-American relations.

N25. Retana y Gamboa, Wenceslao-Emilio. *Aparato bibliografico de la historia general de Filipinas.* Madrid, 1906. 3 v.

4,623 books, intended to include all books printed in the Philippines, about the Philippines, or published by Filipinos, are arranged chronologically, with the date of imprint noted in the margin. The first volume covers the period from 1524 to 1800, the second from 1801 to 1886, and the third , which is in two parts, the period from 1887 to 1905, with an added list of newspapers and periodicals for the period 1801 to 1905. The table of contents is divided into five parts listing principal subjects and anonymous works, periodical publications, collections of Oriental names and idioms, geographical places, and proper names, and items in the bibliography are referred to by number. A key work for the study of Philippine history, but difficult to use. Reprinted in 1964 in Manila.

N26. Welsh,Doris Varner. *A catalogue of printed materials relating to the Philippine Islands,1519-1900, in the Newberry Library.* Chicago, Newberry Library, 1959. 179 p.

A classified list of 1,868 books and periodical articles based on the Edward E. Ayer collection in the Newberry Library. The entries are divided under a general heading and under history, with subdivisions for political, ecclesiastical, economic, social, cultural and local aspects. Author index.

Bibliography after 1900

N27. Mitamura, Ichiro. *Bibliography of the Philippine Islands.* Tokyo, Institute of the Pacific, 1941. 290 p.

3,058 books, periodical articles, letters and official publications, mostly published before 1930, of which some 40% are in Spanish, 30% in Filipino and the remainder in English, French and German. Author arrangement, with a subject index, which refers to the entries by author's name only.

N28. U.S. Army. Office of the Chief of Counter Intelligence. Philippine Research and Information Section. *The Philippines during the Japanese regime, 1942-1945. An annotated list of the literature published in or about the Philippines during the Japanese occupation.* Manila, 1945. 52 p.

185 entries mostly in Tagalog or English, but with a few in romanized Japanese, divided into two sections. The first contains approved and official materials, and periodical articles, including 17 newspapers. The second contains documents of the Resistance movement, but most of these were published by the U.S. Army. Brief annotations, and subject arrangement. Author and title index.

N29. Philippines(Republic). Bureau of Public Libraries. *Books copyrighted, published in the Philippines, 1945-1957.* Manila, 1957. 143 p.

An unannotated list of 1,447 books published and copyrighted in the

Philippines from 1945 to 1957, and excluding non-copyrighted material. Usually arranged by author, but sometimes by publisher, under the year of copyright, and depends for its compilation on the materials actually in the Copyright Office of the Bureau of Public Libraries. It may be supplemented by the monthly list of books and periodicals registered for copyright purposes and appearing in the *Official Gazette*. By no means a complete record of Philippine publications.

N30. Eggan,Frederick Russell. *Selected bibliography of the Philippines, topically arranged and annotated, preliminary edition.* New Haven, Human Relations Area Files, 1956. 138 p. (Behavior science bibliographies)

Some 620 books and periodical articles, mostly in English, arranged under 23 subject headings, including modern history, social and political structure, education, religion, fishing, and industry. Annotated. Author index.

N31. Quezon, Philippines. University of the Philippines. Library. *Classified list of Filipiniana books and pamphlets in the Main Library, as of December 1958.* Quezon City, University of the Philippines, 1958. 358 p.

Over 80% of the 2,959 titles listed are in English, the remainder are in Spanish and other languages. Arranged in a classified order according to the Library of Congress system. No annotations. Author, title and subject index. In spite of the title, books from other private and university libraries are included.

N32. Houston,Charles O.Jr. *Philippine bibliography, I. An annotated preliminary bibliography of Philippine bibliographies, since 1900.* Manila, University of Manila, 1960. 60 p.

155 books and periodical articles in English published to the end of 1957, and arranged in author order. Critical annotations. No index and it is necessary to search through the whole bibliography to find a bibliography on a given subject. Not all entries were inspected by the compiler.

N33. Lopez Memorial Museum, Manila. Eugenio Lopez Collection. *Catalogue of Filipiniana materials in the Lopez Memorial Museum.* Manila, 1962. 262 p.

3,124 books and manuscripts in English, Spanish and Filipino, arranged in a classified order based on the Dewey Decimal Classification. Supplements the University of the Philippines Library *Classified list of Filipiniana...* (1958)

N34. Quezon,Philippines. University of the Philippines. Interdepartmental Reference Service. *Union catalogue of Philippine materials of sixty four government agency libraries of the Philippines.* Manila, 1962. 718 p.

10,277 books, pamphlets, reprints, microfilms and theses on the Philippines, or by Philippine authors and arranged by author. Location symbols show where entries may be found. Subject index. The most comprehensive listing of Filipiniana, and includes those noted in the University of the Philippines Library *Classified list of Filipiniana...* (1958) and Bureau of Public Libraries *Books copyrighted, published in the Philippines, 1945-1957* (1957)

N35. Quezon,Philippines. University of the Philippines. Library. *Philippine bibliography,* 1963- Diliman, Rizal. 1965-

Lists non-governmental and governmental publications on the Philippines, published in the Philippines or elsewhere. First issues of periodicals are included, but music and school textbooks are excluded. Entries held by the University of the Philippines Library are noted. List of Philippine printers and publishers appended. Subject and title index. 1966-1967 issue published 1968 noted.

N36. Saito,Shiro. *The Philippines, a review of bibliographies.* Honolulu, East-West Center Library,1966. 80 p. (Occasional papers of the East-West Center Library,no.5)

Lists 215 bibliographies on the Philippines appearing as books and as periodical articles, and supplements Charles O. Houston *Philippine bibliography...* (1960) bringing his coverage down to 1965, and noting bibliography published before 1957, and not listed by him. Bibliographies in the sciences have not been included. The principal part of this work is an essay, which has a subject arrangement, and contains critical annotation. Author, subject and title index.

N37. Bernardo, Gabriel A. *Bibliography of Philippine bibliographies, 1593-1961.* Quezon City, Ateneo de Manila University, 1968. 192 p. (Occasional papers of the Department of History, Bibliographical series no.2)

1,160 books, articles and sections of books are arranged in chronological order. There is an author and selected subject index.

N38. Quezon, Philippines. University of the Philippines. Library. *Filipiniana 68.* Quezon City, 1969. 2 v.

Represents the holdings of the University of the Philippines libraries, with some 9,843 entries for official and non-official books. Items are arranged in a detailed subject order and subarranged by author. No annotations. Author-title index and subject index. A major list of Filipiniana, revising the Library's *Classified list of Filipiniana books.*

Official publications

N39. Elmer,Emma Osterman. *Checklist of publications of the government of the Philippine Islands, September 1,1900 to December 31,1917.* Manila, Philippine Library and Museum, 1918. 288 p.

A comprehensive listing of some 3,000 government publications arranged under the categories of legislative, executive, judiciary, University of the Philippines, provinces, boards and committees, and then by offices, departments and bureaus. Materials are subarranged by form, including bulletins, reports, gazettes and other publications. Reports are arranged by chronological order. There is an index to government authors and a subject index.

N40. Quezon,Philippines. University of the Philippines. Library. *Checklist of Philippines government documents, 1917-1949.* Quezon City, 1960. 817 p.

This is a continuation of Emma Osterman Elmer *Checklist of publications...* (1918). The materials are arranged by government departments, and the index lists names of authors, titles, subjects and government departments in one sequence. Documents appearing under the Japanese administration are included under a separate heading. Altogether 6,469 entries. A smaller bibliography of 755 items, U.S. Library of Congress *Checklist of Philippine government documents,1950,* 62 p., continues this item.

N41. Quezon,Philippines. University of the Philippines. Institute of Public Administration. Library. *List of Philippine government publications, 1945-1958.* Manila, 1959-60. 2 v.

Part I lists some 2,000 publications for agencies under the Departments of Agriculture and Natural Resources, Commerce and Industry, Education, and Labor. Author and subject index. Part II, reported but not seen, lists publications of agencies under the Departments of Finance, Foreign Affairs, Health and Justice.

N42. Philippines(Republic). Bureau of Public Libraries. *Philippine government publications, 1958-59.* Manila, 1958-59. 2 v.

Issued monthly or bimonthly depending on the number of publications received, and arranged within each issue by department. Items in Philippine languages entered in English translation, with the Philippine language title in parentheses.

N43. Philippines(Republic). Department of Education. National Library. *Checklist of Philippine government publications.* Manila, 1958-

The 1961 issues were quarterly, and listed only those official publications in sufficient numbers of copies for gift or exchange. 1962, 1963, 1964 issues were annual. The 1965-66 issue lists 1,431 publications, and asterisks those items available for exchange.

Periodicals and newspapers

N44. Philippines(Republic). Bureau of Posts. *Annual report...* Manila, 1899-

Over one third of the 1965/66 report is taken up by a listing of periodicals and newspapers, giving date of first issue, language of publication, address, frequency and circulation for each. The report for 1965/66 lists some 1,000 publications, and divides these into those printed in Manila and those printed in the provinces. Certainly the most comprehensive and current accounting of Philippine newspapers and periodicals, but believed to have some entries for defunct publications. First such listing noted in 1946/47 report.

N45. Hart, Donn Vorhis and Quintin A. Eala. *An annotated guide to current Philippine periodicals.* New Haven, Yale University, Southeast Asia studies, 1957. 116 p. (Yale University, Southeast Asia studies. Bibliography series no.4)

312 periodicals, mostly in English, but with a small number in Spanish and Filipino, and excluding Chinese language periodicals and those of a doctrinal nature, arranged in a classified order, followed by an alphabetical list. Frequency, address, subscription cost and circulation information given.

N46. Quezon, Philippines. University of the Philippines. Institute of Public Administration. Library. *Union list of serials of government agency libraries of the Philippines.* Manila, 1960. 911 p.

7,716 serials in 79 Philippine libraries, of which 5,573 are current, arranged by title. Of these 1,024 are Philippine serials of which 403 are current. Locations and holdings stated. Classified list of serials and list of Philippine serials appended.

N47. Golay, Frank H. *Annotated guide to Philippine serial publications in the Cornell University Library.* Ithaca, Cornell University, 1962. 72 p.

Some 200 serials are listed in three groups. The first consists of serials published privately and by institutions, the second of official serials, and the third of United States, and Japanese serials related to the Philippines. Annotated, but no index.

N48. Quezon, Philippines. University of the Philippines. Library. *Union checklist of Filipiniana serials in the libraries of the University of the Philippines, as of 1962.* Quezon City, 1963. 287 p.(University of the Philippines. Library. Research guide no.3)

1,701 serials, with holdings of 26 libraries, are arranged by title. Subject index.

N49. Saito, Shiro. *Philippine newspapers in selected American libraries, a union list.* Honolulu, East-West Center Library, 1966. 46 p. (Occasional papers of the East-West Center Library, no.6)

199 newspapers published in English, Spanish, Philippine languages, Japanese and Chinese, arranged by place of publication. Information on frequency, language of publication, title changes, and holdings by library. Title index.

NEWSPAPER AND PERIODICAL INDEXES

An index to the *Manila Times* from 1946 has been maintained on slips at the University of the Philippines Library. In April 1969 there were approximately 160,000 entries in this index. The *Index to important Philippine periodical literature,* indexing principally newspapers,has been maintained since 1945, and there is a copy of this in manuscript at the National Library in Manila.

N50. Quezon, Philippines. University of the Philippines. Interdepartmental Reference Service. *Index to Philippine periodicals* 1955- Quezon City, 1955-

Indexes some 50-120 periodicals, but does not cover some publications already being indexed in libraries such as the *Official Gazette.* Strong emphasis on the social sciences, agriculture and science, but some literary material is also included. Author and subject arrangement, except that entries under subjects are not repeated. Volume 11, the latest noted, covers 1965-66, and was published in 1967.

N51. *Silliman journal.* Dumaguete City, Silliman University, 1954-

Index to Philippine periodicals was published from volume 3 (1956) the interest is chiefly literary, and authors and subjects are arranged together in one sequence. Some 45 periodicals are indexed, including the weekly supplements of Manila newspapers. No cumulation.

Thesis bibliography

N52. National Science Development Board, Manila. *Compilation of graduate theses prepared in the Philippines, 1913-1960.* Manila, 1964. 437 p.
Arranges 3,943 Masters' and 413 doctoral theses into 65 subject groups. 40 percent are in the field of education, and 12 percent in the field of law. No annotation and no index.

SUBJECT BIBLIOGRAPHY

Social sciences

N53. Quezon, Philippines. University of the Philippines. Social Science Research Center. *An annotated bibliography of the Philippines social sciences, 1956-60.* Quezon city, 1956-60. 3 v.
Based on the materials in the Filipiniana section of the University of the Philippines Library. Volume 1, published in 1956, is on economics, including 2,895 books, periodical articles, laws, proclamations and reports arranged under 31 subject headings, it covers the period from the end of the Spanish occupation and has an author-title index. Volume 2, part I, published in 1957, is on sociology, and has 268 books and reports. Volume 3, part I, published in 1960, is on political science, and has 1,321 books, periodical articles and executive orders.

N54. Cordero, Felicidad V. *An annotated bibliography on community development in the Philippines from 1946-1959.* Diliman, Rizal, Community Development Research Council, University of the Philippines, 1965. 2 v.
2,292 books, periodical articles and reports arranged by subject. Books are given a descriptive annotation. The second volume lists the same materials, but arranges these by author.

N55. Philippines (Republic). Office of Statistical Coordination and Standards. *An annotated bibliography of official statistical publications of the Philippine government.* Manila, 1963. 25 p.
56 Philippine offical publications issued by 10 government agencies, and with statistical information. Annotation gives publisher, frequency, and describes contents.

N56. Manuel, E. Arsenio. *Philippine folklore bibliography, a preliminary survey.* Quezon City, Philippine Folklore Society, 1965. 125 p. (Philippine Folklore Society paper no.1)
An author list of some 1,100 books and periodical articles, almost entirely in English, and mostly Philippine publications. The works of each author arranged by date. Classified ethnographic index.

N57. Virata, Enrique T. *Agrarian reform, a bibliography.* Diliman, Quezon City, Community Development Research Council, University of the Philippines, 1965. 239 p.

1,013 books, unpublished reports and periodical articles, some with extensive annotation, show development of government policy on land reform. Index to authors and subjects.

N58. Saito, Shiro. *Preliminary bibliography of Philippine ethnography.* Manila, Ateneo de Manila, 1968. 388 p.
Approximately 5,000 books and periodical articles are arranged in a detailed subject order. Materials from weekly and popular periodicals are excluded. The most comprehensive bibliography of its kind. Issued in a limited edition for private circulation.

N59. Manila. University of the Philippines. Institute of Planning. *An annotated bibliography of Philippine planning.* Manila, 1968. 203 p.
1,114 entries are arranged by form into books and pamphlets, government publications, periodical and newspaper articles and theses. Entries are annotated. Author index.

Applied sciences

N60. Teves, Juan S. *Bibliography of Philippines geology, mining and mineral resources.* Manila, Bureau of Printing, 1953. 155 p.
2,846 books, reports and periodical articles covering the period 1574-1952 are arranged by author. No annotation and no subject index.

Literature

N61. Yabes, Leopoldo Y. *Philippine literature in English, 1898-1957, a bibliographical survey.* Quezon City, University of the Philippines. 1958. p. 313-434.
386 periodicals and some 900 books and pamphlets in English are arranged alphabetically in two parts, the first for periodicals, and preceded by a short bibliographical essay. The term literature is used broadly, and includes Philippine writing in history. No subject index.

N62. Florentino, Alberto S. *Midcentury guide to Philippine literature in English.* Manila, Filipiniana Publishers, 1963. 96 p.
Some 500 books in English are arranged in a number of sections, but nearly all material is literary, or is related to Philippine literature in English. Not systematic, but quite valuable.

Geography

N63. Pelzer, Karl J. *Selected bibliography on the geography of Southeast Asia, Part II. The Philippines.* New Haven, Yale University, Southeast Asia Studies, 1950. 76 p. (Yale University. Southeast Asia Studies. Bibliography series)
Some 1,100 books, periodical articles, and theses, mostly in English, are arranged under ten broad subject headings. Most entries are not annotated. The term geography is interpreted broadly and the bibliography is intended to supplement John F. Embree *Peoples and cultures of mainland Southeast Asia* (New Haven, Yale University Press, 1950) location of entries in Yale University libraries noted.

N64. Huke, Robert E. *Bibliography of Philippine geography, 1940-1963, a selected list.* Hanover, Department of Geography, Dartmouth College. 1964. 84 p. (Geography publications at Dartmouth, no.1)

Some 1,200 books and periodical articles, almost entirely in English, are arranged in a subject order, with author index. Practically no entries are dated before 1939, and almost all after 1950, thus supplementing Karl J. Pelzer *Selected bibliography on the geography of Southeast Asia, Part II. The Philippines.* (New Haven, Yale University, Southeast Asia Studies, 1950)

History

N65. Philippines (Republic) Bureau of Public Libraries. Research and Bibliography Division. *Manuel L. Quezon, a bio-bibliography.* Manila, 1962. 170 p.

Some 3,000 entries compiled from periodical indexes and newspapers. The first section consists of President Quezon's works and addresses, the second of works and articles by other authors, and the third and major section, of newspaper accounts.

O.THAILAND

The historical foundations of Thailand go back to the mid-13th century with the expulsion of the Thai from Southwest China by the Mongols. Their kingdom was consolidated in the Lower Menam River basin. In recent times territorial adjustments were made in 1941 at the expense of Cambodia, and in 1943 at the expense of Malaya and Burma. These areas were restored to their former countries in 1945. In 1949 the official name of the country was changed from Siam to Thailand.

ENCYCLOPEDIA

O 1. *Saranukrom thai, chabap Ratchabandit Sathan* (Encyclopedia Thai, Royal Institute edition) Phranakhon(i.e. Bangkok), Ratchabandit sathan, B.E. 2498/2499- (1956-)
Compiled by a commission of Thai scholars, with approximately one half of the contents relating to Thailand. Articles are signed, but have no bibliography. V.4 published in 1961 noted.

YEARBOOKS

O 2. *Thailand year book,* 1964/65- Bangkok, Temple Publishing Services, 1964? -
Contains sections on the government of Thailand, banking, social services, income tax, population, international organizations related to Thailand, social welfare services, a listing of temples and a directory of individuals arranged alphabetically. Indexed. 1969/70 issue noted.
O 3. *Thailand official yearbook,* 1964- Bangkok, Government House Printing Office, 1964? -
Review of the history, geography, politics, economy, religion of Thailand, and intended to be issued only on an occasional basis. 1968 issue noted. Index.

DICTIONARIES

O 4. McFarland, George Bradley. *Thai-English dictionary.* Stanford, Stanford University Press, 1956. 1019 p.
A reprint of the 1941 Bangkok edition, including some 16,000 Thai words, with their transliterated and English equivalents and examples of usage.
O 5. Haas, Mary Rosamond. *Thai-English student's dictionary.* Stanford, Stanford University Press, 1964. 638 p.

Some 8,000 Thai words in the 1950 official spelling are transliterated and given English equivalents, with detailed examples of usage. More up to date but less extensive than George Bradley McFarland *Thai-English dictionary.*

O 6. Jumsai, Manich. *Advanced English-Thai dictionary.* Bangkok, Chalermnit Press, 1960. 1504 p.

Some 60,000 English words are given with Thai equivalents, but no examples of usage. Called the sixth unabridged edition, but same pagination as unabridged edition of 1954. Originally published with title *English-Siamese dictionary.*

BIOGRAPHICAL DICTIONARY

O 7. Bangkok. Thammasat Mahawitthayalai. Khana Rathaprasasanasat (Thammasat University. Institute of Public Administration) *Khrai pen khrai nai Prathet Thai 2506* (Who's who in Thailand, 1963) Phranakhon, B.E. 2506(1963) 2 v.

6,000 questionnaires were sent out to prominent persons in government and other fields. Of these 3,204 replied, but 52 could not be used, and the remaining 3,152 are mostly government employees, and some quite prominent people are not included. The only modern Thai biographical dictionary available. Accounts are full, with degrees, date and place of birth, positions held, address, education, specialty and publications.

DIRECTORIES

O 8. *The Siam directory,* 1878- Bangkok, 1878-
Lists the Royal family, members of the government, the foreign diplomatic corps and includes the text of the Constitution. Also listed are universities, newspapers and business firms. Short index. 1880 edition seen. 1969/70 issue last noted.

O 9. U.S. United States Operations Mission to Thailand. Public Administrative division. *Organizational directory of the government of Thailand.* Bangkok, 1960? -
The main part is a directory of government organization, arranged by department, with important officials. This is preceded by two lists, a subject index and a name index. The second part is a directory of provincial officials. 1968/69 issue latest noted.

O10. Thailand. Sapha Wichai haeng Chat (National Research Council) *Directory of natural and social scientific institutions in Thailand.* Bangkok, 1963. 1 v.
Has been brought up to date and supplemented by the National Research Council *Directory of natural scientific institutions in Thailand, 1964.* (Bangkok, Government House Printing Office, 1965. 10 p.) and Jacques Amyot and Robert W. Kickert *Directory of the social sciences in Thai-*

land, 1963. Bangkok, Faculty of Political Science, Chulalongkorn University, 1963? 100 p.

GAZETTEERS

O11. *Akkharanukron phumisat Thai chabap Ratchabandit Sathan.* (Geographical Dictionary of Thailand) Phranakhon, Ratchabandit Sathan, B.E. 2506-09(1963-66) 4 v.
The first volume is a general geography of Thailand, the second and third list geographical names in Thai alphabetical order, with descriptions, history, archeology, resources, economic conditions and statistics. The fourth volume is an appendix arranged by *changwad,* and then by place, with a map of each *changwad.*

O12. U.S. Office of Geography. *Thailand* ... Washington, 1966. 675 p. (Gazetteer no.97)
45,500 entries for place and feature names in Thailand, with longitude and latitude, and classification.

CENSUS AND STATISTICS

O13. Thailand. Samnakngan Sathiti haeng Chat (National Office of Statistics) *Statistical yearbook,* 1915/16- Bangkok, 1916-
Arranged by broad subjects as general information, meteorology, population, public health, education, justice, agriculture, forestry, mining, external trade. Annually to 1930/31, biennially 1931/35 to 1939/44 and then annually again. In English, or in English and Thai.

O14. Thailand. Samnakngan Sathiti haeng Chat (National Office of Statistics) *Thailand population census, 1960. Changwad series.* Bangkok, 1961-62. 71 v.
Carried out with the aid of the United States Technical Assistance Program, and shows the number of inhabitants, their personal, educational and economic characteristics, and has information on fertility. Arranged alphabetically, with a volume for each *changwad* or district. An additional volume, *Thailand population census, 1960. Whole kingdom* (Bangkok, 1962. 57 p.) brings together the information found in the 71 *changwad* volumes. A 1947 census, with 7 v. In 10 reported. In Thai.

BIBLIOGRAPHY

Thai language
O15. *Bannaphiphop* World of books. Phranakhon, 1962-
A quarterly annotated list of current Thai publications added to the National Library. By no means complete in coverage.

O16. Cornell University Libraries. *Catalogue of Thai language holdings in the Cornell University through 1964,* compiled by Frances A. Bernath. Ithaca, Southeast Asia Program, Dept. of Asian Studies, Cornell University, 1964. 235 p. (Data paper no.54)
4,921 entries for the Cornell Thai collection, which now has over 9,000 titles. Full bibliographical information for library purposes. Author arrangement.

Western languages

O17. Sharp, Lauriston. *Bibliography of Thailand, a selected list of books and articles.* Ithaca, Cornell University, 1956. 64 p. (Cornell University. Southeast Asia project, Data paper no.20)
An annotated bibliography of some 315 books and periodical articles, with a stress on sociology. A number of subjects such as history, economy, politics and government, public health and welfare, education, religion, art, literature, language and ethnic groups are covered, but none in great depth. Most entries are in English, but some Thai titles are transliterated and translated. Subject arrangement, but no index.

O18. Mason, John Brown and H. Carrol Parish. *Thailand bibliography.* Gainesville, University of Florida Libraries, 1958. 247 p. (Gainesville, University of Florida Libraries, Bibliographical series no.4)
Over 2,300 books and periodical articles on Thai history, government, archeology, geography, sociology, education, art and natural sciences. Although nine languages are represented, most of the entries are in English. Arranged into two major sections, one for books, in author order, and the other for articles, also in author order. Some entries are annotated. Also contains a useful list of English language newspapers and periodicals published in Thailand.

O19. Bangkok. Chulalongkon Mahawitthayalai. Hong Samut (Chulalongkorn University. Library) *Bibliography of materials about Thailand in Western languages* ... Bangkok, B.E. 2503(1960) 325 p.
Over 4,400 books, periodical articles, microfilms, and films on Thailand are arranged by subject, and then by author, with Thai authors being entered by first name. Philosophy, religion, social sciences, language and literature, science, art, history, travel and biography are included. Compiled from the catalogues of the principal libraries in Thailand and from other bibliographies. No index and no annotation, but easily the most comprehensive bibliography on Thailand.

Official publications

O20. Thailand. Hong Samut haeng Chat(National Library) *List of Thai government publications covering the years 1954,1955,1956.* Bangkok,1958. 31 p.
Some 750 publications, including serials, are arranged by ministry, then by bureau. Titles cited in English, representing the official translation of the Thai title, but only 10% of the publications are actually in English or in English and Thai.

O21. Bangkok. Thammasat Mahawitthayalai. Khana Rathaprasasanasat (Thammasat University. Institute of Public Administration) *List of Thai government publications.* Bangkok, 1958. 43 p.

Continues the National Library *List of Thai government publications covering the years 1954,1955,1956* (Bangkok,1959) with some 1,200 publications arranged by ministry and then by bureau. The titles of publications in Thai, as well as those in English, are all given in English.

O22. Samakhom Hong Samut haeng Prathet Thai (Thai Library Association) *Bannanukrom singphim khong ratthaban Thai* (Bibliography of Thai government publications) Phranakhon, B.E.2505- (1962-)

Does not include the publications of the Department of Fine Arts and Ministry of Culture. Important since it does not provide titles in English translation only, and retains the original Thai, making it possible to more readily identify items described. The first volume, containing some 1,500 entries, is the only one noted. Materials are organized by departments, and there are separate author-title indexes for Thai and English language publications.

O23. U.S. Operations Mission to Thailand. Bangkok. *A compilation of reports and publications.* Bangkok, 1965. 95 p.

Some 300 entries are arranged in broad subjects. A key, unfortunately for one country only, of the principal reporting literature overseas, connected with American programs. Author index, English film index and Thai title index.

Periodical publications

O24. *Rainam nangsuphim khao sung ok pen raya nai Prathet Sayam* (List of newspapers published in Siam) Phranakhon, Ratchabandit Sapha, B.E. 2474 (1931) 22 p.

363 newspapers and periodicals in the National Library, mostly in Thai, but with some in English and Chinese. This is a cremation volume compiled by the Royal Society, and the only source for noting dates of commencing and ceasing publication and frequency for these newspapers and periodicals.

O25. Thailand. Krom kanfukhat khru (Teacher Training Department) *Datchani nittayasan Thai.* Index to articles in Thai periodicals. Phranakhon, B.E. 2500- (1957-) v.1-

Compiled by the Teacher Training Department of the Ministry of Education, and with each volume containing some 6,000 entries from some 30 periodicals. Entries are arranged in each volume by author, title and subject headings. Volume 5, covering 1968, noted.

O26. Thailand. Sathaban Bandit Phatthanaborihansat(National Institute of Development Administration) *Datchani warasan Thai.* Index to Thai periodical literature, 2503-2506, 1960-63. Phranakhon, B.E. 2507-2510 (1964-67) 2 v.

The first volume was published by the Institute of Public Administration of Thammasat University. The second, by its successor, the National Institute of Development Administration, contains over 4,000 periodical articles.

O27. Thailand. Sathaban bandit Phatthanaborihansat (National Institute of Development Administration) *Datchani nangsuphim Thai* Index to Thai newspapers,1964. Phranakhon, B.E. 2511(1965) 710 p.

Some 14,000 entries from three newspapers published in 1964 are arranged by subject.

O28. Thailand. Hong Samut haeng Chat(National Library) *List of current periodical holdings in 1966.* Bangkok, 1967. 46 p.

Lists some 400 periodicals, including official publications, by Thai title order. In addition there is an alphabetical index of daily newspapers, an index to Thai government periodicals, arranged by ministry or office, and a subject index.

Social sciences

O29. Thailand. Samnakngan Sathiti haeng Chat (National Office of Statistics) *Statistical bibliography, an annotated bibliography of Thai goverment statistical publications,* second edition. Bangkok, 1964. 175 p.

Some 375 entries arranged by ministry or office of publication. Titles given in Thai and English, and annotation in English state language of publication and date of latest issue. Paging does not indicate the large number of blank pages. No index.

O30. Amyot, Jacques. *Provisional paper on changing patterns on social structure in Thailand,1851-1965, an annotated bibliography with comments.* Delhi, UNESCO Research Centre, 1965. 171 p.

621 books and periodical articles, mostly in English, but with a few in Thai and French. Most entries are not annotated. The bibliography is arranged in three sections. The first is divided topically, covering geography, history, people, economy, social organization, religion, education and government. The second section is a list arranged alphabetically by author, giving full citations for the materials listed topically under the first section, with a few annotations. The third section evaluates the materials from the standpoint of the social sciences.

O31. Raksasataya, Amara. *Thailand, social science materials in Thai and Western languages.* Bangkok, The National Institute of Development Administration, 1966. 378 p.

1,300 books and periodicals in Western languages are arranged in author order. However the most significant section is a 245-page section of Thai language books on the social sciences, arranged by the Thai alphabet, with some 2,300 entries. The third section lists 109 Thai-language periodicals. Social science is widely interpreted and includes much history.

O32. Thrombley, Woodforth G., William J. Siffin, and Pensri Vayavananda. *Thai government and its setting, a selective annotated bibliography.* Bangkok, The National Institute of Development Adminstration, 1967. 513 p.

In two parts. The first in 93 pages, contains some 500 books and periodical articles in English, in a subject arrangement, with an author index. The second part, in 420 pages, contains some 2,000 items in Thai, and is also arranged by subject with an author index. Annotations are in Thai, but titles are translated into English.

O33. U.S. Operations Mission to Thailand. Bangkok. Technical Library. Document Section. *USOM-Thailand Technical Library Document Section card catalog*. Bangkok, 1967. 580 p.

An author-title and subject catalog of some 5,000 items collected as background materials for projects, and reports written by advisers. Relevant to Thailand's social and economic development, the catalog represents the complete holdings of the Library.

P.EAST ASIA

The East Asia area in this guide will include China, with Chinese Central Asia, Japan, Korea and Mongolia.

HANDBOOK

P 1. Edmunds, William. *Pointers and clues to the subjects of Chinese and Japanese art.* London, Samson Low, Marston and Co., 1934. 725 p.
An encyclopedia of Japanese and Chinese art symbolism, with references in the Chinese and Buddhist sections to the Japanese forms of names. For Japanese art more recent and superior to Henri L. Joly *Legend in Japanese art* (1967, reprint of the 1908 edition)

BIBLIOGRAPHY

P 2. Kerner, Robert J. *Northeastern Asia, a selected bibliography.* Berkeley, University of California Press, 1939. 2 v.
13,884 books, periodicals and periodical articles in this selective bibliography cover the whole of East Asia, including Eastern Siberia, but excluding Southeast Asia. The materials cited are in Chinese, Japanese, Korean, Russian and Western languages, and the titles for all of these are translated. Two thirds of the entries are in non-Western languages. After an initial regional and country division, there is a classified subject arrangement. The best key to the bibliography is the detailed table of contents. There are no annotations. Small subject index.

P 3. Beardsley, Richard K. *Bibliographic materials in the Japanese language on Far Eastern archeology and ethnology.* Ann Arbor, University of Michigan Press for Center of Japanese Studies, 1950. 74 p. (University of Michigan Center of Japanese Studies Bibliographical series number 3)
1,063 books and periodicals articles published after 1900, have been arranged by country and subdivided by topic. The annotations are usually brief and there is little criticism. Library locations are noted. No index.

P 4. Teng, Ssu-yu. *Japanese studies on Japan and the Far East.* Hong Kong, Hong Kong University Press, 1961. 485 p.
Over 4,200 books and periodical articles by 775 living Japanese scholars arranged in subject order. For each scholar there is a short introduction, followed by a list of his books and then his articles. Many older and well known scholars have been omitted, and also writings before 1942. Authors' names are indexed by character. There is a general index.

P 5. Harvard University. Library. *China, Japan and Korea.* Cambridge, Harvard University Library distributed by Harvard University Press, 1968. 494 p. (Widener Library shelflist 14)

In the first two parts Western language books on China, Japan and Korea are arranged in a classifed order. The third part is an author and title index, and the fourth a chronological listing by date of publication. The shelflist represents a rich collection on East Asia of some 15,300 books and periodicals.

P 6. Gillin, Donald G. *East Asia, a bibliography for undergraduate libraries.* By Donald Gillin, Edith Ehrman and Ward Morehouse. Williamsport, Bro-dart, 1970. 130 p.

2,066 books in English. Not annotated but with references to annotations in other bibliographies and to reviews, arranged by country, then by a detailed subject division. Author index.

Q.CHINA

In the modern period China lost major portions of her territory. After the Sino-Japanese war in 1895, Taiwan was seized by Japan. As a result of the 1911 Revolution, Outer Mongolia became independent. In 1932 the Japanese established Manchoukuo, and in 1937 they invaded China proper, and the Nationalist government moved to Chungking. After World War II both Manchuria and Taiwan were recovered. The latter remained in Nationalist hands after 1949, when the Chinese People's Republic was established on the mainland.

REFERENCE WORKS

Q 1. Teng, Ssu-yu and Knight Biggerstaff. *An annotated bibliography of selected Chinese reference works,* revised edition. Cambridge, Harvard University Press, 1950. 326 p. (Harvard-Yenching Institute Studies v.3)
600 entries for selected reference works in Chinese, including 130 additional items mostly published between 1935 and 1948. This book is oriented to the Western student of Chinese studies, and each entry is fully annotated. The annotations are more to help the student use the work cited than to evaluate it. Where there are different editions, the best is indicated by a plus sign. Classified arrangement, with an author and title index. This is a key bibliography and should be used to supplement the listing for Chinese materials before 1948 in this guide.

Q 2. Berton, Peter and Eugene Wu. *Contemporary China, a research guide.* Stanford, Hoover Institution, Stanford University, 1968. 695 p. (Hoover Institution Bibliographical series, v. XXXI)
2,226 general reference works, documentary materials, periodicals, and dissertations in English, Chinese, Japanese and Russian, cover mainland China from 1949, Hong Kong and Taiwan from 1945, and concentrate on social science and humanities aspects. Materials are arranged by topics, with full and critical annotations. There are subject and author-title indexes. A definitive reference work for China from 1949 to 1963, when systematic collection of materials for this work was completed. The second key bibliography for Chinese studies which should also be used to supplement the listing in this guide for the period 1949 to 1963.

ENCYCLOPEDIAS AND HANDBOOKS

Q 3. *Ku chin t'u shu chi ch'eng* (The Chinese encyclopedia) Shang-hai, Shang-hai t'u shu chi ch'eng cheng chu, Kuang-hsu 10(1884) 1,628 v.
This, the greatest of all encyclopedias, was compiled under imperial sponsorship and presented to the Chinese throne in 1725. It contains 10,000

chuan or chapters. The 6,109 items in the encyclopedia are arranged acording to a classified order, and sources are noted. There is an index and description in Lionel Giles *An alphabetical index to the Chinese encyclopedia* (London, British Museum, 1911) this index translates headings and lists the section and *chuan* in which they can be found. Published in a number of editions.

Q 4. Brunnert, Ippolit Semenovich. *Present-day political organization of China.* Shanghai, Kelly and Walsh, 1912. 572 p.

A valuable guide to official positions and organization under the Ch'ing dynasty (1644-1911) to be preferred to William F. Mayers *The Chinese government, a manual of Chinese titles...* (1886). For a fuller treatment of this topic, Orita Yorozu *Shinkoku gyosei ho* (Tokyo, Daian, 1965-66) is a standard reference.

Q 5. Couling, Samuel. *Encyclopedia sinica.* Shanghai, Kelly and Walsh, 1917. 633 p.

A one-volume dictionary of Chinese words, persons and places, mostly written by Samuel Couling but with some articles from other authorities, each article is short. Some bibliographical references are given. No index. Reprinted by the Chinese Materials and Research Aids Center, Taipei, in 1965.

Q 6. Ball, James Dyer. *Things Chinese, or notes connected with China.* Shanghai, Kelly and Walsh, 1925. 766 p.

Another one-volume encyclopedia of China, but with lengthier articles and fuller lists of references than the *Encyclopedia sinica.* There is an excellent index. The work has a Southeast China bias. The 1925 edition is the fifth, and was revised by Edward Theodore Chalmers Werner.

Q 7. Werner, Edward Theodore Chalmers. *A dictionary of Chinese mythology.* New York, Julian Press, 1961. 627 p.

An important reference work for understanding many terms and words which appear in Chinese history and literature. Information is given on gods and goddesses, myths and superstitions. There is an index to myths which refers to related articles, but not to pages. A reprint of an earlier edition, and except for the preface, little different from the 1932 edition.

Q 8. Williams, C.A.S. *Encyclopedia of Chinese symbolism and art motives, an alphabetical compendium of legends and beliefs as reflected in the manners and customs of the Chinese throughout history.* New York, Julian Press, 1960. 468 p.

Consists of articles of varying length arranged alphabetically. The Chinese characters are given for each item, and sources are frequently noted. The book is illustrated and there is an index. Originally published as *Outlines of Chinese symbolism and art motives* (Shanghai, Kelly and Walsh, 1932)

Q 9. Kao, Kuan-lu. *Fo hsueh tz'u tien* (Buddhist dictionary) Shang-hai, Shang-hai i hsueh shu chu. Min kuo 18 (1929) 4 v.

Buddhist classics, books, persons and terms relating to Buddhism are listed in character order. Each entry is followed by an explanation of the term, with a short definition. Many entries are not connected with Buddhism. Index in stroke order.

Q10. Soothill, William Edward and Lewis Hodous. *A dictionary of Chinese Buddhist terms with Sanskrit and English equivalents.* London, Kegan Paul, Trench, Trubner and Co., 1937. 510 p.

8,000 Buddhist terms are arranged in character stroke and then by radical order, and definitions given. There is a Sanskrit and Pali index. Important for reading Chinese Mahayana texts. Reprinted by Buddhist Cultural Service, Taipei, 1962.

Q11. Girard, Marcel. *Nagel's encyclopedia-guide, China.* New York, Cowles Educational Corporation, 1968. 1504 p.

First published in French in 1967, and the product of a team of young French sinologists. Since the most recent guide books of China are now over 40 years old, this represents a unique contribution of great interest to Chinese studies. The first section, in 393 pages, is an introduction to Chinese civilization, surveying geography, language, history, thought, literature, art, the economy, modern culture, games and cooking. The second section, consisting of over two thirds of the book, is a guide covering the whole of China, with much detail and over 120 maps. There is a short index.

YEARBOOKS

English Language

Q12. *China year book,* 1912-39. Shanghai, North China Daily News, 1912-39.

Published by E.P. Dutton, New York, from 1912-19, by the Tientsin Press, Tientsin, from 1921-29, and by the *North China Daily News* from 1931-39. No issues for 1915, 1917 and 1918. The *China year book* was the first to be published in China, and each issue contains much valuable information on social, political and economic conditions. From the second issue, a biographical dictionary and lists of newspapers and periodicals were included. Later issues reflect the Japanese occupation in China. Indexed.

Q13. *Chinese year book,* 1935/36-1944/45. Shanghai, Daily Tribune Publishing Co., 1935-45. 7 v.

Published by the Commercial Press from 1935 to 1941, Thacker in Bombay for 1943, and by the *Daily Tribune* for the 1944/45 issue. No issue for 1942. Was written by outstanding Chinese contributors, and has historical, economic and directory-type information, with lists of central and local Chinese government officials. No biographical section. Indexed. Reprinted by Kraus Reprint Corporation, New York.

Q14. *China annual,* 1943-44. Shanghai, Asia Statistics Co., 1943-44. 2 v.

Only two issues of this yearbook noted. An encyclopedic survey of Chinese history and contemporary political, economic and regional conditions, and includes the texts of laws of the Wang Ching-wei National Government of China established by the Japanese in Nanking. Indexed.

Q15. *China yearbook,* 1937- Taipei, China Publishing Co., 1943-

Earlier issues were published by Macmillan in New York, the 1950 issue was published by Rockport Press, New York, and from 1951, the yearbook was published from Taipei. With the 1957/58 issue, the title was changed from *China handbook.* Surveys political, economic, social and cultural affairs and has a section on the Chinese Communist regime. An extensive biographical section lists some 1,000 personalities. Appendices include the Constitution of the Republic of China, important laws passed during the previous year, and other official documents. Indexed. 1966/67 last issue noted.

Q16. *Communist China,* 1955- Hongkong, Union Research Institute. 1956-
Each issue contains a number of commentaries and essays on subjects as the Communist Party, finance, education, political development. Based on documentation from Chinese Communist newspapers.

Japanese language

Q17. *Shina nenkan,* 1916-42(China yearbook, 1916-42) Tokyo, Toa dobunkan, Taisho 5 - Showa 17(1916-42) 7 v.
An encyclopedic yearbook, the 1942 issue having 1,210 pages, surveying China's geography, peoples, cities and villages, economy, politics and government, foreign relations, communications, the Chinese Communist Party, and overseas Chinese. Detailed table of contents, but not indexed.

Q18. *Chugoku nenkan,* 1955-60(China yearbook,1955-60) Tokyo, Ishigaki shoten, Showa 30-30(1955-60)
Relies heavily on the *Jen min shou ts'e* (People's handbook) published in Peking. Stresses foreign relations of Communist China, Sino-Japanese relations and trade. Arrangement is by subject, with sections for geography, foreign relations, economics, culture, politics, and education. In appendices will be found texts of laws, lists of organizations and statistics. Subject and names indexes arranged by the Japanese syllabary. Continued by the *Shin Chugoku nenkan* (New China yearbook,1962-)

Q19. *Shin Chugoku nenkan,* 1962- (New China yearbook,1962-) Tokyo, Kyokuto shoten, Showa 37- (1962-)
Arranged by subject, and includes foreign relations, land and people, politics and government, economy, social affairs, culture, and statistics. There is a who's who of government officials and Communist Party members. A separate appendix includes directories and a traveller's guide with maps of major cities. Detailed table of contents and subject and name indexes.

Chinese language

Q20. *Shen pao nien chien,* Min kuo 22-33(Shen pao yearbook,1933-44) Shang-hai, Shen pao, Min kuo 22-33(1933-44) 6 v.
Arranged by subject, and including population, home and foreign events, politics and government, finance, industry, labor, education, transportation, and based on information from official and other publications. Laws and regulations are included. Statistical information is frequently unreliable.

Q21. *Jen min shou ts'e*, 1950- (People's handbook,1950-) Pei-ching, Ta kung pao, 1950-
Contents are largely compiled from the Peking *Jen min jih pao* (People's Daily) and are arranged by subject, frequently stressing the most outstanding topic of the previous year. The 1964 issue, for example, stresses Sino-Soviet relations. Other subjects include population, government, foreign relations, finance, culture and sports. No issue for 1954. 1965 issue last noted.

Q22. *Chung hua min kuo nien chien*, 1951- (Yearbook of the Republic of China,1951-) T'ai-pei, Chung hua min kuo nien chien she, Min kuo 40- (1951-)
Records political, economic, education, social and general events for the previous financial year, from July 1 to June 30, and gives some coverage for events on the China mainland. Detailed table of contents, but not indexed. 1968 issue last noted.

DICTIONARIES

Q23. Mathews, Robert. *Chinese-English dictionary,* revised American edition. Cambridge, Harvard University Press, 1956. 1226 p.
Arranged by romanization, with an index to some 7,800 characters arranged by radicals. This dictionary is rich in compounds, but less consistent than others in its romanization. A revision of the 1931 edition. Reprinted by the Cheng wen shu chu, Taipei, in 1964.
There is a *Revised English index* published in 1954 in 186 pages, which is valuable as an abridged key to some 20,000 English words in the dictionary.

Q24. Fenn, Courtenay. *The five thousand character dictionary.* Cambridge, Harvard University Press, 1966. 696 p.
Arranged by romanization, with an index in radical order. This dictionary is useful for establishing a consistent romanization, but has fewer compounds than others. A reprint, without revision, of the 1940 edition.

Q25. *Kuo yu tzu tien* (Dictionary of the national language) T'ai-pei, Shang wu yin shu kuan, Min kuo 42(1953) 4 v.
The first comprehensive and scholarly dictionary to include spoken language forms, and arranged by the *Chu yin fu hao,* a Chinese phonetic alphabet, which was first published in 1918. Each character also has an accompanying *Gwoyeu romatzyh* romanization which represents both pronunciation and tones through spelling. The first volume was originally published in 1937. A revised and abridged edition *Han yu tz'u tien* (Dictionary of the Chinese language)(Pei-ching, Shang wu yin shu kuan,1957) omits the *Gwoyeu romatzyh.*

Q26. Chung wen ta tz'u tien pien tsuan wei yuan hui. *Chung wen ta tz'u tien* Encyclopedic dictionary of the Chinese language. T'ai-pei, Min kuo 51-57(1962-68) 40 v.
Based on Morohashi Tetsuji *Dai kanwa jiten* (Tokyo, 1955-60) 13 v. With

some supplementation and changes, and with definitions in Chinese. Certainly the most comprehensive dictionary of Chinese now available.

Q27. Shu, Hsin-ch'eng. *Tz'u hai* (Chinese encyclopedic dictionary) T'ai-pei, Chung hua shu chu, Min kuo 51(1962) 2 v.

Arranged by stroke order, with brief but excellent definitions. There is no index. In the second volume a number of appendices give the Constitution of the Republic of China, a world chronology to 1962, a listing of mainland administrative units, and western proper names in the dictionary. George Kennedy *ZH Guide* (New Haven, 1953) 185 p. is a useful guide to this dictionary.

Q28. *Chinese-English dictionary of modern Communist usage,* second edition. Washington, Joint Publications Research Service, 1963. 845 p. (JPRS 20,904 OTS 63-31674)

A valuable and more official guide to current usage translated from *Chinesisch-Deutsches Worterbuch* (Han te tz'u tien)(Peiching Shang wu yin shu kuan, 1960) 789 p., with 35,000 words and phrases arranged alphabetically in the *p'inyin* romanization officially employed in Mainland China, with characters and translation into English. There is a Wade-Giles and *p'inyin* conversion table.

Q29. *Modern Chinese-English technical and general dictionary.* New York, McGraw-Hill, 1963. 3 v.

Includes most of Mathews *Chinese-English dictionary* and other dictionaries, but is twice the size of Mathews, with 212,000 entries, of which 80% are scientific and technical. The third or main volume is arranged in the *p'inyin* romanization, with characters noted as in the standard telegraphic code. The first two volumes are concerned with tables showing characters and their telegraphic code equivalents.

Q30. Huang, Yen-kai. *Chung hua ch'eng yu ts'u tien* A dictionary of Chinese idiomatic phrases. Hongkong, Eton Press, 1964. 1291 p.

Arranged in romanized order, according to the Wade-Giles system, this dictionary lists 30,000 phrases with some 4,700 initial characters. The phrase is first given in characters, followed by the romanization, then its translation and source when known. Unfortunately only the title of the work is given and this is usually insufficient to locate the context. The romanization contains many errors.

Q31. Yale University. Institute of Far Eastern Languages. *Dictionary of spoken Chinese.* New Haven, Yale University Press, 1966. 1071 p.

A revised edition of the War Department Technical Manual TM 30-933 *Dictionary of spoken Chinese* (1945) and for use by students of the colloquial language at the intermediate level. In two parts, Chinese-English, arranged by the Yale system of romanization, with some 3,000 entries, and a second part, with English into Chinese. Characters and examples of usage are stated. Index from Wade-Giles romanization to the *p'inyin* and Yale system.

BIOGRAPHICAL DICTIONARIES

Q32. Giles, Herbert. *A Chinese biographical dictionary.* Taipei, Literature House, 1962. 2 v.(in case)

A reprint of the 1898 edition containing 2,579 entries for prominent persons in Chinese history, and arranged in alphabetical order, with the names followed by characters and dates of birth and death, which are sometimes unreliable. Biographies are usually short. A number of revisions have been suggested by Paul Pelliot and others but these are ignored in this reprint. Also reprinted by Burt Franklin, New York, 1966.

Q33. Fang, I. *Chung-kuo jen ming ta tzu tien* Cyclopedia of Chinese biographical names. Shang-hai, Shang wu yin shu kuan, Min kuo 27(1938) 1808 p.

Over 40,000 persons are listed by stroke order of the Chinese characters, and covering the period from earliest times to 1912, but with weaker representation from 1644. Persons included are those mentioned in the official histories, and others important for literary or classical studies. Non-Chinese associated with Chinese history are also included, but legendary names are not. The annotation includes the dynasty in which the person lived, his home town, various names by which he was known and a brief biography. The dating by dynasty is often not helpful, since a single dynasty may cover a number of centuries.

Q34. Liu, Ping-li. *Chung wai jen ming tz'u tien* (Biographical dictionary of Chinese and foreigners) Shang-hai, Chung hua shu chu, Min kuo 29(1940) 1300 p.

Useful for identification of non-Chinese names found in Chinese texts. Arranged in stroke order, with an alphabetical index for some 5,000 Western names, representing one third of the entries.

Q35. Tan, Cheng-pi. *Chung-kuo wen hsueh chia ta tzu tien* (Biographical dictionary of Chinese literary figures) Shang-hai, Kuang ming shu chu, Min kuo 30(1941) 1746 p.

Lists 6,848 authors who lived to about 1940. The arrangement is chronological. For each his various names, home area, dates of birth and death, and biographical and bibliographical information are given. There is an index in stroke order.

Ch'ing dynasty,1644-1911

Q36. U.S. Library of Congress. Asiatic Division. *Eminent Chinese of the Ch'ing period.* Washington, 1943-44. 2 v.

800 biographies of Ch'ing dynasty personalities, excluding all who died after 1912. In addition to the sources quoted, personal impressions from Western residents in China have been used. Edited by Arthur Hummel.

Republican China, 1912-

Q37. *Who's who in China,* 1918-50. Shanghai, China Weekly Review, 1918-50. 6 v. and 3 supplementary volumes.

Short biographies of several thousand of China's prominent business, political and professional men, with information gathered from question-naires, newspapers and interviews. Names are listed alphabetically, followed by characters. Character indexes.

Q38. *Chung hua min kuo jen shih lu* (Biographical dictionary of the Republic of China) T'ai-pei, Chinese Science Commission, Min kuo 42(1953) 470 p.

Lists some 4,500 men and women, with names arranged in stroke order, and who were living at the time of publication. Communists are excluded. Accounts are short, and include the popular name if used, age, place of birth, schools attended, occupation, and membership in the Kuomintang. More recent, in English, but more selective is the biographical listing in the *China annual* with some 1,000 entries.

Q39. Perleberg, Max. *Who's who in modern China.* Hong Kong, Ye Olde Printerie, 1954. 428 p.

Max Perleberg, a German who lived in China for 25 years as a scholar and translator, compiled this biographical dictionary of 2,019 biographies of persons prominent in the period from 1911 to the end of 1953. Useful appendices include a history of Chinese political parties and a description of the government organization in mainland China and in Taiwan.

Q40. Boorman, Howard L., and Richard C. Howard. *Biographical dictionary of Republican China.* New York, Columbia University Press, 1967-

Projected to be a four to five volume dictionary listing over 600 persons prominent in China from 1911 to 1949, including some still living. Biographies are scholarly and substantial in length. It continues Arthur Hummel *Eminent Chinese of the Ch'ing period.*

Communist China, 1949-

Q41. U.S. Department of State. Bureau of Intelligence and Research. *Directory of Chinese Communist officials.* Washington, 1966. 621 p.

The latest of a series with previous issues appearing in 1960 and 1963 with similar titles. It is based on published information available at the end of February 1966. In the first part (464 pages) officials are listed according to their positions, and the second part is an alphabetical index of approximately 1,000 names. Through its arrangement the directory also provides a valuable guide to the organization of the Communist Party, Chinese central and local government, the mass organizations, armed forces, diplomatic and consular corps, and scientific institutions.

Q42. Kazan-kai, Tokyo. *Gendai Chugoku jimmei jiten,* 1966 nemban(Biographical dictionary of modern China, 1966 edition) Tokyo, Gaiko jihosha, Showa 41(1966) 1209 p.

A revision of *Gendai Chugoku, Chosenjin meikan* (Biographical dictionary of modern China and Korea) 1953, which appeared in revised editions in 1957 and 1962 as *Gendai Chugoku jimmei jiten.* 15,000 personalities are arranged in the Japanese syllabic order, with a Wade-Giles romanization and character key. The date and place of birth, personal history, occupation and present position are noted. Persons who died before 1960 are excluded unless their names are still very prominent.

Overseas Chinese are included. The previous editions are still important since they include less prominent persons now dead and not included in the current publication.

Q43. *Chung kung jen ming lu* (Biographical record for Communist China) T'ai-pei, Chung hua min kuo kuo chi kuan hsi yen chiu so, Min kuo 56(1967) 756 p.

Containing some 2,000 biographies, this list is significant in that it was compiled in Taiwan. Arranged in stroke order.

Q44. Yu lien yen chiu so, Hongkong (Union Research Institute) *Who's who in Communist China.* Hongkong, 1969-70. 2 v.

Over 3,000 personalities are included. Some of those noted have died recently, but none who died before 1949 included. The date for last inclusion of entries for volume 1 was September 1968, and for volume 2 was May 1969. Character index.

DIRECTORIES

Q45. Chuang, Wen-ya. *Handbook of cultural institutions in China,* by W. Y. Chyne, Shanghai, Chinese National Committee on Intellectual Coopera- tion, 1936. 282 p.

Lists some 450 organizations, mostly with a research function, giving for each their history, finances, activities and publications. A classified index lists organizations in broad subject categories, and then alphabetically. Each entry in the index is followed by the organization's name in charac- ters. Reprinted by the Chinese Materials and Research Aids Service Cen- ter, 1967.

Q46. Kun, Joseph C. *Higher educational institutions of Communist China, 1953-1958, a cumulative list.* Cambridge, Massachusetts Institute of Technology, Center for International Studies, 1961. 50 p.

227 institutions are listed by field of study, and then by the six major geographical divisions of China. Each entry lists the latest name in En- glish, followed by the characters. Other earlier names are noted. Not all institutions are noted, and this list is becoming increasingly dated. Indexed.

Q47. Wang, Chi. *Mainland China organizations of higher learning in science and technology and their publications, a selected guide.* Washington, U.S. Government Printing Office, 1961. 104 p.

Some 700 societies, organizations, universities, institutes, and libraries are grouped into sections, and information is given on their officials, loca- tion, activities, and publications. There are indexes by romanized title to the organizations, to English titles of organizations, and to serial publica- tions.

Q48. Chung yang t'u shu kuan. Taipei(National Central Library) *Directory of the cultural organizations of the Republic of China.* Taipei, 1963. 142 p.

Some 260 learned societies, libraries, museums, universities, colleges, re- search institutions and research departments of official and commercial organizations are arranged by type of institution. For each body the name is listed, followed by the name in characters, address, officers, publications, and if a library, the size of the collection. First published in 1961. No index.

Q49. Ajia kenkyujo, Tokyo (Asia Research Institute) *Chugoku kogyo kojo soran* (Guide to industry and factories in China) Tokyo, 1965. 1200 p.
Lists some 4,000 factories in China, arranged by product and subdivided by province. The source for the information is cited. Alphabetical index giving the name of the factory in *p'inyin* romanization, with kind of factory stated in English.

Q50. Nielsen, Robert R. *Academic and technical research organizations of mainland China, a selective listing, revised.* Washington, Aerospace Technology Division, Library of Congress, 1966. 172 p.
Consists of four lists, each arranged by name of organization in the Wade-Giles romanization. The romanized name is followed by the characters and translation. Some 1,260 organizations, including libraries are listed, but 220 of these are affiliated with the Chinese Academy of Sciences. Index in the *p'inyin* romanization. First published in 1965.

ATLASES

Q51. Herrmann, Albert. *An historical atlas of China.* Chicago, Aldine Publishing Company, 1966. 88 p.
A revision by Professor Norton Ginsburg of the *Historical and commercial atlas of China* originally published 1935 and reprinted in 1964 in Taipei. The 64 pages of maps, most of which are colored, are arranged chronologically, commencing with prehistoric sites and extending down to the contemporary period. For this latest period there are also a number of valuable subject maps. Appendices contain a selected bibliography of some 300 items, an index of geographical and proper names, and a list of Chinese characters. An important part of the atlas is a major review of Chinese historical geography by Paul Wheatley.

Q52. U.S. Central Intelligence Agency. *China, provisional atlas of Communist administrative units.* Washington, 1959. 14 p.
Contains 29 maps, of which 25 are reproductions of the provincial maps appearing in the *Chung-kuo fen sheng ti t'u* (Provincial atlas of China) 1956. The first four maps depict China as a whole, with administrative units as of March 1959. Chinese characters are romanized and there is an index to administrative names. Valuable for showing changes in administrative areas in mainland China.

Q53. *National atlas of China.* Taipei, The National War College in cooperation with the Chinese Geographical Institute, 1959-62 5 v.
Written in Chinese and English. The first volume is concerned with Taiwan, the second with the border areas, the third with North China, the fourth with South China. The last covers China as a whole, with maps of population, topography, climate, forestry, etc. Only the first four vol-

umes have an index. Useful for locating places and administrative units noted in Nationalist publications, but does not recognize the various changes that have taken place on the mainland since 1949. V.2-3 have title *Atlas of the Republic of China.*

Q54. *Kung fei ch'ih chu hsia ti Chung-kuo ta lu fen sheng ti t'u* (Atlas of areas of mainland China under Communist control) T'ai-pei, Kuo fang yen chiu yuan, Chung-kuo wen hua hsueh yuan, Min kuo 55(1966) 146 p.
A reprint of the 1964 edition of *Chung-kuo fen sheng ti t'u* (Provincial atlas of China) with an additional five articles on administrative units, industry, agriculture, communications and transportation, and minorities, bringing the atlas up to date to the end of 1965. The descriptive matter of the original has been reproduced with only slight changes.

GEOGRAPHICAL DICTIONARIES AND GAZETTEERS

Q55. Playfair, G.H.M. *The cities and towns of China, a geographical dictionary,* second edition. Shanghai, Kelly and Walsh, 1910. 582 p.
Over 9,000 entries for place names, many of which are references, arranged in alphabetical order, stating locations. Lists of cities are also arranged by provinces. There is an index arranged by radicals. Both contemporary names and historical names are included. The second edition has added rivers and lakes, and claims to have eliminated inaccuracies of the first edition. Reprinted by Literature House, Taipei, 1965.

Q56. Liu, Chun-jen. *Chung-kuo ti ming ta tz'u tien* (Chinese geographical names dictionary) T'ai-pei, Wen hai chu pan she, Min kuo 56(1967) 1118 p.
Some 16,000 placenames are arranged by stroke order, with a romanized form for each entry. Indexed by the Chinese Post Office romanization system. Some duplication with the *Chung-kuo ku chin ti ming ta tz'u tien.* The 1930 edition has a similar pagination.

Q57. Tsang, Li-ho. *Chung-kuo ku chin ti ming ta tz'u tien* (Chinese historical geographical dictionary) Shang-hai, Shang wu yin shu kuan, Min kuo 20(1931) 1410 p.
Lists over 40,000 place names, including mountains and rivers, arranged in stroke order. For modern names, reference is given to older forms. For about half of the places sources are cited, location is often difficult owing to lack of detail.

Q58. U.S. Office of Geography. *Hong Kong, Macao, Sinkiang, Taiwan and Tibet* ... Washington, U.S. Government Printing Office, 1955. 390 p. (Gazetter no. 5)
27,295 entries for place and feature names, including 1,225 for Hong Kong, 70 for Macao, 5,900 for Sinkiang, 17,800 for Taiwan, and 2,300 for Tibet. Longitude and latitude for all names given, together with their classification.

Q59. U.S. Office of Geography. *China...* Washington, U.S. Government Printing Office, 1956. 2 v. (Gazetteer no. 22)

37,600 place and feature names, exclusive of those names already cited in *Hong Kong, Macao, Sinkiang, Taiwan and Tibet.* For each name its classification, longitude and latitude are given. The introduction warns of variations of as much as a degree in these coordinates.

Q60. Tien, H.C. *Gazetteer of China.* Hong Kong, Oriental Book Co., 1961. 237 p.
2,457 localities are listed, and of these 1,963 are *hsien* (county) names. Older names in use are also noted. For each place name its Chinese Post Office romanization, romanization according to the Wade-Giles system, Chinese characters, province or region, longitude and latitude are given. An index by stroke order lists characters in place names.

Q61. U.S. Office of Geography. *Mainland China, administrative divisions and their seats...* Washington, U.S. Government Printing Office, 1963. 253 p. (Gazetteer no. 70)
Divided into three parts, a general list of about 11,900 entries for administrative divisions at the province, sub-province and *hsien* (county) level, the names of Communist and Nationalist seats, with Nationalist names and conventional names cross referenced to Communist names. The second part has 2,560 names for administrative seats, and the third part 2,156 province, sub-province and *hsien* level administrative areas. Both parts are divided by the 28 provinces and major city areas. Taiwan is excluded. Communist names are based on the *Chung hua jen min kung ho kuo hsing cheng ch'u hua chien ts'e* (Administrative divisions of the People's Republic of China)(Pei-ching, 1960). Locations for names are stated by longitude and latitude.

CHRONOLOGY AND CHRONOLOGICAL TABLES

Q62. Moule, Arthur Christopher. *The rulers of China, 221 B.C.-A.D. 1949...* London, Routledge and Kegan Paul, 1957. 131 p.
The most useful and detailed guide to Chinese chronology in English. W. Perceval Yetts has written an introductory section on the earlier rulers, c. 2100-249 B.C. Indexes to year titles, and to Emperors by their temple titles, memorial titles, styles, and family names.

Q63. Chung-kuo k'o hsueh yuan. Tzu-chin-shan t'ien wen tai (Chinese Academy of Sciences. Purple Mountain Observatory) *1821-2020 nien erh pai nien li piao* (Chronological tables for two centuries, 1821-2020) Pei-ching, K'o hsueh ch'u pan she, 1959. 477 p.
A comparative Western and Chinese calendar, making possible the rapid conversion of Chinese and Western dates.

Q64. Tung, Tso-pin. *Chung-kuo nien li tsung p'u* Chronological tables on Chinese history. Hong Kong, Hong Kong University Press, 1960. 2 v.
An exhaustive collection of tables enabling conversion of dates from the Chinese to Western systems. The first volume emphasizes the period from 2674 to 1 B.C., the second the period from 1 A.D.. There are indexes to the tables in both stroke and alphabetical order. A knowledge of Chinese is requisite to use these two volumes.

STATISTICAL SOURCES

Q65. China. Chu chi ch'u (Directorate General of Budget, Accounts and Statistics) *Chung hua min kuo t'ung chi t'i yao* Statistical abstract of the Republic of China. T'ai-pei, Min kuo 44- (1955-)
There are four kinds of statistical data in this yearbook. The first concerns China as a whole, the second refers to the achievements of the Nationalist government, the third refers to Taiwan province, and the fourth to recent surveys. The 1968 edition has 308 tables and 47 charts, and most of the information covers a ten years' span when there are changes to report. Current issues are in Chinese and English, but some explanatory matter only in Chinese. First appeared in 1935 in Nanking.

Q66. China (People's Republic of China, 1949-) Kuo chia t'ung chi chu (State Statistical Bureau) *Ten great years, statistics of the economic and cultural achievement of the People's Republic of China.* Peking, Foreign Languages Press, 1960. 223 p.
A series of official statistical tables for the period 1949 to the end of 1958 showing growth of population, development of socialist reorganization of industry and agriculture, capital construction, industrial production, growth of agricultural production, transportation, commerce and cultural and educational affairs.

Q67. Chen, Nai-Ruenn. *Chinese economic statistics, a handbook for mainland China.* Chicago, Aldine Publishing Co., 1967. 539 p.
Includes the economic data from *Ten great years...* And supplements these from a wide variety of Chinese Communist sources. Over 600 tables cover area and population, national income, capital formation, industry, agriculture, communications, trade, prices and living standards, public finance and employment. Statistics are restricted to the period 1949-59. More recent economic statistical estimates may be found in U.S. Joint Economic Committee *An economic profile of mainland China* (Washington, U.S. Government Printing Office, 1967) 2 v.

BIBLIOGRAPHY

Q68. *Revue bibliographique de sinologie,* v. 1- 1955- Paris, Mouton, 1957-
Selected books and periodical articles on China in the social sciences and the humanities, and not restricted to materials in Chinese, are arranged by subject and reviewed in English or French. There is a list of periodicals from which articles have been analyzed, and an author index. A gap of several years now exists between the publications and the date of their review, reducing the value of this bibliography.

Chinese language

BIBLIOGRAPHY OF BIBLIOGRAPHIES
Q69. Liang, Tzu-han. *Chung-kuo li tai shu mu tsung lu* (A catalog of Chinese bibliographies) T'ai-pei, Chung hua wen hua ch'u pan chih yeh wei yuan

hui, Min kuo 42(1953) 484 p. (Hsien tai kuo min chi pen chi shih tsung shu)

Some 2,000 bibliographies are included in this work which has replaced Shao Jui-peng *Shu mu ch'ang pien* (Catalog of bibliographies) (Pei-p'ing, 1928). Entries are arranged by categories, no index.

PRE-1912 PUBLICATIONS

Q70. Chi, Yun and others. *Ssu k'u ch'uan shu tsung mu, ch'in ting* (Catalog of the collection of the Four Libraries) Shang-hai, Ta tung shih yin, Min kuo 19(1930) 44 v.

The *Ssu k'u ch'uan shu* was a collection of over 10,000 Chinese books, of which 3,461 were reprinted, and another 6,793 were extant when it was compiled, but not part of it. The catalog is annotated, but difficult to use, and for this reason Yu Ping-yao and I.V. Gillis *Title index to the Ssu k'u ch'uan shu* Peiping, 1934, 420 p. is useful.

Q71. Katsura, Isoro. *Kanseki kaidai* (Annotated catalog of selected Chinese books) Tokyo, Meiji shoin, Meiji 41(1908) 980 p.

An annotated bibliography of some 3,000 Chinese books arranged in the traditional Chinese book classification. Books selected on the basis of the author's judgement of their importance and of their use in Japan. Collectanea, when cited, have listing of contents. Title index by stroke, and author index in Japanese syllabic order.

Q72. Liu, I-cheng. *Chiang-su sheng li kuo hsueh t'u shu kuan tsung mu* (Catalog of the Kiangsu Provincial Sinological Library) Nanching, Min kuo 22-24(1933-35) 24 v.

Lists 37,002 titles in 198,222 volumes, and arranged in the traditional Chinese book classification. Three additional sections were added for gazetteers, maps and collectanea. Each section is further divided. No annotations and no index. The ... *Pu pien* (... Supplement) published in 1937 (6 v.) adds another 18,000 entries, but these are principally contents of collectanea. Books listed now reported to be part of the Nanking Library.

Q73. Wang, Chung-min. *Kuo hui t'u shu kuan ts'ang Chung-kuo shan pen shu lu.* Descriptive catalog of rare Chinese books in the Library of Congress. Washington, Library of Congress, 1957. 2 v.

1,777 works are listed, of which all but 70 are pre-Ch'ing. The books are arranged in the traditional Chinese book classification, and there are separate author and title indexes. The entries are annotated. Rarity is defined as being published before the Ch'ing dynasty, or having been proscribed in the Ch'ing dynasty. Does not include the rare books of the National Library of Peking, for which one listing is the manuscript *Kuo li Pei-ching t'u shu kuan shan pen shu chuang hsiang shu mu* (Packing list of rare Chinese books of the National Library of Peking, 1941. 151 double leaves). These books are on microfilm.

REPUBLICAN AND CONTEMPORARY PUBLICATIONS

Q74. Tohogakkai, Tokyo (Institute of Eastern Culture) *Kin hyaku nen rai Chugoku bun bunken genzai shomoku* (Catalog of books published in

Chinese in the past century and located in Japanese libraries) Tokyo, Showa 32(1957) 838 p.

Some 20,000 books and periodicals published from 1851 to 1954, and in major Tokyo libraries, are arranged in Japanese syllabic order, with bibliographical and location information. No character index, making use of the list difficult for non-Japanese reader.

Q75. Ajia keizai kenkyujo, Tokyo (Institute of the Developing Economies *Gendai Chugoku kankei Chugokugo rombun sogo mokuroku* Union catalogue of Chinese literature on modern China. Tokyo, 1967-68. 8 v.

36,000 different titles, based on 110,000 cards from 22 Japanese libraries, cover the period from 1912 to 1965, are arranged in 6 volumes, the first three on the social sciences, the fourth on the natural sciences, and the fifth and sixth on the humanities. V. 7 is an index by authors, and v. 8 an index in three sections(Chinese romanization, Japanese romanization and stroke). The Japanese *toyo kanji*, or simplified standard characters, have been used even when this has meant a departure from the original. Older characters are used only when these are not listed in the *toyo kanji*.

Q76. Yang, Chia-lo. *T'u shu nien chien* (Book yearbook) Nan-ching, Chung kuo t'u shu ts'u pen chi kuan, Min kuo 22(1933) 2 v. (Chung kuo t'u shu ta tz'u tien pai chung ti 67 chung)

The first volume contains sections on Chinese bibliography, library and publication law, libraries in China arranged by province and a list of publishing firms. The second lists some 8,000 books published between 1912 and 1933, first by subject, then alphabetically by title. No publication dates are given, and there is no index. The entries are annotated. In the copy noted the two volumes were bound in one.

Q77. P'ing Hsin. *Sheng huo ch'uan kuo tsung shu mu* (Sheng huo cumulated catalog of Chinese publications) Shang-hai, Shang-hai sheng huo shu tien, Min kuo 24(1935) 716 p.

20,000 titles published in China from 1912 to 1935 are arranged by subjects. Title, author and price given, but no date of publication. The original title and author of books translated into Chinese noted. Four corner index to titles.

Q78. *Quarterly bulletin of Chinese bibliography.* Shanghai, Chinese National Committee on Intellectual Cooperation, 1934-47.

A quarterly list of selected periodical articles and books compiled originally from the holdings of the National Library of Peiping. Divided into sections for Chinese books, Western language books, Chinese periodical articles and Western language articles. The sections are subdivided by subject. Characters and romanization are given for all Chinese entries, and each issue contains about 300 articles and 150 books. No mention of the basis of selection. V. 1-4 were issued from 1934 to 1937, and a new series commenced in 1939 and continued to v.7 in 1947. The Chinese edition *T'u shu chi k'an* has a different content, and only the 1934 issues were combined. Reprinted by Kraus Reprint Corporation, New York.

Q79. *Philobiblon, a quarterly review of Chinese publications,* no. 1-7, June 1946-September 1948. Nanking, 1946-48.

Each issue is a classified listing of books and periodicals issued during the three months under review. Chinese author names are transliterated and titles translated. From December 1946, extremely select with annotations. The issue for July 1947, the last noted, contains some 180 books and periodicals. Reprinted by Kraus Reprint Corporation, New York.

Q80. *Ch'uan kuo hsin shu mu*, 1950- (National catalog of new books, 1950-) Pei-ching, Wen hua pu ch'u pan shih yeh kuan li chu, 1951-

The most continuous bibliographical record for mainland Chinese publications from 1950, arranged by broad subjects and giving full bibliographical information, and sometimes a short annotation. Books in minority and Western languages are cited by their Chinese titles. Original titles and authors of books translated into Chinese noted. Issued on an annual basis for 1950(published 1951), semi-annually for 1951 and 1952, annually for 1953; and monthly from 1954 to August 1958 when its frequency changed to three times a month. Now appearing semimonthly, with last issues noted for 1966. Translations of no. 8-11, May and June 1965, published as *National bibliography of new books, selected issues* (Honolulu, East-West Center Research Translations, 1966. 2 v.)

Q81. *Ch'uan kuo tsung shu mu*, 1949-1954- (National cumulated catalog of books, 1949-1954-) Pei-ching, Wen hua pu ch'u pan shih yeh kuan li chu, 1956-

Arranged by a detailed subject classification based on the People's University Classification system. The first volume covers publications for the period 1949-54, but includes, presumably, only those still in print in 1954. Succeeding volumes are for publications issued in 1955, 1956, 1957 and 1958, the last noted, and listing 26,414 books. These annual volumes are more than a cumulation of the *Ch'uan kuo hsin shu mu*, since they contain 40% more titles. A wide range of publications are included such as periodicals, textbooks, books for the blind, books in minority and Western languages. There is an index of titles. An outstanding bibliographical achievement, which appears to have ceased publication with the volume for 1958. Available on microfilm.

Q82. Kuo li chung yang t'u shu kuan, Taipei (National Central Library) *Monthly list of Chinese books*, v.1- 1960- Taipei, 1960-

A select list of current Chinese publications arranged by subject. Authors and titles are romanized, and the title translated into English. Author index to the issues of the previous year. Basis of selection not stated, and lagging badly in its coverage. Publication suspended in July 1967 and resumed in 1969 with title *Kuo-li chung yang t'u shu kuan hsin shu mu lu.*

Q83. Kuo li chung yang t'u shu kuan, Taipei (National Central Library) *Chung hua min kuo ch'u pan t'u shu mu lu hui pien* (Catalog of publications of the Republic of China) T'ai-pei, Min kuo 53 (1964) 2 v.

14,500 books received through copyright deposit at the National Central Library from 1949 to 1962, and published in Taiwan, Hong Kong and Macao. Most books are in Chinese, but some are in English. Entries are arranged by subject, and full bibliographical information is given. No index. The most complete statement we have for Taiwan publications.

OFFICIAL PUBLICATIONS

Q84. Kuo li chung yang t'u shu kuan, Nanking (National Central Library) *Kuo li chung yang t'u shu kuan ts'ang kuan shu mu lu, ti i chung* (Catalog of official publications in the National Central Library, first part) Nanching, Min kuo 23(1934) 318 p.

Some 2,000 central and local official publications in the National Central Library. The main text lists publications issued from 1926 to 1932, and an appendix lists those issued from 1911 to 1925. Arrangement follows the Chinese government structure. Chinese title and western language index.

SELECTED BIBLIOGRAPHY

Q85. Fairbank, John King and Kwang-ching Liu. *Modern China, a bibliographical guide to Chinese works, 1898-1937.* Cambridge, Harvard University Press, 1961. 608 p.

1,500 annotated entries are arranged in a subject order, covering historical materials, government and law, foreign affairs, economic data, social problems, culture and education, intellectual and literary history. All books are to be found in the Harvard-Yenching Institute. Noted that "some corrections have been made to the 1950 edition, but this work is not noted as revised." Index to authors, compilers, titles and subjects.

Q86. Kuo li chung yang t'u shu kuan, Taipei (National Central Library) *Select bibliography of the Republic of China.* Taipei, 1957. 59 p.

1,200 titles, judged to be the most important published from 1947 to 1957, but mostly from 1952 to 1956, are divided into 8 major subject divisions. Titles are translated into English. No index.

PROHIBITED BOOKS

Q87. Yao,Chin-kuang. *Ch'ing tai chin hui shu mu ssu chung* (Catalog of books prohibited in the Ch'ing dynasty, 1644-1911) Shang-hai, Shang wu yin shu kuan, Min kuo 26(1937) 180 p. (Wan yu wen k'u 2 chi 700 chung)

Many of the approximately 2,500 entries, in addition to title, size and statement of contents, have short critical comments. No index.

Periodicals and newspapers

Q88. *China publishers' directory, a practical guide to newspapers and periodicals for China advertisers.* Shanghai, Commercial Advertising Agency, 1934. 123 p.

Some 540 newpapers and periodicals, with an emphasis on those in Chinese, are listed by province, noting their date of establishment, frequency of publication, circulation, format and size. Supplementary list (4 p.) includes another 35 newspapers.

Q89. Ssu-ch'uan sheng t'u shu kuan, Chengtu (Szechwan Provincial Library) *Ssu-ch'uan sheng ke t'u shu kuan kuan ts'ang Chung wen chiu ch'i k'an lien ho mu lu(shao kao) 1884-1949* (Union catalog of Chinese language periodicals in libraries in Szechwan, first draft, 1881-1949) n.p. 1959. 4 v. And index volume.

Lists 9,788 periodicals in 19 libraries, and is important since only two of these libraries are surveyed in the *Ch'uan kuo Chung wen ch'i k'an lien ho mu lu, 1833-1949,* and includes wartime publications not noted elsewhere.

Q90. *Ch'uan kuo Chung wen ch'i k'an lien ho mu lu, 1833-1949.* (National union catalog of Chinese language periodicals, 1833-1949) Pei-ching, Pei-ching t'u shu kuan, 1961. 1522 p.

19,115 periodicals in 50 major Chinese libraries are arranged by stroke order of titles. Information given is full, including the date of first issue, frequency of publication, publisher, library locations and holdings. When periodical has ceased publication, this is noted.

Q91. Hsien tai wen hsueh ch'i k'an lien ho tiao ch'a hsiao tsu. *Chung-kuo hsien tai wen hsueh ch'i k'an mu lu, shao kao.* Contemporary Chinese literature, a list of periodicals, 1902-1949. Shang-hai, Shang-hai wen i chu pan she, 1961. 110 p.

Some 1,700 periodicals are arranged in broad chronological periods, with some periodicals further subdivided. For each, dates of commencing and ceasing publication, frequency, editors, place of publication and publisher are given. Holdings in the Shanghai Library are also noted. Many of the periodicals noted are not listed in any other bibliography, including the *Chuan kuo Chung wen ch'i k'an lien ho mu lu, 1833-1949.* Title index. Reprinted by the Center for Chinese Research Materials, Association of Research Libraries, Washington, 1968.

LIBRARIES OUTSIDE CHINA

Q92. Hervouet, Yves. *Catalogue des periodiques chinois dans les bibliotheques d'Europe.* Paris, Mouton, 1958. 102 p. (Le monde d'outre mer, passe et present, 4 ser. Bibliographies 2)

Some 600 periodicals are arranged in alphabetical order of their Chinese title, with information on place of publication, publisher, date of first issue, and location of library holdings. Periodicals which ceased publication before 1911 are omitted.

Q93. Toyo bunko, Tokyo. Chugoku kenkyu iinkai (Oriental Library. Seminar on modern China) *Chugoku-bun shimbun zasshi sogo mokuroku. Nihon shuyo kenkyu kikan toshokan shozo* (Union catalog of newpapers and periodicals in Chinese, in libraries of important Japanese research institutions) Tokyo, Showa 34 (1959) 171 p.

Some 3,000 newspapers and periodicals are located in 23 Japanese libraries. Holdings stated.

Q94. *Chinese periodicals in British libraries, handlist no.2.* London, Trustees of the British Museum, 1965. 102 p.

Lists 1,603 Chinese periodicals in 16 British libraries. For each periodical the place of publication, location and extent of holdings is given, together with dates of first issue and when publication ceased, if known. *Handlist no. 1* was a preliminary union catalog of Chinese language periodicals in British libraries.

Q95. U.S. Library of Congress. *Union card file of Oriental vernacular serials.*

Chinese, Japanese and Korean. Chinese file. Washington, 1966.
Contains 27,479 cards and is available on microfilm, or on electrostatic
enlargement in card size from the Library of Congress. 17 major Chinese
collections in the United States made their serial records available for
microfilming in 1964 and 1965, and are represented.

CONTEMPORARY CHINA

Q96. *Shang-hai shih pao k'an t'u shu kuan Chung wen ch'i k'an mu lu,
1949-1956* (Catalog of Chinese language periodicals in the Shanghai Mu-
nicipal Newspapers and Periodicals Library,1949-1956) Shanghai, Shang-
hai shih pao k'an t'u shu kuan, 1956. 138 p.
1,393 Chinese language periodicals published between 1949 and 1956 are
listed in title stroke order. Frequency of publication, place of publication,publisher and holdings stated. Subject index.

Q97. Nunn,G.Raymond. *Chinese periodicals, international holdings,
1949-1960.* Ann Arbor, 1961. 85 p.
Lists over 1,700 Chinese periodicals in an attempt to compile a comprehensive listing, but did not use the *Shang-hai shih pao k'an t'u shu kuan
Chung wen ch'i k'an mu lu,1949-1956.* For each entry the romanized
form of the title, the characters, translation of the title and location of
library holdings are stated. The emphasis is on holdings in the United
States. *Indexes and supplement* (1961, 107 p.) lists additional holdings,
and provides Wade-Giles and *p'inyin* indexes.

Q98. Shih,Bernadette P.N. *International union list of Communist Chinese
serials, scientific, technical and medical, with selected social science titles.*
Cambridge, Massachusetts Institute of Technology Libraries, 1963. 75 p.
A later list than G.Raymond Nunn *Chinese periodicals, international
holdings,1949-1960,* and notes only 874 titles, with holdings for 601.
Entries for 100 selected social science titles.

Q99. Yu lien yen chiu so, Hongkong (Union Research Institute) *Catalogue of
mainland Chinese magazines and newspapers held by the Union Research
Institute,* third edition. Hongkong, 1968. 149 p.
Divided into two parts, the first containing 716 periodicals, with romanized title, characters, translation of title, frequency and holdings, and the
second with similar information for 426 newspapers. Copies of materials
listed available from the Institute in microfilm.

Q100. U.S. Library of Congress. *(Draft listing of Communist newspapers held
by the Library of Congress)* Washington, 1964-65. 2 v.
366 Chinese newspapers, mostly representative of the provincial press are
listed with holdings. Intended for issue in sheets for binding in ring
binders, and given no formal title by the Division of Orientalia repsons-
ible for the compilation.

Q101. Irick,Robert L. *An annotated guide to Taiwan periodical literature,
1966.* Taipei, Chinese Materials and Research Aids Service Center, 1966.
102 p.
Lists 519 periodicals out of some 700 currently registered publications,
and arranges these by 73 subjects. Entries are annotated. Title index by
stroke and by romanization.

WESTERN LANGUAGE PERIODICALS AND NEWSPAPERS

Q102. King,Frank H.H., and Prescott Clarke. *A research guide to China Coast newspapers, 1833-1911.* Cambridge, Harvard University Press, 1965. 235 p. (Harvard East Asia monographs 18)

235 newspapers are listed, with information on holdings for 125 in 46 libraries. In addition to the listing there is a great deal of information concerning the development of the China-Coast newspaper. Japanese newspapers published in China are noted in an appendix. This account can be brought down to 1930 by Thomas Min-heng Chao *The foreign press in China* (Shanghai, China Institute of Pacific Relations,1931, 114 p.)

Q103. Birch, Garnett Elmer. *Western language periodical publications in China, 1828-1949.* Honolulu, 1967. 166 p.

Master's thesis at the University of Hawaii, 1967. 861 periodicals issued from 1828 to 1949 are listed in alphabetical order. The most comprehensive listing available. Holdings not stated. Chronological index to periodicals by date of first issue. The main part of the text is a discussion of the development and distribution of the Western language periodical publishing in China.

CHINESE LANGUAGE PERIODICALS INDEXES

Q104. T'an,Cho-yuan. *Chung wen tsa chih so yin* (Index to Chinese periodicals) Kuang-tung. Ling-nan ta hsueh t'u shu kuan. Min kuo 24 (1935) 2v.

105 periodicals published from the beginning of the Republic to 1929 are indexed in a similar system to that of the *Reader's guide to periodical literature,* and under each heading titles of articles, author's name, periodical, volume, issue, pagination and date are given. Although only a small number of the total number of periodicals for the period are covered this is a most valuable source.

Q105. Columbia University. East Asian Library. *Index to learned Chinese periodicals.* Boston, G.K.Hall and Co., 1963. 215 p.

Contains 4,500 entries from 13 Chinese periodicals published for the most part from the mid-twenties to 1950. The first part is arranged by author, and the second by subject. Titles are translated, but not romanized. No index.

Q106. *Jen wen yueh k'an* (Humanities monthly) v.1-8, 1930-37, v.9, 1947. Shang-hai, Jen wen yueh k'an she, Min kuo 19-36(1930-47) 9 v.

Articles from 250 Chinese periodicals are indexed by subject. Entries give title, author's name, periodical, volume, page and date. New books are listed in a book section. For v.9, issues 1-3 only noted, published in 1947 after a break of ten years.

Q107. *Ch'i k'an so yin* The current Chinese magazine essays index, v.1-8. Nanching, Nan-ching Chung-shan wen hua chiao yu kuan, Min kuo 22-26(1933-37) 8 v.

More comprehensive than the *Jen wen yueh k'an.* V.5 indexes some 450 periodicals. A number of subject arrangements are used. V.5 uses the Dewey Decimal Classification system.

Post-1949 Chinese language periodical indexes

Q108. Kuo li T'ai-wan ta hsueh, Taipei(National Taiwan University) *Chung wen ch'i k'an lun wen fen lei so yin,* ti i chi- Classified index to articles in Chinese language periodicals. T'ai-pei, Min kuo 49- (1960-)
The number of periodicals indexed has increased from the original 30 for the period 1945-57 to 75 for 1961, in the third issue. The third issue also contains a list of some 450 periodicals published in Taiwan, and arranged in classified order.

Q109. *Ch'uan kuo chu yao pao k'an tzu liao so yin* (National index to materials in important periodicals and newspapers) no.1-38, 1955-58. Shang-hai, Shang-hai shih pao k'an t'u shu kuan, 1955-58. 38 nos.
Arranged by subjects, then by the newspaper and periodical title in which the article appeared. Date of publication, name of author, pagination, and volume are stated. A representative issue will cite some 5,000 articles from some 40 newspapers and 260 periodicals. In 1959 divided into two sections *Che hsueh she hui k'o hsueh pu fen* (Philosophy and social sciences section) no.39- 1959- and *Tzu jan chi shu k'o hsueh pu fen* (Natural and applied sciences section) no.1- 1959- available on microfilm, including nos. 1-12 of *Tzu jan chi shu k'o hsueh pu fen* and nos. 39-57 of *Che hsueh she hui k'o hsueh pu fen.*

WESTERN LANGUAGE PERIODICAL INDEXES

Q110. Lust,John. *Index sinicus, a catalogue of articles relating to China in periodicals and other collective publications, 1920-1955.* Cambridge, Heffer, 1964. 663 p.
Supplements Yuan T'ung-li *China in Western literature,* and has 19,734 Western language articles in periodicals, memorial volumes, symposia and congress proceedings. Some 840 periodicals, 150 collective works and 25 congresses were surveyed to make the compilation. The subject arrangement of Dr. Yuan's work is followed. All items were personally examined by the contributors.

Q111. Sorich, Richard. *Contemporary China, a bibliography of reports on China published by the United States Joint Publications Research Service.* New York, Prepared for the Joint Committee on Contemporary China of the American Council of Learned Societies and the Social Science Research Council, 1961. 99 p.
The reports on China published from the end of 1957 to July 1960 are listed by JPRS number. The contents of each number is stated. Subject index.

Q112. Kyriak,Theodore E. *Catalog cards in book form to United States Joint Publications Research Service translations, 1957-* Annapolis,Research and Microfilm Publications,1962-
Worldwide in scope, including the Soviet Union, Eastern Europe, Southeast Asia, North Korea, as well as mainland China. For each area the JPRS reports are listed numerically, referring to a reproduction of a card outlining contents. Beyond this rudimentary regional approach there is no subject approach, and this listing is a slight improvement on that in

the *Monthly Catalog of United States Government Publications,* which lists the reports by number.

Q113. Kyriak, Theodore E. *China, a bibliography,* v.I, nos 1-12, v.II, Jul. 1962-Jun.1964. Annapolis, Research and Microfilm Publications, 1962-64.

After a break from August 1960 to the end of June 1962, this new indexing of JPRS reports continues the work of Richard Sorich *Contemporary China ...,* but with the same defect of not indexing the individual articles within each report. Subject index. Continued by *China, bibliography - index to U.S. JPRS Research translations,* v.III, nos.1-12, Jul.1963-Jun.1965, and v.IV, *China and Asia (exclusive of Near East) bibliography-index to U.S. Research translations,* Jul.1965-)

NEWSPAPER INDEXES

Q114. *Jih pao so yin* The leading Chinese newspapers index, a book of record. V.1-7 Min kuo 23-26 (1934-37) Shang-hai, Chung-shan wen hua chiao yu kuan, Min kuo 23-26 (1934-37) 7 v.

12 leading Chinese newspapers are indexed in a detailed classified arrangement. Each monthly issue contains some 12,000 entries.

Q115. *Jen min jih pao so yin* (Index to the People's Daily) 1950- Pei-ching, Jen min jih pao, 1950-

A monthly subject index to the *Jen min jih pao,* with copies noted through September 1959. Other newspapers as the *Kuang ming jih pao* (Enlightenment Daily) and *Ta kung pao* (L'Impartiale) also published monthly indexes. Newspapers are also indexed in the *Ch'uan kuo chu yao pao k'an tzu liao so yin.*

Q116. Yu lien yen chiu so, Hongkong (Union Research Institute) *Index to the material on Communist China held by the Union Research Institute.* Hongkong, 1962. 197 p.

Microfilm copies of the files of the Union Research Institute's newspaper clippings are now held at three centers in the United States: the Center for Research Libraries; the Center for Chinese Studies, University of California, Berkeley; and the University of Hawaii Library. The index is a key to these files, which are particularly valuable for the period from 1956.

Q117. Cheng chi ta hsueh, Taipei. She hui k'o hsueh tzu liao chung hsin (Chengchi University. Social Science Materials Center) *Chung wen pao chih lun wen fen lei so yin* Classified index to Chinese newspapers,1962-T'ai-pei, Min kuo 52- (1963-) annual.

Each issue contains some 7,000 entries for articles from Taiwan newspapers, arranged in a detailed subject order.

Collectanea or Chinese series

Q118. *Chung-kuo ts'ung shu tsung lu* (Comprehensive bibliography of Chinese series) Shang-hai, Chung hua shu chu, 1959-62. 3 v.

A Chinese collectanea or *ts'ung shu* is to be distinguished from a publisher's series where books may continue to be added from time to time. The collected works of a writer is one form of *ts'ung shu,* but the emphasis may be on works concerning a family or an area. The first of these series was issued in 1202, and this form of publication has led to the preservation of possibly over one-half of early Chinese works, which would otherwise have been lost. Chinese bibliographies of *ts'ung shu* date from 1799, but this is the most comprehensive, listing more *ts'ung shu* and more individual titles than others which it now supersedes. The first volume is a classified arrangement of 2,797 collectanea, giving their locations among 41 mainland Chinese libraries. The second arranges 38,891 titles found in these *ts'ung shu* in a similar traditional order of classics, history, philosophy and belles lettres. The third indexes titles and authors by the four corner system. Buddhist collectanea and collectanea published after 1842 are not included. Editions are noted, and the more reliable indicated. Conversion tables as key to the four corner system included.

Essay bibliography

Q119. Kyoto daigaku. Toyoshi kenkyukai (Kyoto University. Oriental History Society) *Chugoku zuihitsu sakuin* (Index to Chinese essays) Tokyo, Nihon gakujutsu shinkokai, Showa 29 (1954) 1018 p.

The tables of contents of 157 collections of Chinese essays are indexed in the Japanese syllabic order. Stroke index.

Q120. Saeki, Tomi. *Chugoku zuihitsu zatcho sakuin* Index to Chinese essays and miscellaneous writings. Kyoto, Kyoto daigaku Toyoshi kenkyukai, Showa 35 (1960) 1144 p. (Toyoshi kenkyu sokan 7)

A supplement to the *Chugoku zuihitsu sakuin,* indexing the tables of contents of an additional 46 collections.

Western languages

Q121. Cordier, Henri. *Bibliotheca sinica, dictionnaire bibliographique des ouvrages relatifs a l'Empire chinois,* Paris, E. Guilmoto, 1904-8. 4 v. and *Supplement et index,* Paris, 1922-24.

Some 26,000 books, periodicals and periodical articles in Western languages, and published from the 16th century to 1924. Cordier's French annotations are critical and reflect his great knowledge of China. The main work is divided into five parts, of which the first deals with China as a whole, and comprises the first two and a half volumes. The second part deals with foreigners in China, the third with relations between China and foreigners, the fourth with Chinese in foreign countries, and the fifth with tributary countries of China. Difficult to use since there is no comprehensive index, a need partly met by the *Author index to the Bibliotheca sinica of Henri Cordier* (New York, East Asiatic Library, Columbia University Libraries, 1953, 84 p.) which lists 7,700 author entries with page references. A key bibliography of China for Western language materials, but contains much that is now superseded. Reprinted by the Cheng wen Publishing Co., Taipei, 1966.

Q122. Toyo bunko, Tokyo(Oriental Library) *Catalogue of the Asiatic Library of Dr. G. E. Morrison, now a part of the Oriental Library, Tokyo, Japan.*

Tokyo, 1924. 2 v.

Dr. G. E. Morrison was once adviser to the President of China and Peking correspondent of *The Times*. From 1892 to 1917 he collected all available books on China and adjacent areas. The collection contains some 13,530 books in many Western languages, but nearly two-thirds are in English, and one-sixth is in French. Entries are arranged in author order, and there is no annotation and no subject index. Since a large proportion of these entries are to be found in Henri Cordier *Bibliotheca sinica ...*, the principal importance of this catalog is the location of an extant copy.

Q123. Yuan, T'ung-li. *China in Western literature, a continuation of Cordier's Bibliotheca sinica*. New Haven, Far Eastern Publications, Yale University Press, 1958. 802 p.

Dr. T. L. Yuan was Director of the National Library of Peiping from 1926 to 1948. He has listed some 18,000 books in English, French, German and Portuguese published between 1921 and 1957 in broad subject divisions, with detailed breakdown. There are divisions for areas as Manchuria, Mongolia, Tibet, Sinkiang, Taiwan, Hong Kong and Macao, which are treated separately. It is not annotated, and all items have been examined by the compiler. Author index. Since books only are included, John Lust *Index sinicus...* which includes periodical articles and excludes books, supplements this bibliography.

Q124. Hucker, Charles O. *China, a critical bibliography*. Tucson, University of Arizona Press, 1962. 125 p.

A selected annotated list of 2,285 books, periodical articles and sections of books on traditional and modern China. Many entries are repeated. The bibliography has a subject arrangement and within each subject division the compiler has grouped his materials from the most authoritative to the less, and the more general in scope to the more narrow. Entries are mostly in English, although there are some French and German items. Each subject division has a short introduction. Author index. A valuable introductory bibliography.

Q125. Sinor, Denis. *Introduction a l'etude de l'Eurasie centrale*. Wiesbaden, Otto Harrasowitz, 1963. 371 p.

A bibliographical essay, with 4,403 entries, mostly periodical articles published in the 20th century to 1961, with only a few in English. Important since it is concerned with a number of peoples on China's borderland where they have often played a major role in Chinese history. Author index to pages, not items.

Q126. Leslie, Donald, and Jeremy Davidson. *Author catalogues of Western sinologists*. Canberra, Department of Far Eastern History, Research School of Pacific Studies, Australian National University, 1966. 257 p. (Guide to bibliographies on China and the Far East)

Some 500 Western writers on China and related areas are arranged in alphabetical order, with references to sources where listings of their works may be found. Altogether 286 periodicals, nearly all of them Western, were analyzed. A further 100 are noted as not being analyzed. Short subject index.

Japanese language

Q127. Fairbank, John King and Masataka Banno. *Japanese studies on modern China, a bibliographical guide to historical and social science research on the 19th and 20th centuries.* Tokyo, Charles E. Tuttle, 1955. 331 p.

Lists over 1,000 Japanese books and periodical articles on modern China, arranging them by major subjects in modern Chinese history, and then by author. Critical annotations, with notes on the existence of book reviews have been added. The index lists authors and titles in one sequence. There is a character index to authors. Only hints at the vast amount of work carried out by Japanese scholars in the field of Chinese Studies.

Russian language

Q128. Skachkov, Petr. Emelianovich. *Bibliografiia kitaiia.* Moskva, Izdaltelstvo Vostochnoi Literaturi, 1960. 690 p.

19,951 books and periodical articles published in Russian up to 1957, and covering the period 1730 to 1957, are arranged under 25 broad subjects and further divided into books and articles. A revised edition of the 1932 bibliography which contains only 10,000 entries. Ideally the two should be used together to avoid missing material not in the second edition. Articles include reviews of major books in Russian, listed by the title of the book. The second edition has an author index only, where the first has both an author and subject index.

Q129. Yuan, T'ung-li. *Russian works on China, 1918-1960, in American libraries.* New Haven, Yale University, Far Eastern Publications, 1961. 162 p.

1,348 entries are divided into main geographical areas: China Proper, Manchuria, Mongolia, Sinkiang, Tibet and Taiwan, and further subdivided by subjects. Only the latest edition is cited, with earlier editions noted in brief annotations. While this bibliography is small compared with that of Skachkov, it is important for locating materials.

Subject bibliography

RELIGION AND THOUGHT, MISSIONS

Q130. Pfister, P. Louis. *Notices biographiques et bibliographiques sur les Jesuites de l'ancienne Mission de Chine, 1552-1773.* Chang-hai, Imprimerie de la Mission Catholique, 1932-34. 2 v. (Varietes sinologiques no. 59-60)

Lists 463 Jesuits arranged in chronological order, and commencing with St. Francis Xavier, with their biographies and publications. In addition there is a short bibliography of some 250 entries. Detailed subject and name index.

Q131. Wylie, Alexander. *Memorials of Protestant missionaries to the Chinese, giving a list of their publications and obituary notices of the deceased with copious indexes.* Shanghae, American Presbyterian Mission Press, 1867. 330 p.

338 missionaries are listed in chronological order, with a short account of

their lives and lists of their publications in Chinese and English. Index to missionaries and to titles of Chinese and English publications. Reprinted in Taipei, 1967.

Q132. Chu, Clayton H. *American missionaries in China, books, articles, and pamphlets extracted from the subject catalogue of the Missionary Research Library*. Cambridge, Harvard University Press, 1960. 509 p. (Research aids for American Far Eastern policy studies no. 2)

Some 7,000 entries for materials in English, published to 1959, but with a stress on publications issued before 1941. The entries are arranged under 464 subject headings, following the arrangement in the Missionary Research Library. Author and organization index.

Q133. Chan, Wing-tsit. *An outline and an annotated bibliography of Chinese philosophy*. New Haven, Far Eastern Publications, Yale University, 1959. 127 p.

Revises an earlier mimeographed bibliography published in 1955 to which annotations and an additional 100 titles have been added. Altogether there are some 400 entries, divided into three sections. The first is a chronological arrangement with books listed in a brief form under appropriate headings, and graded into essential, supplementary and optional reading. The second is a list by author giving fuller bibliographical information, a brief annotation and noting whether the books should be in a basic library. The third section consists of author-subject indexes. Materials are in Chinese and Western languages.

Q134. Chan, Wing-tsit. *Chinese philosophy, 1949-1963, an annotated bibliography of mainland China publications*. Honolulu, East-West Center Press, 1965. 290 p.

Divided into two sections, the first containing 213 books, and the second 756 periodical and newspaper articles. Each section subdivided chronologically by period. Authors' names in romanization and characters, and titles in romanization, characters and translation. Brief annotations. Name index to authors and to persons cited.

SOCIAL SCIENCES

Q135. U.S. Bureau of the Census. *Bibliography of social science periodicals and monographs series, mainland China, 1949-1960*. Washington, U.S. Government Printing Office, 1961. 32 p. (Foreign social science bibliographies series P-92 no. 3)

107 periodicals and 35 monograph series in the Library of Congress are arranged under 14 social science fields and bibliography. Separate subject and title indexes.

Q136. U.S. Bureau of the Census. *Bibliography of social science periodical and monograph series, Republic of China, 1949-1961*. Washington, U.S. Government Printing Office, 1962. 24 p. (Foreign social science bibliographies P-92 no. 4)

57 periodicals and 27 monograph series are arranged into 15 social science fields. Annotation covers frequency, contents and holdings of the Library of Congress. Separate indexes to subjects, titles, authors and issuing agencies.

Economics

Q137. Wu, Yu-chang. *Chung-kuo ho tso wen hsien mu lu* (Bibliography on cooperation in China) Shang-hai, Nan-ching Chung-kuo ho tso she, Min kuo 25(1936) 110 p.

840 books and periodicals, almost entirely in Chinese on cooperation in China and elsewhere, arranged by publisher and including both official and commercial publications. No annotation and no index.

Q138. U.S. Bureau of the Census. *Population and manpower of China, an annotated bibliography.* Washington, Government Printing Office, 1958. 132 p. (International population reports ser. P. 90, no. 8)

Some 650 books and serials in Chinese, Japanese and Western languages are arranged in subject order, with annotations. Author index.

Q139. Chen, Nai-ruenn. *The economy of mainland China, 1949-1963, a bibliography of materials in English.* Berkeley, Committee on the Economy of China, Social Science Research Council, 1963. 297 p.

Contains 10,000 entries for materials published between 1949 and July 1963, including translations. Approximately 160 periodicals were surveyed to make this compilation. The first part, of 256 pages, includes materials originating in mainland China, and consists mainly of translations from the American Consulate General in Hong Kong. P. 257-97 are for materials originating outside mainland China, mostly from the United States and Hong Kong. There are 297 subject divisions.

Political science and law

Q140. Jiang, Joseph. *Chinese bureaucracy and government administration, an annotated bibliography.* Honolulu, Research Translations, East-West Center, 1964. 157 p.

561 Chinese books and periodical articles, published since 1911, of which only one half have been inspected and annotated. Divided by subjects, and has author and subject indexes.

Q141. Lin, Fu-shun. *Chinese law, past and present, a bibliography of enactments and commentaries in English text.* New York, East Asian Institute, Columbia University, 1966. 419 p.

Divided into two sections: the first, on Communist Chinese law, is some two thirds of the book; the second section is on non-Communist Chinese law. Altogether there are 3,500 books, periodical articles, statutes, documents and newspaper articles surveying Chinese law from earliest times. Author index. No annotations.

Q142. Hsia, Tao-t'ai. *Guide to selected legal sources of mainland China, a listing of laws and regulations and periodical legal literature with a brief survey of the administration of justice.* Washington, Library of Congress, 1967. 357 p.

The first part consists of a translation of two statutory collections the *Chung yang jen min cheng fu fa ling hui pien* (Collection of laws and decrees of the Central People's Government) (v.1-5, 1952-55) and the *Chung hua jen min kung ho kuo fa kuei hui pien* (Collections of laws and regulations of the People's Republic of China)(v.1-13, 1956-64). The second part consists of 940 legal articles from some 58 mainland Chinese periodicals, with titles in translated form only. The second part has an author index and a 71-page introductory survey of the mainland Chinese legal system.

Q143. *Preliminary union list of materials on Chinese law.* Cambridge, Harvard Law School, 1967. 919 p. (Studies in Chinese law no.6)

A union list of approximately 9,000 items, mostly in Chinese and located in 19 libraries, 17 of which are in the United States. The principal section is arranged by subject, and is followed by a list of some 100 periodicals, and a listing of statutory materials.

NATURAL AND APPLIED SCIENCES

Q144. Chao, Chi-sheng. *K'o hsueh chi shu ts'an kao shu t'i yao* (Essentials of scientific and technical reference books) Pei-ching, Shang wu yin shu kuan, 1958. 539 p.

1,554 books in Chinese, mostly published since 1950, are arranged in a classified order, and with the exception of a few items in the initial general section, all are concerned with the natural and applied sciences. Under each subject books are arranged according to their form, and entries are annotated. Separate title and author indexes arranged by stroke.

Q145. U.S. Library of Congress, Reference Department. Science and Technology Division. *Chinese scientific and technical serial publications in the collections of the Library of Congress,* revised edition. Washington, 1961. 107 p.

Some 1,900 entries, mostly from mainland China, are divided into seven major topic groups, and further subdivided. Entries give the romanized title, characters, translation of title, former titles and Library of Congress holdings. There are romanized and Western language title indexes.

Q145.1. Lee, Amy C., and D.C. Dju Chang. *A bibliography of translations from mainland Chinese periodicals in chemistry, general science and technology published by the U.S. Joint Publications Research Service, 1957-1966.* Washington, National Academy of Sciences, 1968. 161 p.

Identifies some 2,000 reports translated into English by the Joint Publications Research Service, with an emphasis on the sciences. These reports are not indexed in detail through any other source.

MEDICINE

Q146. Taki, Mototane. *Chung-kuo i chi k'ao* (Chinese medical books) Pei-ching, Jen min wei sheng chu pan she, 1956. 1404 p.

3,800 books on traditional Chinese medicine are arranged in subject order, and entries are fully annotated. There is a list of titles in the expanded table of contents, and an index to titles by stroke order. Reprint of a Tokugawa period Japanese bibliography.

Q147. Manshu ika daigaku, Mukden(Manchurian Medical University) *Chugoku igaku shomoku* (Catalog of Chinese medical books) Hoten (i.e. Mukden) Showa 6-16(1931-41) 2 v.

Some 2,800 books are arranged in classified order, with a title and author index by strokes for each volume. Full bibliographical information and contents note for each entry.

AGRICULTURE

Q148. Wang, Yu-hu. *Chung-kuo nung hsueh shu lu* (Catalog of books on Chinese agriculture) Pei-ching, Nung yeh ch'u pan she, 1964. 351 p.

Some 500 books on traditional Chinese agriculture are arranged in chronological order, with annotations. Separate subject, title and author indexes.

Q149. Logan, William J.C. *Publications on Chinese agriculture prior to 1949.* Washington, National Agricultural Library, United States Department of Agriculture, 1966. 148 p. (Library List no. 85)

888 books and 186 periodicals in Chinese, Japanese and Western languages, many entries with brief annotations, are arranged in subject order. The materials are in the National Agricultural Library. Author and title indexes.

Q150. Kuo, Leslie Tse-chiu and Peter B. Schroeder. *Communist Chinese periodicals in the agricultural sciences.* Washington, United States Department of Agriculture National Agricultural Library, 1963. 33 p. (Library List no. 70 revised)

132 periodicals arranged in alphabetical order, with holdings in the National Agricultural Library. 19 new titles have been added to the 1960 edition. Title, publisher and subject indexes.

Q151. Kuo, Leslie Tse-chiu. *Communist Chinese monographs in the U.S.D.A. Library.* Washington, U.S. Department of Agriculture Library, 1961. 87 p. (Library List no. 71)

Some 900 monographs are arranged in a detailed subject order, and nearly all entries are annotated. Author index.

Q152. Logan, William J.C. *Chinese agricultural publications from the Republic of China since 1947.* Washington, National Agricultural Library, United States Department of Agriculture, 1964. 55 p. (Library list no.81)

58 periodicals and 257 monographs published in Taiwan since 1947 are arranged by major subjects. For most entries there are brief annotations. Author and title indexes.

MINING AND GEOLOGY

Q153. Pei-ching k'uang yeh hsueh yuan. T'u shu kuan, *Chung-kuo k'uang yeh ch'i k'an lun wen so yin* (Index to periodical articles on Chinese mining engineering) Pei-ching, Ko hsueh ch'u pan she, 1960. 366 p.

Over 8,000 articles from 102 periodicals published from 1917 to 1959, on mining engineering and associated fields, are arranged in detailed subject order.

CHINESE LANGUAGE, LITERATURE, DRAMA AND MUSIC

Chinese language

Q154. Teng, Maurice H. *Recent Chinese publications on the Chinese language.* New Haven, Yale University, Institute of Far Eastern Languages, 1961. 45 p.

110 books are arranged into 7 major sections, and in the sections by title according to the Yale Romanization system. Brief annotations for all entries. No index.

Q155. Yang, Winston L.Y., and Teresa S. Yang. *A bibliography of the Chinese language.* New York, American Association of Teachers of Chinese Language and Culture, 1966. 171 p.

Some 1,500 books, periodical articles and theses in Western languages are arranged under 18 major subject groups. Author index. No annotation.

Q156. U.S. Department of State. Office of External Research. *List of Chinese dictionaries in all languages.* Washington, D.C. 1967. 44 p.

A list of 412 Chinese dictionaries in use in U.S. Government organizations, entered under title and arranged by subject, except for 75 general dictionaries in the humanities, and the social science section which are arranged by language. Only 34 dictionaries have a pre-1950 publication date, and the value of this bibliography, particularly for developments in the sciences, is evident. Author index, but no Chinese characters.

Chinese literature

Q157. Davidson, Martha. *A list of published translations from Chinese into English, French and German.* Ann Arbor, published for the American Council of Learned Societies, by J.W. Edwards, 1952-57. 2 v.

The first part contains 1,493 entries, arranged under subjects. Novels, drama and folktales included, but not poetry. The second part, with entries numbered 1494 to 5391, covers poetry arranged by dynasty, then by author, to the end of the Sung dynasty.

Q158. Hightower, James Robert. *Topics in Chinese literature, outlines and bibliography,* revised edition. Cambridge, Harvard University Press, 1953. 128 p. (Harvard-Yenching Institute Studies v.3)

A select bibliography arranged under 17 different literary styles. Each section has an introduction, followed by short bibliographies, divided into authorities and translations. Index to authors and to Chinese titles.

Q159. Sun, K'ai-ti. *Chung-kuo t'ung su hsiao shuo shu mu* (Catalog of Chinese popular novels) Pei-ching, Tso chia ch'u pan she, 1957. 323 p.

Some 800 novels are arranged in a broad classified order, and indexed by the *chu yin fu hao* system. For most entries annotations and locations are given, but some are noted as not having been inspected by the compiler.

Q160. Schyns, Joseph. *1500 modern Chinese plays and novels.* Hong Kong, Lungmen Bookstore, 1966. 484 p. (Scheut editions. Ser.1. Critical and literary studies, v.3)

Summarizes the contents of 1500 modern plays and novels, with special attention to their moral content. There are sections for fiction, ancient fiction, present-day drama, drama translated into Chinese and ancient drama. There is also a biographical section for 202 writers, giving information on birth date, education and works. Stroke index. Reprint of the 1948 edition published by Catholic University Press, Peiping.

Drama

Q161. Huang, Wen-ying. *Ch'u hai tsung mu t'i yao* (Bibliography of Chinese drama) Shang-hai, Ta tung shu chu, Min kuo 19(1930) 19 v.

Over 770 entries arranged by title, with little information other than a synopsis of the plot, and date of publication and publisher. If drama is extant or not is not mentioned. No index. Supplemented by Pei Ying *Ch'u hai tsung mu t'i yao pu pien* (Supplement to the Bibliography of Chinese drama) (Pei-ching, Jen min ch'u pan she, 1959. 298 p.) which adds another 72 dramas and makes a large number of corrections to the original work. The supplement contains a title index to the original work by stroke order.

Q162. Fu, Hsi-hua. *Yuan tai tsa chu ch'uan mu* (Catalog of Yuan Northern drama) Pei-ching, Tso chia ch'u pan she, 1957. 429 p. (Chung- kuo ku ten hsi chu tsung lu chih 3)

737 entries, of which 550 are identified with authors, are arranged under a broad period order. Annotated. Author and title indexes.

Q163. Fu, Hsi-hua. *Ming tai tsa chu ch'uan mu* (Catalog of Ming Northern drama) Peiching, Tso chia ch'u pan she, 1958. 328 p. (Chung-kuo ku ten hsi chu tsung lu chih 4)

523 entries, of which 349 are identified with authors, are arranged in broad period order. Annotated. Indexes for authors and titles.

Q164. Fu, Hsi-hua. *Ming tai ch'uan ch'i ch'uan mu* (Catalog of Ming dramatic romances) Pei-ching, Jen min wen hsueh ch'u pan she, 1959. 580 p. (Chung-kuo ku ten hsi chu tsung lu chih 5)

950 Ming dramatic romances, of which 618 are identified with authors, are listed, with full annotations. Indexes to authors and titles.

Q165. Yang, Daniel Shih-p'eng. *An annotated bibliography of materials for the study of the Peking theatre.* Madison, University of Wisconsin, 1967. 98 p.

162 reference books and plays, mostly in Chinese, and partly representing material held by the University of Wisconsin. Annotated. Index to personal names, titles and terms.

Music

Q166. Yuan, T'ung-li. *Chung-kuo yin yueh shu p'u mu lu* Bibliography on Chinese music. T'ai-pei, Chung hua kuo yueh hui, Min kuo 45 (1956) 24, 49 p.

Reproduces the eleventh instalment of Richard A. Waterman *Bibliography of Asiatic music* and adds another 56 entries. The remainder of the bibliography consists of 323 books in Chinese. Not annotated.

Q167. Chung yang yin yueh hsueh yuan, Tientsin. Chung-kuo yin yueh yen chiu so(Central Academy of Music. Chinese Music Institute) *Chung kuo ku tai yin yueh shu mu* (Catalog of books on early Chinese music) Pei-ching, Yin yueh ch'u pan she, 1962. 142 p.

Some 1,400 books of Chinese music from earliest times to 1840 are listed in three major groups: extant works, possibly extant works and lost works. Entries are subarranged by categories. Title index in alphabetical order.

GEOGRAPHY

Q168. Wang, Yung and Mao Nai-wen. *Chung-kuo ti hsueh lun wen so yin* (Index to articles on Chinese geography) Pei-p'ing, Kuo li Pei-p'ing shih han ta hsueh, Min kuo 23-25(1934-36) 4 v.

11,000 articles selected from 180 Chinese periodicals published from 1902 to 1935, arranged in a detailed subject order in 2 two-volume sections. Each section has a separate place name index. Citations do not give dates of publication or page number.

Q169. *Translations on the geography of mainland China.* Washington, U.S. Department of Commerce Joint Publications Research Service, 1968. 232 p. (Translations on Communist China, no.10, Bibliography of Joint Publications Research Service. JPRS 45,174)

The first section is arranged by topic and the second by area. Approximately 1,500 entries, many of which are entered under both topic and area.

HISTORY

Q170. Sun, I-tu(Jen) and John De Francis. *Bibliography of Chinese social history, a selected and critical list of Chinese periodical sources.* New Haven, Institute of Far Eastern Languages, Yale University, 1952. 150 p.

176 periodical articles are arranged under 14 subjects. Each entry has a full citation, together with an annotation. Author and subject entry index.

Q171. *Chung-kuo shi hsueh lun wen so yin* (Index to articles on Chinese history) Pei-ching, K'o hsueh ch'u pan she, 1957. 2 v.(in 4)

Over 30,000 articles on Chinese history from 1,300 Chinese periodicals published from 1900 to 1937, and arranged in four major subject divisions, further subdivided. Based on the *Kuo hsueh lun wen so yin* (Index to articles on Chinese studies) 1928-36 in 4 parts, and containing some 12,000 articles. The revision is largely based on additional material located in Peking libraries. No author index, but an index of subjects and proper names. Pagination not cited in entries.

Q172. Hua tung shih fan ta hsueh, Shanghai. Li shi hsi (East China Normal University. History Department) *Chung-kuo ku tai chi shih chi shih pao k'an lun wen tzu liao so yin* (Index to newspaper and periodical articles on early and medieval Chinese history) Shang-hai, 1959. 197 p.

Approximately 6,000 articles from periodicals and newspapers published from 1949 to 1959. Divided into two parts, the first by subject, and the second by dynasty to the end of the Ch'ing dynasty, then subdivided by subjects. Date of issue of article given, but no pagination. No index.

Q173. Yu, Ping-kuen(Yu Ping-chuan) *Chinese history, index to learned articles, 1902-1962, compiled in the Fung ping Shan Library, University of Hong Kong.* Hong Kong, East Asia Institute, 1963. 572 p.
10,325 articles selected from 355 periodicals, covering Chinese history to the end of the Ch'ing dynasty. Articles are arranged by author to show evolution of his ideas and interests. Index by stroke order giving subjects referred to in the text. Only one-third of the number of entries of *Chung-kuo shih hsueh lun wen so yin* (Pei-ching, 1957) but bibliographical information more detailed.

TO THE END OF THE MING DYNASTY

Q174. Frankel, Hans Herman. *Catalogue of translations from the Chinese histories, for the period 220-960.* Berkeley, University of California Press, 1957. 295 p.
Over 2,000 translations which may be extensive or may be only a few lines, arranged in the order of the *Po-na* edition of the Chinese dynastic histories, citing locations. Index to subjects and translators.

Q175. Hartwell, Robert. *A guide to sources of Chinese economic history, A.D. 618-1368.* Chicago, University of Chicago, Committee on Far Eastern Civilizations, 1964. 257 p.
1,119 entries referring to collected works for the T'ang through Yuan dynasties, but emphasizing the Sung dynasty. Annotated. Index for place names, and personal names, and general index.

Q176. Yamane, Yukio. *Mindai shi kenkyu bunken mokuroku* (Catalog of research materials on the Ming dynasty) Tokyo, Toyo bunko Mindai shi kenkyushitsu, 1960. 258 p.
2,373 periodical articles and 128 books in Japanese and Chinese are arranged in detailed classified order covering Japanese-Ming relations, biography, social, economic, political, religious, intellectual, literary, art and science history. Indexes to authors' names and prominent Chinese and non-Chinese of the Ming period.

Q177. Franke, Wolfgang. *An introduction to the sources of Ming history.* Singapore and Kuala Lumpur, University of Malaya Press, 1968. 397 p.
Over 800 major works are annotated and arranged in chapters for historical works, biographies, memorials, political institutions. Foreign affairs and military organization, geographical works and local histories, economics, technology, encyclopedias and collectanea. Locations of copies noted in many cases.

Ch'ing dynasty,1644-1911

Q178. Irick, Robert L, Yu Ying-shih and Liu Kwang-ching. *American-Chinese relations, 1784-1941, a survey of Chinese language materials at Harvard.* Cambridge, Harvard University Press, 1960. 296 p. (Research aids for American Far Eastern policy studies, no.3)
Some 2,800 entries are arranged in a detailed subject order, under reference works and surveys, documentary collections, periodicals, libraries and archives, economic and cultural relations, missions, education, social

reform and diplomatic relations. Intended to be a practical guide for students. Author index.

Q179. Feuerwerker, Albert and Cheng S. *Chinese Communist studies of modern Chinese history.* Cambridge, East Asian Research Center, Harvard University, 1961. 287 p. (Chinese economic and political studies, Special series)

430 books and 18 periodicals are arranged in a classified order, with most entries fully and critically annotated. Each major subject division has a lengthy introduction. The principal divisions are: General, Ming and Ch'ing dynasties, the Republic, economic history, intellectual and cultural history, and reference works. Author, subject and title index. Includes a short essay on Chinese Communist historiography.

Q180. Teng, Ssu-yu. *Historiography of the Taiping rebellion.* Cambridge, East Asian Research Center, Harvard University, distributed by Harvard University Press, 1962. 180 p. (Harvard East Asian monographs)

A bibliographical essay surveying T'aiping, Ch'ing, Japanese, Western and Russian sources. Titles are noted in the index-glossary.

Q181. Liu, Kwang-ching. *Americans and Chinese, a historical essay and a bibliography.* Cambridge, Harvard University Press, 1963. 211 p.

Lists over 1,500 sources for the study of American non-governmental relations with China. Materials are in English, and are arranged under manuscripts, archives, biography, memoirs and published letters, newspapers and periodicals, and reference works. Preceded by a short historical essay on American Chinese contacts.

Republican and Communist china

Q182. Wu, Eugene. *Leaders of twentieth century China, annotated bibliography of selected Chinese works in the Hoover Library.* Stanford, Stanford University Press, 1956. 106 p. (Hoover Institute and Library, Bibliographical series 4)

More than 500 entries with descriptive annotations are arranged in 8 parts, for collective biography, political, military, intellectual, industrialist and businessmen biographies, overseas Chinese, school yearbooks and serials. Index for authors, titles and biographees.

Q183. Uchida, Naosaku. *The overseas Chinese, a bibliographical essay based on the resources of the Hoover Institution.* Stanford, Hoover Institution on War, Revolution and Peace, Stanford University, 1959. 134 p. (Hoover Institution Bibliographical series 7)

679 books and periodicals are discussed under the following subjects: Amoy merchants, Kongsi system, coolie trade, anti-Chinese immigration policies, assimilation problems, social institutions, economic problems, the Communist Chinese and the overseas Chinese. Half the book an essay on overseas Chinese. No index.

Q184. Chou, Ts'e-tsung. *Research guide to the May Fourth movement, intellectual revolution in modern China, 1915-1924.* Cambridge, Harvard University Press, 1963. 297 p. (Harvard East Asia series 13)

1,479 books, periodicals and periodical articles are arranged into three major parts. The first is a listing of periodicals and newpapers, mostly established from 1915 to 1923, arranged by year and annotated. The second is a bibliography of books and periodical articles in Chinese and Japanese, and the third is a bibliography of periodical articles in Western languages. Index to authors, titles and terms.

Q185. Liu, Chun-jo. *Controversies in modern Chinese intellectual history, an analytical bibliography of periodical articles, mainly of the May Fourth and post-May Fourth era.* Cambridge, Harvard University Press, 1964. 207 p.

Over 500 articles in Chinese from 17 periodicals are arranged in classified order with full annotations. Author and subject index.

Q186. Hsueh, Chun-tu. *The Chinese Communist movement...* Stanford, Hoover Institution, 1960-62. 2 v. (Hoover Institution, Bibliographical series, VIII, XI)

359 books and periodicals in the first volume cover the period from 1921 to 1937, and 863 in the second volume cover the period from 1937 to 1949. Entries are annotated and arranged by subject. Each volume has its own title and author index.

Q187. Israel, John. *The Chinese student movement, 1927-1937, a bibliographical essay on the resources of the Hoover Institution.* Stanford, Stanford University Press, 1959. 29 p. (Hoover Institution Bibliographical series 6)

46 books and 81 newspapers and periodicals are discussed.

Q188. Young, John. *The research activities of the South Manchurian Railway Company,1907-45, a history and bibliography.* New York, East Asian Institute, Columbia University, 1965. 730 p.

The first part is a study of South Manchurian Railway research activities and the second consists of 6,284 books, studies, or periodicals arranged in 46 categories. Each entry is entered under title, which is romanized and translated. Library locations stated. No index.

Q189. Mote, Frederick W. *Japanese sponsored governments in China, 1937-45, an annotated bibliography compiled from materials in the Chinese collection of the Hoover Library.* Stanford, Stanford University Press, 1954. 68 p. (Hoover Institute and Library, Bibliographical series 3)

383 annotated entries for books, periodicals and newspapers divided into 7 sections: reference and general background, books published in areas under puppet governments, non-puppet publications, prominent puppet leaders, postwar publications, serials and newspapers. Annotations are brief and descriptive. Author and title index.

Q190. Rhoads, Edward J.M. *The Chinese Red Army, 1927-1963, an annotated bibliography.* Cambridge, Harvard University Press, 1964. 188 p. (Harvard East Asian monographs 16)

Some 600 books, periodical articles, mimeographed papers, and unpublished manuscripts, mostly in Chinese and English, arranged under 19 subject headings, and annotated. The selection of Chinese language materials is selective, attempting to avoid Communist and nationalist bias. Author index.

Local history
   A valuable guide to bibliographies and library catalogs, referring to Chinese
local gazetteers, is Donald Leslie and Jeremy Davidson *Catalogues of Chinese
local gazetteers* (Canberra, Department of Far Eastern History, Research
School of Pacific Studies, Australian National University, 1967. 125 p.) in
which 111 items are described. Only the 7 most important bibliographies and
catalogs are listed here. For important American holdings outside the Library
of Congress, the reader is referred to Ch'iu K'ai-ming *A classified catalogue of
Chinese books in the Chinese-Japanese Library of the Harvard-Yenching Institute at Harvard University* (Cambridge, 1938-40, 3 v.) for a list of 1,200 local
gazetteers. Another important holding of over 1,400 local gazetteers is to be
found in the East Asian Library of Columbia University, but this and other
American collections have yet to be recorded in a union list.

Q191. Tan, Ch'i-hsiang. *Kuo li Pei-p'ing t'u shu kuan fang chih mu lu* (Catalog
   of local histories in the Peiping Library) Pei-ching, Pei-ching t'u shu kuan,
   Min kuo 22(1933)-1957. 6 v.
   Volume 1-4 contain some 5,200 gazetteers in 3,800 different editions
   arranged by province, with a stroke order index to places. Volume 5,
   which is noted as Supplement II, was published in 1936, and lists 862
   gazetteers acquired from 1933 to 1936. Volume 6, or Supplement III,
   contains an additional 2,357 titles.
Q192. Chu, Shih-chia. *Kuo hui t'u shu kuan ts'ang Chung-kuo fang chih mu
   lu* Catalogue of Chinese local histories in the Library of Congress. Washington, U.S. Government Printing Office, 1942. 552 p.
   Nearly 3,000 local gazetteers are arranged by province. Gazetteers in
   ts'ung shu are included. Romanized and stroke order index to places.
   Does not include gazetteers published in the Ming period and earlier
   among the rare books of the National Library of Peking, and microfilmed
   by the Library of Congress. The best listing of these is to be found in the
   manuscript *Kuo li Pei-ching t'u shu kuan shan pen shu chuang hsiang shu
   mu* Packing list of rare Chinese books of the National Library of Peking,
   March 1941 (151 p.)
Q193. Tenri toshokan, Tenri(Tenri Library) *Chubun chishi mokuroku* (Catalog of local histories in Chinese) Tenri, Tenri daigaku shuppanbu, Showa
   30(1955) 138, 276 p. (Tenri toshokan sosho dai 19 shu)
   Some 2,500 entries, of which over one half are local gazetteers, are
   arranged in a number of categories such as maps, early gazetteers, later
   gazetteers, with province subdivisions in most cases. Alphabetical index
   to entries by their Japanese pronunciation, with a character key. Books
   listed are not to be found in the Toyo bunko *Chugoku chihoshi rengo
   mokuroku* (Tokyo, 1964)
Q194. Hervouet, Yves. *Catalogue des monographes locals chinoises dans les
   bibliotheques d'Europe.* Paris, Mouton, 1957. 100p. (Le monde d'outre-
   mer, passe et present, 4 ser. Bibliographies 1)
   2,590 local histories in 1,434 different editions are arranged by province,
   with locations in 25 libraries. Index to names of places. Not exceptional

in numbers of gazetteers, and useful only in terms of availability.

Q195. Kuo li chung yang t'u shu kuan, Taipei(National Central Library) *T'ai-wan kung ts'ang fang chih lien ho mu lu* (Union catalog of local histories in public libraries in Taiwan) T'ai-pei, Sheng chung chu chu, Min kuo 46(1957) 107 p.

Some 3,300 gazetteers, published to 1954, arranged by provinces. Includes the holdings of 11 libraries. But excludes useful modern gazetteers for Taiwan.

Q196. Chu, Shih-chia. *Chung-kuo ti fang chih tsung lu tseng ting pen* (Catalog of Chinese local histories, revised edition) Shang-hai, Shang wu yin shu kuan, 1958. 318 p.

A union list of the holdings of 22 libraries noting some 7,000 gazetteers, an increase of approximately 1,000 over the 1935 edition. Bibliographical information given is slight, with title, date and edition only noted. Arranged by province, with a stroke order index for personal names and for titles.

Q197. Toyo bunko, Tokyo. Toyogaku bunka senta renraku kyogikai (Oriental Library. Oriental culture center cooperation conference) *Chugoku chihoshi rengo mokuroku* (Union catalog of Chinese local histories) Tokyo, Showa 39(1964) 267 p.

Some 3,500 titles arranged by provinces, and held by four major Japanese libraries, excluding the Tenri Library. Stroke order index to titles.

Hong Kong

Q198. U.S. Bureau of the Census. *Bibliography of social science periodicals and monograph series, Hong Kong, 1950-61.* Washington, 1962. 13 p. (Foreign social science bibliographies, series P-92, no. 7)

27 periodicals and 22 monograph series in the Library of Congress are arranged under 14 social science fields and bibliography. Each entry is annotated. Separate title and subject indexes.

Q199. Braga, Jose Maria. *A Hong Kong bibliography,1965.* Hong Kong, Government Press, 1965. 17 p.

Some 300 books and reports are arranged by broad topics, but with no annotation and no index. Useful lists of English and Chinese newspapers and periodicals published in Hong Kong are appended.

Manchuria

Q200. Berton, Peter. *Manchuria, an annotated bibliography.* Washington, Library of Congress, Reference Department, 1951. 187 p.

843 books and periodicals in English, Russian, Chinese, and Japanese, but mostly in Japanese, arranged in a classified order, with an author and subject index. Annotated. Highly selective since the Library of Congress has over 2,000 titles in Western languages, and over 10,000 books in Japanese on Manchuria.

Sinkiang

Q201. Yuan, T'ung-li and Watanabe Hiroshi. *Shinkyo kenkyu bunken moku-roku, 1866-1962, Nihon bun* Classified bibliography of Japanese books and articles concerning Sinkiang. Tokyo, 1962. 92 p.

1,166 books and periodical articles are arranged in a classified order, with separate author and subject indexes. No annotation.

Taiwan

Q202. Cordier, Henri. *Bibliographie des ouvrages relatifs a l'ile Formose.* Chartres, Imprimerie Durand, 1893. 59 p.

Some 300 books, periodical articles and maps are arranged in a broad subject order, represent the earlier Western literature on Taiwan. No table of contents and no index.

Q203. *T'ai-wan wen hsien tzu liao mu lu* (Catalog of materials on Taiwan) T'ai-pei, T'ai-wan sheng wen hsien wei yuan hui, Min kuo 47 (1958) 163 p.

Approximately 3,000 books, almost entirely in Japanese, arranged by subject. An appendix lists some 120 books in Western languages.

Q204. *T'ai-wan wen hsien fen lei so yin,* Min kuo 48 nien- Classified index to Taiwan materials, 1959- T'ai-pei, T'ai-wan sheng wen hsien wei yuan hui, Min kuo 49- (1960-)

Annual bibliography for articles from some 200 newspapers and periodicals, arranged by a detailed subject classification. No index. 1964 issue published 1966 noted.

Q205. Chung-kuo wen hua hsueh yuan, T'ai-wan yen chiu so (China Cultural Council. Taiwan Institute) *T'ai-wan wen hsien mu lu* (Bibliography of materials on Taiwan) T'ai-pei, Min kuo 54(1965) 264 p.

Some 4,000 books and reports in Japanese and Chinese in a detailed subject arrangement. No index.

Tibet

Q206. Hsu, Ginn-tze(Hsu, Chin-chih) *A bibliography of the Tibetan highland and its adjacent districts* Ch'ing kang tsang kao yuan chi pi lien ti ch'u hsi wen wen hsien mu lu. Peking, Science Press, 1958. 462 p.

The compiler claims that this bibliography of some 5,000 articles from 384 Western and Russian language periodicals comprises approximately four-fifths of the total published literature. Arranged under broad subject headings as geology, seismology, history, general works, climatology, maps, languages, and geographical areas as Himalayas, Pamirs, Kashmir, and Nepal. Author and subject index.

R.JAPAN

The first step of territorial expansion for modern Japan was in 1875, with the acquisition of the Kurile Islands. In 1879 the Ryukyus became Okinawa Prefecture. In 1895, following the Sino-Japanese War, Japan acquired Taiwan, and in 1906, the Liao-tung peninsula in Manchuria and Southern Sakhalin. Korea formally became a part of the Japanese Empire in 1910. In 1945 the territory of Japan was once again restricted to the four main islands. In 1954 the northern islands of the Ryukyus were returned to Japan, and in 1968, the Bonins.

REFERENCE BOOKS

R 1. *Guide to Japanese reference books* Nihon no sanko tosho. Chicago, American Library Association, 1966. 303 p.

A translation into English of *Nihon no sanko tosho,* kaitei ban (Japanese reference books, revised edition) (Tokyo,1965) 2,475 books and periodicals published to September 1964 have been cited, but older and out-of-print materials have been excluded to a large extent from the selection. Divided into four parts: general works, humanities, social sciences, and science and technology, with about one third of the entries in the last part. In spite of translation, this is still a book designed for the Japanese audience, a bibliography of books published in Japan, and almost entirely in Japanese. Important Western reference works on Japan have been ignored, even when superior to Japanese works cited. Nevertheless this is a major step forward in the development of reference literature.

ENCYCLOPEDIAS AND HANDBOOKS

Traditional Encyclopedias

R 2. Jingu shicho, Tokyo(Office of the Great Shrine) *Koji ruien* (Encyclopedia of ancient matters) Tokyo, Yoshikawa kobunkan, Showa 42- (1967-)

A reprint of the 51-volume edition. Each volume or group of volumes represents a major subject as astronomy, government, law, etc., and consists of collections of sources from diaries, records, and myths, published to the end of the Tokugawa period. V.51 will be a table of contents and an index in the order of the Japanese syllabary. A valuable selection for the student of Japanese cultural history.

R 3. Mozume, Takami. *Kobunko* (Comprehensive anthology) Tokyo, Kobunko kankokai, Showa 2(1927) 20 v.

Collection of texts from Japanese and Chinese books noted in the

Gunsho sakuin (Index to Japanese classical literature). Texts are arranged by subject and emphasize literature, but since the number of selections listed in the *Gunsho sakuin* is five times greater than those in the *Kobunko*, for fuller treatment of a subject reference should be made to this source. Traditional *kana* spelling is used. Each volume has its own table of contents.

General and subject encyclopedias

R 4. Mochizuki, Shinko. *Bukkyo daijiten* (Buddhist encyclopedia dictionary) Kyoto, Sekai Seiten Kanko Kyokai, Showa 35-38(1960-63) 10 v.

The main body of the dictionary consists of some 15,000 entries in the first 5 volumes, and while it refers to Buddhism in general, there is an emphasis on Japan. Each entry has a bibliography, and is arranged by the Japanese syllabary. Volume 6 is a chronological table of Buddhism, indexed for personal names, dynastic reigns, and book titles. Volume 7 is an index, with separate parts for Japanese and Chinese terms, Pali terms, and Sanskrit terms. The index for Japanese and Chinese terms is arranged by the Japanese syllabary and has an index by characters as a key to the Japanese pronunciation. V.8 is a supplement and v.9 and 10 published in 1963 contain approximately 3,000 additional entries. First edition published 1909-31.

R 5. *Nihon rekishi daijiten* (Encyclopedia dictionary of Japanese history) Tokyo, Kawade shobo, Showa 31-35 (1956-60) 20 v., and 2 supplementary volumes.)

A broad and objective coverage, reflecting post-war research, including foreign persons and subjects when related to Japan. Entries are signed and arranged in Japanese syllabic order. Volume 19 is supplementary, and volume 20 is a subject index, arranged under 12 major headings, then subdivided. The supplementary volumes are *Nihon rekishi nempyo* (Chronological table of Japanese history) 1960, 373 p. and *Nihon rekishi chizu* (Japanese historical atlas) 1961, containing 60 principal maps and a 58-page index of subjects, personal and placenames.

R 6. Heibonsha *Sekai daihyakka jiten* (World encyclopedia) Tokyo, Showa 39-43 (1964-68) 26 v.

A major encyclopedia with world-wide coverage where only 25 per cent of the 80,000 items refer to Asia, and only one half of these refer directly to Japan. Articles are signed, but have no bibliographies. The first atlas volume is for Japan, has 114 maps and an index for some 60,000 placenames. The second atlas volume covers the rest of the world. Revision of the 1955-63 edition.

Handbooks

R 7. Chamberlain, Basil Hall. *Things Japanese.* London, Kegan Paul, Trench, Trubner, 1939. 584 p.

The author was Emeritus Professor of Japanese and Philology at Tokyo University. This is a combination of a brief introduction to Japanese culture, an encyclopedia and a dictionary. Treatment is popular and the number of revisions since 1890 is a reflection of changing times and attitudes in Japan. Reprinted by University Books, New Hyde Park, New York, 1966.

R 8. Papinot, Edmond. *Historical and geographical dictionary of Japan.* New York, Ungar, 1964. 2 v.

A reprint of the 1910 translation of the 1906 French edition. A dictionary of historical and geographical names, including historical geographical names, together with considerable information on the customs, feasts and other aspects of Japanese culture. Useful lists appended include tables of provinces and departments, tables of fiefs, lists of emperors, genealogical tables, tables for computation of years, months and days, and tables of weights and measures.

R 9. Nihon Yunesuko kokunai iinkai (Japan. National Commission for UNESCO) *Japan, its land, people and culture,* revised edition . Tokyo, Ministry of Finance Printing Bureau, 1964. 885 p.

Developed as a result of UNESCO's major project on mutual appreciation of East and West cultural values. The signed articles have been written by Japanese authorities and translated into English. It is intended to give an encyclopedic coverage of Japan, with geographical, historical, social, economic and cultural information. An alphabetical index provides ready access.

R10. Kobata, Atsushi. *Dokushi soran* (Handbook of Japanese history) Tokyo, Jimbutsu oraisha, Showa 41(1966) 1864 p.

A valuable and entirely new guide to Japanese historical studies, with a topical arrangement, and a first name index in Japanese syllabic order. All aspects of history are well covered, the emphasis being however on illustration and tables rather than description. Chronology and genealogy well developed.

R11. Joly, Henri L. *Legend in Japanese art.* Rutland, Tuttle, 1967. 623 p.

Over 1,118 entries, of which over 300 are cross references, referring to the history, legend, folklore, and religion in the art of Japan, with over 700 illustrations. Less reliable than William Edmunds *Pointers and clues to the subjects of Chinese and Japanese art* (London, Sampson Low, 1934)

R12. Goodertier, Joseph M. *A dictionary of Japanese history.* New York, Walker/Weatherhill, 1968. 415 p.

The first of a projected trilogy of reference works written for the Western reader of Japanese history and literature, and having over 1,100 entries on important events, major clans, government and social structure, styles of architecture and painting, works of literature, and religious and social developments. Biographical and geographical materials will be found in the later volumes. Subject and character indexes.

YEARBOOKS

R13. *The Japan yearbook,* 1905-31. Tokyo, Japan year book office, 1905-1931.

Arranged by subject, with a detailed table of contents, and indexed from the 1926 issue. Later issues have a biographical section. Becomes *The Japanese Empire, yearbook of Japan*, 1932, 1 v. *The Japan Times year book*, 1933, 1 v. *The Japan-Manchoukuo year book*, 1934, 1935, 1937, 1938-41, and the *Orient yearbook*, 1942. Issues for 1908-9, 1919-20, 1921-22, 1924-25 were combined.

R14. *Asahi nenkan*, 1925- (Asahi yearbook, 1925-) Tokyo, Asahi shimbunsha, Taisho 13- (1924-)
The finest general yearbook for Japan, arranged by subjects, with sections on world affairs and Japanese affairs, including land and people, law, labor, economy, statistics, transportation, local affairs and culture.

R15. *The Japan yearbook*, 1933-52. Tokyo, Foreign Affairs Association, 1933-52.
Arranged by subject, with a detailed table of contents, and excellent index. Coverage of not only prewar years, but of wartime Japan and Japan under the occupation. Criticized for attempting too much and lacking in reliability. All issues to 1944 republished by the Interdepartmental Committee for the acquisition of foreign publications.

R16. *The Japan annual*, 1954-58. Tokyo, Japan annual publications, 1954-58. 3 v.
Each issue has four parts, on national affairs, international affairs, the economy, and social and cultural affairs, further subdivided by subjects. The 1954 and 1955 issues have tables of contents and indexes, but the 1958 issue lacks both. Information supplied by government and private industry and written by authorities.

DICTIONARIES

R17. Shimonaka, Yasaburo. *Daijiten* (Great dictionary) Tokyo, Heibonsha, Showa 28-29(1953-54) 26 v.(in 13.)
The most comprehensive Japanese dictionary published with some 730,000 words arranged in Japanese syllabary order. Volume 26 contains an extensive index of characters difficult to read and arranged in stroke order. Of the total number of entries, 280,000 are for place names and personal names and 40,000 are dialect words. A reprint in reduced format of the 1934-37 edition in 26 volumes with some revisions.

R18. Shimmura, Izuru. *Kojien* (Comprehensive dictionary) Tokyo, Iwanami shoten, Showa 30(1955) 2359 p.
A standard one-volume dictionary representative of many similar works of this kind, with some 100,000 works covering a wide range of Japanese culture, and arranged in the Japanese syllabic order. Entries are followed by characters and meanings in Japanese. Short index by stroke order to characters difficult to read.

Japanese character dictionaries
R19. Morohashi, Tetsuji. *Dai Kanwa jiten* (Great Chinese-Japanese dictionary) Tokyo, Taishukan shoten, Showa 30-35(1955-60) 13 v.

50,000 different characters, with some 500,000 compounds, arranged in radical order, then by strokes. Characters given in variant forms, with both early and modern Chinese and Japanese pronunciation stated. The dictionary is based on a number of Chinese sources as the *Pei wen yun fu* and the *K'ang hsi tz'u tien* and has been developed for the Japanese sinologist. Volume 13 has stroke indexes, Japanese readings, four corner indexes. A major work now published in a Chinese edition as *Chung wen ta tz'u tien.*

R20. Ueda, Kazutoshi. *Daijiten* (Great dictionary) Tokyo, Kodansha, Showa 38(1963) 2821 p.

A standard one volume dictionary, important for the large number of characters represented, some 15,000. These are arranged in radical order. For each pronunciation is given, and meaning stated in Japanese. Indexes arrange characters by stroke, and by Japanese pronunciation, and a useful select list of characters in grass style or *sosho* forms. Widely known through its 1942 reprint by Harvard University Press.

Japanese-English, English-Japanese dictionaries

R21. Takahashi, Morio. *Romanized English-Japanese, Japanese-English dictionary.* Tokyo, Taiseido, 1958. 457, 1226 p.

One of the few, and certainly one of the most comprehensive modern Japanese dictionaries giving romanized Japanese equivalents for English words. The first part is for English-Japanese, with 10,000 English words and phrases, and the second has 50,000 Japanese words and phrases. The entries in both parts have been selected on the basis of their usefulness for daily use. Japanese characters follow the romanized forms.

R22. *Kenkyusha's new English-Japanese dictionary on bilingual principles* Kenkyusha shin Ei-Wa daijiten. Tokyo, Kenkyusha, 1960. 2204 p.

Contains over 190,000 words, including abbreviations and proper names, with their Japanese equivalents in characters. No romanization of the Japanese since this is intended for the Japanese reader.

R23. *Kenkyusha's new Japanese-English dictionary* Kenkyusha shin Wa-Ei daijiten. Tokyo, Kenkyusha, 1962. 2136 p.

Some 85,000 works, with character equivalents and numerous examples of use in Japanese, followed by translations in English.

R24. Nelson, Andrew. *Modern reader's Japanese-English character dictionary.* Rutland, Tuttle, 1963. 1048 p.

Now replacing as a standard dictionary the older Arthur Rose-Innes *Beginner's dictionary of Chinese-Japanese characters.* 5,446 characters, including 671 variants, arranged in radical order, and with readings and translations followed by some 70,000 compounds with translation. Valuable appendices, including a list of Japanese standard characters or *toyo-kanji.*

BIOGRAPHICAL DICTIONARIES

R25. Haga, Yaichi. *Nihon jimmei jiten* (Japan biographical dictionary) Tokyo, Ogura shoten, Taisho 3(1914) 1174 p.
Some 50,000 historical figures are arranged by their personal names in the order of the Japanese syllabary. Each entry has characters for the name, and a brief identifying biographical note. Two indexes, one arranged by strokes for the characters of the personal name, and the second by the Japanese syllabic order for the family name. A valuable and extensive one-volume listing.

R26. Heibonsha. *Dai jimmei jiten* (Biographical dictionary) Tokyo, Showa 28-30(1953-55) 10 v.
The first six volumes list some 50,000 Japanese and volume 9, 8,000 living Japanese. Volumes 7-8 list 8,000 foreigners, of whom very few live in Japan. Volume 8 has an alphabetical index. Volume 10 is an index in stroke order. Earlier edition with title *Shinsen dai jimmei jiten,* (Tokyo, 1937-41. 9 v.)

R27. *Seiyo jimmei jiten* (Biographical dictionary of Westerners) Tokyo, Iwanami shoten, Showa 31(1956) 1962 p.
A greatly expanded revision of the 1932 edition, important for giving notice to Westerners and Asians prominent in Japanese history, but otherwise not noteworthy. Some 20,000 persons are listed in Japanese syllabic order, with indexes to names in their original spelling. No Chinese or Koreans included.

R28. *Japan biographical encyclopedia and who's who,* 1964-65. Tokyo, Rengo Press, 1965. 2377 p.
The third edition, the first being published in 1958, lists 15,730 names, including prominent persons in Japanese history, from Jimmu Tenno, whose dates are given as 711-585 B.C., to the present day, where the range of selection is wide, including important public and business personalities. All cabinet officials from 1885 are included. Each entry is followed by the family name, personal name, Japanese characters, a one-word classification, and an account varying from five lines to one and a half columns. Principal works of the biographee noted. An inconvenience is the arrangement of names in one major and two minor alphabetical sequences, but the names index is cumulated.

Contemporary biography

R29. *Nihon shinshiroku* (Japan who's who) Tokyo, Kojunsha, Meiji 22- (1889-)
Recent issues list some 80,000 Japanese prominent in politics, business, government, education and culture, and arranged in the Japanese syllabic order. Information includes occupation, place and date of birth, education, address, and telephone number. Lists many persons not found in other collective biography sources. Appendices include directories of major firms, public offices and educational institutions.

R30. *Jinji koshinroku* (Japan who's who) Tokyo, Jinji koshinjo, Meiji 36-
(1903-)
Appears irregularly every two or three years and is the most comprehensive listing of prominent Japanese. The 24th issue published in 1968 lists
some 80,000 and gives personal information as date and place of birth,
education, address, and a brief account , about twice the length of that
found in the *Nihon shinshiroku*. The entries are arranged in the Japanese
syllabic order and there is a character key.

R31. *Who's who in Japan*, 1912-1940/41. Tokyo, Who's who in Japan publishing office, 1912-40. 21 v.
Lists some 6,000 living persons with a short biographical note on their
age, education, careers and addresses. Prominent foreigners in Japan are
also noted. Becomes *Who's who in Japan and Manchoukuo*, 1941/42
Noted as the 21st annual edition with some 4,800 names.

R32. *Japan who's who and business directory*, 1948-51. Tokyo, Tokyo news
service, 1948-51. 2 v.
The 1950-51 volume contains some 3,200 biographies of living Japanese,
some 1,200 more than in the 1948 edition, and is based on questionnaires.

R33. Nihon chosakuken kyogikai (Japanese Copyright Council) *Bunkajin
meiroku* (Who's who in culture) Tokyo, Showa 26- (1951-)
A classified arrangement of some 45,000 copyright holders, compiled
from questionnaires distributed to authors. The author index is arranged
by characters. Useful for identifying the correct pronunciation of an
author's name, and also for brief summaries of the salient facts of his life,
with important works. Title on spine *Chosakuken daicho* (Register of
copyright holders) regarded by compilers as the correct name for this
directory.

R34. *The Japan Times foreign residents, business firms, organizations, directory*, 1951- Tokyo, Japan Times, 1951-
An annual directory originally issued with title *Directory of foreign residents*. Arranged by cities, then alphabetically. Some 8,000 entries, including information on firms arranged by kind of business.

R35. Nihon Yunesuko kokunai iinkai, Tokyo (Japan. National Commission
for Unesco) *Who's who among Japanese writers*. Tokyo, 1957. 140 p.
Includes some 300 contemporary literary authors still actively engaged in
writing. For each author his name, special field, background and education and description of his principal works noted. Appendices contain
lists of literary organizations and prizes.

Names Dictionaries

R36. Gillis, Irvin and Pai Ping-ch'i. *Japanese surnames*. Peking, 1939. 173,
171 p.
A listing of 9,335 names arranged by stroke order, with an index to these
names arranged alphabeticaly. Valuable as a tool for locating standard
romanization of Japanese family names, but not sufficiently comprehensive, and assistance has to be sought from other sources such as the
Bunkajin meiroku and the *Jinji koshinroku* for contemporary persons

and the *Dai jimmei jiten* for historical persons. Reprinted by Edwards Brothers, Ann Arbor, 1942.

R37. Gillis, Irvin and Pai Ping-ch'i. *Japanese personal names.* Peking, 1940. 70, 70 p.

A companion volume to the authors' *Japanese surnames* with 3,511 personal names arranged by stroke order, with an alphabetical index. Reprinted by Edwards Brothers, Ann Arbor, 1942.

DIRECTORIES

Official

R38. *Shokuinroku,* Meiji 19- (Register of civil officials, 1886-)

A directory of official organizations in Japan, listing officials by name under the appropriate departments and bureaus. The first part is concerned with the national officialdom, the second with that of the prefectures and local governments. Many valuable charts show the relationship of government organizations, but it contains no index to officials by name. Earlier issues from 1886 to 1943 and 1946 have now been published on microfilm by Yushodo, Tokyo.

R39. U.S. Embassy. Japan. *The government organization of Japan, with names of bureau, division and section chiefs, as of November 20,1962.* Tokyo, Translation Services Branch, Political Section, American Embassy, 1962. 232 p.

An issue of a list published from time to time by the U.S. Embassy and valuable since it gives a comprehensive survey of English language equivalents to Japanese official names. A shorter and even more dated list may be found in Kenkyusha's *New Japanese-English dictionary* (Tokyo, 1954) p. 2116-2121.

Commercial

R40. *Nihon shokuinroku,* Showa 22- (Japan who's who in government, schools, organizations, banks and companies, 1947-) Tokyo, Jinji koshinjo, Showa 22- (1947-)

More a directory to some 30,000 firms and organizations than a who's who. There are four parts for government organization, universities, academic and professional associations, and business and industrial firms. Large stockholders and principal officers noted for commercial firms. No index.

R41. *Standard trade index of Japan,* 1950- Tokyo, The Japan Chamber of Commerce and Industry, 1950-

An index to commodities and services in the 1967/68 issue lists over 28,000 items and identifies 8,600 Japanese firms which deal with these commodities. Short informative notes are given for each company including address, date of establishment and kind of business. Index to companies. Title varies: 1950, 1955 and 1956 issues *Japan register of merchants, manufacturers and shippers.* 1969/70 last issue noted.

Academic

R42. National Committee of Japan on Intellectual Cooperation. *Academic and cultural organizations in Japan.* Tokyo, Kokusai bunka shinkokai, 1939. 525 p.

Lists some 600 organizations as academic and cultural societies, institutions of higher learning at the end of 1938, giving addresses, officers, year of establishment, membership, objects, history, expenditures and publications. Organizations are listed in their romanized form, followed by the form in characters and translation into English.

R43. Japan. Mombusho. Daigaku gakujutsukyoku(Ministry of Education. Higher Education and Science Bureau) *Scientific and technical societies in Japan,1962.* Tokyo, Japan Society for the Promotion of Science,1962. 109 p. (Directory of research institutions in Japan. Natural and applied sciences,v.1)

334 scientific and technical societies, including agricultural and medical, are arranged by subject under the English form of the name, followed by the romanized form. Address, date of establishment, membership and publications noted. Indexes to names of societies, to periodicals and to subjects. Superseded by later lists in the Japanese language but still useful.

R44. Japan. Mombusho. Daigaku gakujutsukyoku(Ministry of Education. Higher Education and Science Bureau) *List of universities and colleges in Japan, natural and applied sciences.* Tokyo, Japan Society for the Promotion of Science, 1963. 107 p. (Directory of research institutions in Japan, natural and applied sciences v.3)

Some 140 universities are arranged in alphabetical order, and under each there is a listing of science departments and institutes. There is an index of institutes and laboratories under eight major headings, and list of periodical publications also arranged under broad subject headings.

R45. Japan. Mombusho. Daigaku gakujutsukyoku(Ministry of Education. Higher Education and Science Bureau) *Directory of research institutions and laboratories in Japan.* Tokyo, Japan Society for the Promotion of Science, 1964. 379 p. (Directory of research institutions in Japan. Natural and applied sciences v.2)

1,326 research institutions are listed in alphabetical order, with addresses, statement of research objectives, and publications, where applicable. University institutes are not included, the list being restricted to official, other non-profit organizations and industrial firms. Title index to periodicals and a subject index to research activities included.

R46. *Japanese universities and colleges,1965-6, with national research institutes.* Tokyo, Japan Overseas Advertiser Co., 1965. 475 p.

Arranged in five sections. The first surveys scientific research in Japan, the second lists 324 universities and colleges arranged by region, the third lists junior colleges, the fourth 67 research institutes attached to national universities, and the fifth 75 national research institutes arranged by ministry. Information is given on publications, staff, background and activities for each institution.

R47. Nihon gakujutsu kaigi, Tokyo(Science Council of Japan) *Zenkoku gaku kyokai soran.* Directory of the learned societies in Japan. Tokyo, Okurasho insatsukyoku, Showa 41(1966) 337 p.

1,061 learned societies are arranged by subject, with information noted for membership,background, and publications. Index to English forms of journal and society names.

R48. Nihon gakujutsu kaigi, Tokyo(Science Council of Japan) *Zenkoku kenkyukikan soran,* Showa 42 nemban. Directory of the research institutes and laboratories in Japan. Tokyo, Okurasho insatsukyoku, 1967. 759 p.

1,478 institutes and laboratories are arranged in terms of their affiliation. Each organization has an English translated title, statement of objects, staff, library resources and publications. Indexes to institutes and universities under the Japanese and English forms of their names, subject indexes also in English and Japanese, indexes to serials in English and Japanese and an index to firms in English and Japanese.

ATLASES

R49. Zenkoku kyoiku tosho kabushiki kaisha. *Nihon keizai chizu.* The economic atlas of Japan. Tokyo, Showa 29(1954) 166 p.

An atlas of economic activity in Japan, data as of the fifties, which has been made more accessible to the non-Japanese reader by Norton Ginsburg and John D.Eyre *The economic atlas of Japan,* (Chicago, University of Chicago Press,1959) which translates the Japanese language sections of the atlas. Physical geography, land use and farming, mineral resources, industry, communications, and urban and regional development are shown under 61 major colored maps.

R50. Zenkoku kyoiku tosho kabushiki kaisha. *Nihon rekishi chizu* (Historical atlas of Japan) Tokyo, Showa 31(1956) 482 p.

A valuable atlas of Japanese history arranged in chronological order and containing 75 principal colored maps, and many insets. Type on maps and in introductions rather small but clear. Place name index. Republished in 1966.

R51. Teikoku shoin. *Complete atlas of Japan.* Tokyo,1964. 55 p.

The most detailed atlas of Japan available with place names in romanized form and text in English. Most of the maps are large, clear, colored, physical maps of parts of Japan with railroads and place names. Nearly 5,000 names noted in index.

R52. Nihon chiiki kaihatsu senta, Tokyo(Japan Center for Area development research) *Nihon retto no chiiki kozo* Regional structure of Japanese archipelago. Tokyo, Showa 42(1967) 1 v.

Statistical data for Japan under 114 heads, in the form of colored maps and tables. Use has been made of 5-kilometer squares to develop presentation of data independent of existing political units. Interesting and unusual schematic diagrams are employed to present data. Physical features, climate, population, distribution, labor force, capital assets, water use, agriculture, industry, urban business, income, transportation, communication and housing are covered. Compiled by a leading geographer and Japan's leading architect.

GEOGRAPHICAL DICTIONARIES AND GAZETTEERS

R53. Gerr, Stanley. *A gazetteer of Japanese placenames.* Cambridge, Harvard University Press, 1942. 269, 225 p.
   4,500 placenames are listed, and over one third are for physical features. The area covered includes Japan, Korea, Formosa and mandated territories, but excludes China. In two parts, the first arranged by radicals and the second alphabetically. Approximate longitude and latitude given.

R54. U.S. Office of Geography *Japan ...* Washington, U.S. Government Printing Office, 1955. 731 p. (Gazetteer no.13)
   Approximately 28,700 places and physical features are listed in alphabetical order, with their longitude and latitude. The Ryukyus are included, and the Kuriles excluded.

R55. *Nihon chimei jiten* (Dictionary of placenames for Japan) Tokyo, Asakura shoten, Showa 30(1955) 4 v.
   Placenames, with descriptions, are arranged regionally with an index in the Japanese syllabic order. Altogether some 19,000 places listed. A recent and concise reference work. A new edition, *Nihon chimei daijiten* (Tokyo, Asakura shoten, 1967-) of which three volumes have now appeared out of a projected seven, reflects the important changes of the past ten years, and is arranged by place in the Japanese syllabic order. The Japan atlas volume in the *Sekai daihyakka jiten* which notes 60,000 placenames in its index should also not be overlooked.

R56. Japan. Jichicho. Gyoseikyoku(Local autonomy Office. Administrative Bureau) *Zenkoku shichoson yoran,* 39 nemban. The national directory of cities, towns and villages. Tokyo, Dai ichi hoki, Showa 39(1964) 361 p.
   3,398 local administrative units are arranged in regional order, with name of unit, population, date of establishment, and changes, including former names. Prefectural maps show location of units. Index. Issued annually from 1956 to 1966. No issue for 1965.

CHRONOLOGY AND CHRONOLOGICAL TABLES

R57. Hioki, Shoichi. *Kokushi dai nempyo* (Japanese history chronology) Tokyo, Heibonsha, Showa 10-12(1935-37) 7 v.
   A detailed chronology of Japanese history, emphasizing political events and arranged by era names, with no indications of the Western date. The first three volumes cover the period to 1868, volumes 4-6, from 1868 to 1934. Volume 7 is an index in two parts, the first dealing with names, the second with events.

R58. Toyo keizai kenkyujo, Tokyo (Oriental Economic Research Institute) *Sakuin seiji keizai dai nempyo* (The economic and political chronology of Japan, with index) Tokyo, Toyo keizai shimposha, Showa 28(1943) 2 v.
A detailed chronology for the period from 1841 to 1943 , in 1,080 pages, with a detailed index in 808 pages. Includes lists of members of the House of Peers and the House of Representatives, both arranged in Japanese syllabic order.

R59. Tsuchihashi, Yachita. *Japanese chronological tables from 601 to 1872 A.D.* Tokyo, Sophia University Press, 1952. 128 p. (Monumenta Nipponica monographs no.11)
Tables permit conversion into the Western date of the first day of each Japanese month. Appendices contain tables for counting days of the year and for computing cyclical characters. The author has compiled a list of errors in William Bramsen "Japanese chronological tables..." *Transactions of the Asiatic Society of Japan,* v.37,no.3,1910, p.1-131, and in Tsuji Zennosuke *Dai Nihon nempyo* (1941)

R60. Nishioka, Toranosuke. *Shin Nihonshi shi nempyo* (New Japanese history chronological tables) Tokyo, Chuo koronsha, 1955. 633 p.
A chronology of Japanese history from 48 A.D. to 1955, with a comparative column for world history. Japanese era, Western calendar, Chinese sexagenary cycle dates are also noted. Appendices contain a chronological table for archeology, and chronological tables for local rulers in Japan. Index.

CENSUS

Annual estimates of the population of Japan may be found in the *Nihon teikoku tokei nenkan* for the period from 1872 to 1897. For following years figures were based on the quinquennial registration of the population from 1903 to 1918. From 1920 a new quinquennial series commenced which has continued to the present day.

R61. Japan. Naikaku. Tokeikyoku (Bureau de la statistique imperiale) *Taisho kyunen kokusei chosa hokoku* (Report on the 1920 census) Tokyo, Taisho 13-Showa 4(1923-29)
appeared in four parts. The fourth part was in 47 prefectural volumes.
Taisho juyonen kokusei chosa hokoku (Report on the 1930 census) Tokyo, Showa 6-10(1931-35)
in four parts, the last in 47 prefectural volumes.
Showa gonen kokusei chosa hokoku (Report on the 1930 census) Tokyo, Showa 6-10(1931-35)
in five parts, the third in two sections, and the fourth in 47 prefectural volumes.
Showa junen kokusei chosa hokoku (Report on the 1935 census) Tokyo, Showa 11-14(1936-39)
in two parts, the second in 47 prefectural volumes.

These prewar censuses were of high quality, but were written completely
in Japanese, making them less accessible than the postwar series. The
mid-decade censuses in 1925 and 1935 were less complete than the decennial censuses. All available on microfilm, from the Library of Congress.
R62. Japan. Sorifu. Tokeikyoku (Prime Minister's Office. Statistical Bureau)
1940 population census of Japan. Showa 15-nen kokusei chosa hokoku.
Tokyo, 1961-62. 2 v.
The first volume covers total population, sex, age, marital status, race and
nationality, and the second industry and employment status.
R63. Japan. Sorifu. Tokeikyoku(Prime Minister's Office. Statistical Bureau)
Population census of 1950. Showa 25-nen kokusei chosa hokoku. Tokyo,
1951-55.
Appeared in eight volumes, with volume 3 in two parts. The seventh
volume was divided into 46 prefectural divisions.
1955 population census of Japan. Showa 30-nen kokusei chosa hokoku.
Tokyo, 1956-59.
In five parts, of which the fifth was divided by prefectures.
1960 population census of Japan. Showa 35-nen kokusei chosa hokoku.
Tokyo, 1961-64.
In four parts, of which the fourth part was divided by prefectures.
1965 population census of Japan. Showa 40-nen kokusei chosa hokoku.
Tokyo, 1966-67.
In six parts, of which the fourth part was divided into 46 prefectural
volumes.
There are 2 subseries, the large scale decennial census and the simplified
mid-decade census. An extremely reliable and valuable census, much im-
proved over the excellent prewar series. In English and Japanese.

STATISTICAL YEARBOOKS

R64. Japan. Naikaku. Tokeikyoku(Bureau de la statistique imperiale) *Nihon
teikoku tokei nenkan* (Statistical yearbook for the Japanese Empire)
Tokyo, Tokyo tokei kyokai, Meiji 15-Showa 26(1882-1951) 59 v.
Covers the period from 1868 to 1940, and based on reports from ministries. Each volume consists of a large number of tables arranged by subject. Index to subjects by the Japanese syllabic system. Entirely in Japanese. Available on microfilm. An abstract in Japanese and French is
entitled *Resume statistique de l'empire du Japon* Nihon teikoku tokei
tekiyo, 1887-1940.
R65. Japan. Sorifu. Tokeikyoku (Prime Minister's Office. Statistical Bureau)
Nihon tokei nenkan, Showa 24-nen- Japan statistical yearbook, 1949-
Tokyo, Showa 24- (1949-)
Continues the prewar statistical annual series, but differs from it in offer-
ing data in both English and Japanese. The first volume covers statistical
information from 1941. Data is collected from official and private agen-

cies, and the tables are grouped by subjects, and explanations and re-
marks accompany each table. The data cover land, climate, population,
labor force, agriculture, forestry, fisheries, mining, manufacturing, construction, utilities, transportation, trade, finance, prices, wages, housing,
elections, education, religion, health and justice.

BIBLIOGRAPHY

Bibliography of bibliographies

R66. Amano, Keitaro. *Hompo shoshi no shoshi* (Bibliography of Japanese
bibliographies) Osaka, Mamiya shoten, Showa 8(1933) 370 p.
Divided into 2 sections. The first contains 177 bibliographies published
before 1858, arranged in chronological order, and the second, 4,373
arranged by subject. Most of the bibliographies, which include materials
published separately as books and also in books and periodicals, are in
Japanese separate indexes for subjects and authors arranged in the Japanese syllabic order. The most comprehensive listing of Japanese bibliographies.

Bibliography of books in Japanese, published to 1890

R67. Samura, Hachiro. *Kokusho kaidai,* zotei kaihan (Bibliography of Japanese books, revised edition) Tokyo, Rikugokan, Taisho 15(1926) 2 v.
Some 25,000 books published to 1867, arranged in the Japanese syllabic
order, with author, subject, stroke and collected work indexes. Short and
excellent descriptive annotations, often include biographical information
on the authors. A list of all collected works published up to 1926 is
appended.
R68. Takaichi, Yoshio. *Meiji bunken mokuroku* (Catalog of Meiji books)
Tokyo, Nihon hyoronsha, Showa 7(1932) 316 p.
A list of some 5,400 Japanese books published from 1868 to 1891,
divided into two groups. The first has 12 subjects which are further
divided, and the second is an author index, arranged in the Japanese
syllabic order. No annotations.
R69. Iwanami shoten, Tokyo. *Kokusho somokuroku* (Catalog of Japanese
books) Tokyo, Showa 38- (1963-)
A union catalog of 500,000 extant books published before 1868 in some
450 public and private libraries. It is arranged in the Japanese syllabic
order, with the title in Japanese characters, with subject classification,
author, date of publication, and whether manuscript or printed. Printed
books represent some 40% of the titles. Library locations also stated.
Eight volumes projected, and volume 5, published in 1967 noted. Since

the basic compilation was carried out before World War II many of the locations stated have now changed.

Trade bibliography

R70. Tokyo shosekisho kumiai, Tokyo. *Tokyo shosekisho kumiai tosho somokuroku* (Tokyo booktrade association catalog of books in print) Tokyo, Meiji 26-Showa 15(1893-1940) 9 v.

Includes only the materials listed in the catalogs issued by the members of the association, but easily the most comprehensive trade listing available. Catalogs were issued in 1893, 1898, 1906, 1911, 1918, 1923, 1929, 1933 and 1940, with the number of entries increasing. A very valuable supplement to the catalogs of the Imperial Library.

R71. *Shuppan nenkan,* Showa 5-16 nemban (Publication yearbook, 1930-41) Tokyo, Tokyodo, Showa 5-16(1930-41) 12 v.

Tokyodo was a major Tokyo book wholesaler before World War II and this yearbook is based on its monthly *Tokyodo geppo* (1927-41). The most significant section of this yearbook consists of a catalog of books published in the previous year arranged by subject, with full bibliographical description and a short annotation. Other sections list deposits at the Naimusho (Ministry of Home Affairs) other than those in section three, and classified lists of periodicals. There is no index which makes the location of a particular title difficult. Compared to the Tokyo shosekisho kumiai *Shuppan nenkan,* Showa 4-15 nempan, coverage was as much as one-third more complete, classification was more complete, more consistent and easier to follow.

R72. *Shoseki nenkan,* Showa 17 nemban (Book yearbook, 1942) Tokyo, Kyodo shuppansha, Showa 17(1942) 1426 p.

Supersedes the Tokyodo *Shuppan nenkan* and supplements a yearbook for periodicals, the *Zasshi nenkan* (1939-42) published by the same company. The yearbook follows, in general, the arrangement of contents of the Tokyodo yearbook, except that all book titles were brought together in one sequence. There is no index, and only part of the entries are annotated. For the 1943 issue there was a title change *Nihon shuppan nenkan,* Showa 18 nemban, 1260 p. Periodicals are again included. The 1944-46 and the 1947-49 issues were published by the Nihon shuppan kyodo kabushiki kaisha. No annotations and no indexes are included in these 2 issues.

R73. *Shuppan nyusu* Showa 21-nen 11-gatsu- (Publication news, Nov. 1946-) Tokyo, Shuppan nyususha, 1946-

Issued three times a month, this contains the only trade record we have for the period from the beginning of 1948 through 1949. Arranged according to the Nihon Decimal Classification. Currently entries are annotated.

R74. *Shuppan nenkan,* 1951 nemban- (Publication yearbook, 1951-) Tokyo, Shuppan nyusu-sha, Showa 26- (1951-)

Similar in contents to the Tokyodo *Shuppan nenkan,* which it regards as its direct predecessor, with the exception that the listing of books is now arranged according to the Nihon Decimal Classification. Indexing of author, titles and subjects commences from the 1952 issue. Periodicals also listed.

Imperial library catalogs

R75. Teikoku toshokan, Tokyo (Imperial Library) *Teikoku toshokan wakan tosho bunrui mokuroku* (Classified catalog of the Japanese and Chinese books in the Imperial Library) Tokyo, Meiji 33-40 (1900- 1907) 9 v.

The Imperial Library received one of the two copies of all Japanese publications deposited at the Ministry of Home Affairs. Each volume covers a major subject field, and is further subdivided, and has its own index to titles. Continued by the *Teikoku toshokampo* (Imperial Library bulletin) issued from 1908 to 1944, which has a subject arrangement and was issued as a quarterly, and monthly from 1931.

R76. Teikoku toshokan, Tokyo (Imperial Library) *Teikoku toshokan wakan tosho shomei mokuroku* (Title catalog of the Japanese and Chinese books in the Imperial Library), Tokyo, Meiji 32- Showa 37 (1899-1962) 12v.

Series 1 covers accessions from 1875 to 1893, series 2 from 1894 to 1899, series 3 from 1900 to 1911, series 4 in three parts, from 1912 to 1926, series 5, in four parts, from 1927 to 1935, and series 6, in two parts, from 1936 through 1940. Each series is arranged by title. Series 7, from 1941 to 1949, published in 1966, reported.

R77. Kokuritsu kokkai toshokan, Tokyo (National Diet Library) *Teikoku toshokan kokuritsu toshokan wakan tosho bunrui mokuroku,* Showa 16-nen 1-gatsu - 24-nen 3-gatsu (A classified catalog of Japanese and Chinese books in the Imperial Library, Jan. 1941-Mar. 1949) Tokyo, Showa 39(1964) 1144 p.

32,890 entries are arranged by the Nihon Decimal Classification. No index.

National Diet Library catalogs

R78. Kokuritsu kokkai toshokan, Tokyo (National Diet Library) *Zen Nihon shuppambutsu somokuroku,* Showa 23 nemban. Japanese national bibliography, 1948- Tokyo, Showa 26- (1951-)

An annual compilation based on the *Nohon shuho* (weekly accessions report) (1955-) of the National Diet Library, but with wider coverage. It includes trade publications, central and local official publications, periodicals, newspapers, Western language materials published in Japan. Publications issued from 1948 are covered, and official publications were included from 1959, at first in separate volumes, but are now incorporated in the single annual volumes. Arranged by type of publication, and subdivided by the Nihon Decimal Classification. 1968 last volume noted.

R79. Kokuritsu kokkai toshokan, Tokyo (National Diet Library), *Kokuritsu kokkai toshokan zosho mokuroku,* Showa 23-33 nen National Diet Library catalog, 1948-58. Tokyo, Showa 34-43(1960-68) 6v.(in 7.)

140,000 titles acquired by the National Diet Library from 1948 to 1958, of which nearly 100,000 are in Japanese, and are arranged in four volumes by the Nihon Decimal Classification. Each volume has an alphabetical author index. The fifth volume in two parts has over 40,000 non-Japanese books and periodicals, arranged by the Dewey Decimal Classification, with an author index in the second part. A title index to v.1-4 was published in 1968.

R80. Kokuritsu kokkai toshokan, Tokyo (National Diet Library) *Kokuritsu kokkai toshokan zosho mokuroku, wakansho no bu,* Showa 34- (Catalog of the National Diet Library, Japanese and Chinese book section, 1959-) Tokyo, Showa 35- (1960-)

An annual publication continuing *Kokuritsu kokkai toshokan, zosho mokuroku,* Showa 23-33 nen, and containing Chinese, Japanese and Korean books received after 1958, arranged by the Nihon Decimal Classification. There is a title index. Originally this publication was entitled *Shusho tsuho* (Acquisition list) issued from 1948 to 1957, when it became an annual with that title. Valuable as a guide to catalogers, since from 1965 it has been based on offset reproduction of catalog cards.

Official publications

R81. Japan. Naikaku insatsukyoku (Cabinet Printing Office) *Kancho kanko tosho mokuroku,* Showa 2-12 (Catalog of government publications, 1927-37) Tokyo, Showa 2-12(1927-37)

Includes both central and local official publications, together with publications from Taiwan and Korea, and arranged in two sequences, the first by issuing body, and the second by subject. Continued by *Kanko kancho tosho geppo,* Showa 13-18 nen (Government publications monthly, 1938-43) Tokyo, Showa 13-188 (1938-43)

R82. Kokuritsu kokkai toshokan, Tokyo (National Diet Library) *Kancho kankobutsu sogo mokuroku* (Catalog of official publications) Tokyo, Showa 27-35(1952-60) 8 v.

Bibliography of central government publications issued from 1945 to 1958, issued annually from 1953. From 1959 recording of official publications was continued by *Zen Nihon shuppambutsu mokuroku* as separate volumes for 1959 and 1960, and from the 1961 issue incorporated in the main volume. Each volume is arranged by the Nihon Decimal Classification, and indexed by issuing agency.

R83. Kokuritsu kokkai toshokan, Tokyo (National Diet Library) *List of Japanese government publications in European languages,* revised and enlarged edition. Tokyo, 1959. 82 p.

Includes Japanese government publications issued from August 1945 to December 1958, and materials published by the Supreme Commander of the Allied Powers to 1952. The publications are almost entirely in English, although some are bilingual in Japanese and English, and are arranged by ministry and bureau. There are approximately 1,200 government publications and 270 Supreme Commander of the Allied Powers materials. A revision of the 1956 edition.

Selected bibliography
R84. Michigan. University. Center for Japanese Studies. *Bibliographical series, no.1-* Ann Arbor, 1950-
The following bibliographies have been issued in this series, the number of entries in each stated in parentheses:
1. *Political science,* second edition,1961. 210 p. (1,759)
2. *Japanese dialects,* 1950. 75 p. (995)
3. *Far Eastern archeology and ethnology,* 1950. 74 p. (1,063)
4. *Japanese history,* 1954. 165 p. (1,551)
5. *Japanese economics,* 1956. 91 p. (1,191)
6. *Japanese geography,* 1956. 128 p. (1,254)
7. *Japanese religion and philosophy,* 1959. 102 p. (902)
8. *Japanese literature of the Showa period,* 1959. 212 p.(1,248)
9. *Japanese language studies in the Showa period,* 1961. 153 p. (1,473)
Bibliographies of Japanese language materials, arranged in detailed subject classification. Entries are selected and annotated, and each subject group will commence with an introduction to the subject and its materials. Series 1,6, and 9 have author indexes. An *Index for Japanese history, a guide to reference and research materials* was published by the School of Oriental Studies, Canberra University College, in 33 pages. All have detailed tables of contents. These are excellent introductory guides to the Japanese literature of the fields represented. The inconsistency in providing indexing of authors and titles makes it difficult to determine whether or not a given book has been included.
R85. Kokusai bunka shinkokai, Tokyo(Society for International Cultural Relations) *K.B.S. Bibliography of standard reference books for Japanese studies, with descriptive notes.* Tokyo, 1959-
The following bibliographies have been issued in this series
1. *Generalia,* 1959. 110 p.
2. *Geography and travel,* 1962. 164 p.
3. *History and biography, Part I,* 1963, 197 p. *Part II,* 1964, 218 p. *Part III,* 1965, 236 p.
4. *Religion,* 1963. 181 p.
5a. *History of thought, Part I,* 239 p. *Part II,* 1965,167 p.
5b. *Education,* 1966. 186 p.
6a. *Language,* 1961. 155 p.
6b. *Literature, Part I,* 1962, 122 p. *Part II,* 1966, 249 p. *Part III,* 1967, 150 p. *Modern period, Part I,* 1967, 153.
7a. *Arts and crafts,* 1959. 170 p.
7b. *Theatre,dance and music,* 1960. 182 p.
8. *Manners, and customs and folklore,* 1961. 101 p.
The term reference books has been used in a wider sense than the usual use of the word, referring to standard works in the subject field. Annotations are critical and descriptive. Each volume has further subject division, but have no index. A number of volumes have added listings of materials in Western languages. Valuable as an introduction to the Japanese-reading Western student.

Translated works

R86. Kokuritsu kokkai toshokan, Tokyo(National Diet Library) *Meiji Taisho Showa honyaku bungaku mokuroku* (Catalog of translated literature from 1868 to 1955) Tokyo, Kazama shobo, Showa 34(1959) 779 p.

A bibliography of Japanese translations of Western and Russian language literary works listed in two parts. The first includes 26,600 entries published from 1912 to 1955, arranged by the original authors in Japanese transliteration and in the Japanese syllabic order. The second part has 3,200 translations and adaptions published from 1911 to 1968, arranged in order of date of publication. Two author indexes, one for 1,895 Western authors, and the other for 294 Russian authors.

Prohibited publications

R87. Saito, Shozo. *Gendai hikka bunken dai nempyo* (Chronological listing of banned modern materials) Tokyo, Suikodo, Showa 7(1932) 432 p.

Lists over 5,000 periodical and newspaper issues and books which have been banned during the Meiji and Taisho periods(1868-1926) index in the Japanese syllabic order.

R88. Japan. Mombusho. Shakai kyoikukyoku(Ministry of Education. Social education bureau) *Rengokokugun soshireibu kara bosshu o meizerareta senden-yo kankobutsu somokuroku* (Catalog of propaganda publications whose confiscation was ordered by the Supreme Commander of the Allied Powers) Tokyo, 1948. 418 p.

Over 7,700 books arranged by title in the Japanese syllabic order. Author, publisher, and date of publication given for each title.

R89. Odagiri, Hideo and Fukuoka Seikichi. *Showa shoseki zasshi shimbun hakkin nempyo,* jo.(Chronological tables of books, periodicals, and newspapers prohibited in the Showa period,volume 1) Tokyo, Meiji bunken, Showa 40(1965) 676 p.

Some 8,300 entries for materials published through 1933, arranged by chronological order and divided into books, newspapers, periodicals and non-Japanese publications. The reason for prohibition is stated.

Periodicals and newspapers

R90. Tokyo teikoku daigaku. Hogakubu(Tokyo Imperial University. Department of Law) *Totenko, Meiji shimbun zasshi bunko shozo mokuroku* (Totenko, catalog of the Meiji newspaper and periodical library) Tokyo, Naigai tsushinsha shuppambu, Showa 5-16(1930-41) 3 v.

Some 4,000 Japanese newspapers and periodicals published from 1868 to 1912 arranged by the Japanese syllabic order by volume. Entries give title, issuing body, subject, date of first issue, frequency and holdings. Index by prefecture, then by date.

R91. Teikoku toshokan, Tokyo(Imperial Library) *Teikoku toshokan zasshi shimbun mokuroku, Showa 10-nen matsu genzai* (Catalog of the periodicals and newspapers in the Imperial Library at the end of 1935) Tokyo, Migensha, Showa 12(1937) 157 p.

The newspaper section lists 240 Japanese language newspapers, a few of which were published outside Japan, and the periodical section some 2,800 Japanese language periodicals. Information given on publisher and holdings of the Imperial Library. Both sections arranged in the Japanese syllabic order. *Teikoku toshokan zasshi shimbun zoka mokuroku, Showa 23-nen 6-gatsu matsu genzai* (Catalog of the periodicals and newspapers in the Imperial Library, supplemented, at the end of June 1948) continues the coverage.

R92. *Zasshi nenkan* , Showa 14-17 nen(Periodical yearbook,1939-42) Tokyo, Kyodo shuppansha, Showa 14-17(1939-42) 4 v.

Some 2,400 to 3,000 general periodicals arranged under a large number of headings, with some annotations, together with lists such as yearbooks and other categories. The 1942 issue records Japanese periodicals published overseas, periodicals published in East Asia, local and academic periodicals. Index to titles in Japanese syllabic order.

R93. *The Japanese press,* 1949- Tokyo, Nihon shimbun kyokai, 1948-
The most bibliographically significant section is one tenth of the publication, and lists 99 daily newspapers, and nine specialized papers in the 1965 issue, with circulation, address and brief notes for each. 1949,1951,1952,1955-65 issues noted.

R94. Japan. Mombusho. Daigaku gakujutsukyoku (Ministry of Education. Higher Education and Science Bureau) *Gakujutsu zasshi sogo mokuroku* (Union catalog of learned periodicals) Tokyo, Nihon gakujutsu shinkokai, Showa 32-37(1957-62) 7 v.

Of the seven volumes only the *Jimbun kagaku wabunhen, 1959 nemban* (Humanistic sciences, Japanese language section,1959) and including holdings in Japanese, Chinese and Korean for 48 scholarly libraries in 1957, and the *Shizen kagaku wabunhen 1959 nemban* (Natural sciences, Japanese language section,1959) including the holdings up to 1957 of 61 scholarly libraries, are of significance for Japanese bibliography. Other volumes relate to Western language periodical holdings in Japan. The collection of the National Diet Library and the Hibiya Public Library in Tokyo are not included. In each volume titles are arranged alphabetically by title, and locations and holdings are given.

R95. Japan. Mombusho. Daigaku gakujutsukyoku(Ministry of Education. Higher Education and Science Bureau) *Bibliographical list of Japanese learned journals, natural sciences, humanities and social sciences,* second edition. Tokyo, 1959-62. 2 v.

The first volume covers the humanities and social sciences, the second natural and applied sciences. A supplement to v.2 was issued in 1964, and the volume was replaced by the *Directory of Japanese scientific periodicals,1964, natural sciences medical sciences, and industry* (1964, 283 p.) revised by the *Directory of Japanese scientific periodicals,1967* (1967, 670 p.

R96. Nihon shiryo kenkyukai, Tokyo (Japan materials research society) *Nihon nenkanrui somokuroku* (Catalog of Japanese yearbooks) Tokyo, Seiwado, Showa 39(1964) 236 p.

Based on the *Sengo Nihon nenkanrui somokuroku,* but with 600 additional titles. The 2,477 current titles are arranged by the Nihon Decimal Classification. Bibliographical information is given, but no annotation. Where possible the latest issue has been examined. Title index in the Japanese syllabic order.

R97. U.S. Library of Congress. *Union card file of Oriental vernacular series, Chinese, Japanese and Korean. Japanese file.* Washington, 1966.

45,242 holdings cards have been microfilmed from the periodical checklists of the principal East Asian collections in the United States. Copies of the microfilm have been made available by the Library of Congress in film or electrostatic copies. More than one card may be used to report a given title, and each title may be reported by one or more libraries.

R98. Shuppan nyususha. *Nihon zasshi soran,1967* (Directory of Japanese periodicals,1967) Tokyo, Showa 42(1967) 485 p.

9,775 current periodicals are listed, and these are divided into six groups: general periodicals(2,487 titles), scholarly periodicals(1,916 titles), government official bulletins(1,210 titles), organization bulletins(1,571 titles), privately published periodicals(1,289 titles), and public relations periodicals and company bulletins(1,302 titles). Within each group titles are further subdivided by subject. Title index and list of publishers with addresses. The 1963 edition listed 7,380 titles.

PERIODICAL INDEXES

R99. Kokuritsu kokkai toshokan, Tokyo (National Diet Library) *Zasshi kiji sakuin,* Showa 23- Japanese periodical index, 1948- Tokyo, Kinokuniya shoten, Showa 23- (1948-)

Although a *Zasshi sakuin* (Periodical index) was compiled by Shimotomae Shigamatsu from 1922 to 1941, this was the first serious attempt to develop a comprehensive index, and reliance for much of the control of earlier periodical publications has to be placed on indexes issued by the periodicals themselves. The best guide to these is Amano Keitaro *Zasshi somokuji sakuin shuran* (Collection of indexes to periodicals) (Tokyo, Nihon kosho tsushinsha, Showa 41(1966)) which contains 1,334 indexes to periodicals and newspapers published to 1964, arranged by subject. In 1950 the index was divided into two parts, *Jimbun kagakuhen* (Humanities section) and *Shizen kagakuhen* (Natural sciences section). The latter commenced with a new number series, and from 1960 to 1964 was translated into English *Japanese periodicals index, natural science.*

Originally organized by subject headings, but since 1963 by a classified arrangement. Difficult to use since the index is not cumulated, and there have been changes in frequency and arrangement. Nethertheless this survey of some 1,000 current Japanese periodicals is a major contribution to bibliographical control.

R100 Japan. Mombusho. Jimbun kagaku Obun mokuroku henshu iinkai (Ministry of Education. Committee for the compilation of a catalog in Western languages of the humanistic sciences) *Bibliography of the humanistic studies and social relations,* no.1-1952-Tokyo, 1955-

Lists books and articles from some 600 Japanese scholarly periodicals, arranging these by broad subject groups. Authors and titles are given in romanized and character forms, and titles are also translated.

R101. Nihon gakujutsu kaigi, Tokyo(Science Council of Japan) *Bunkakei bunken mokuroku* (Catalog of materials related to culture) 1946- Tokyo, Showa 27- (1952-)

Volumes I-X published from 1952 to 1960 were published with the title *Bungaku, tetsugaku, shigaku bunken mokuroku* . Includes books, periodical and newspaper articles published since 1945, and each issue is arranged around a central subject, and organized by topics, with an author index. Coverage is extensive, with several thousand entries in each issue. No.18,of 1965 published 1966 noted.

R102. Morris, I.I., and Paul C. Blum. *The Transactions of the Asiatic Society of Japan, comprehensive index.* Tokyo, The Asiatic society of Japan, 1958. 96 p.

V.6 of the 3rd series of the *Transactions of the Asiatic society of Japan*, published in December 1958, and is a valuable guide to the contents of this major source on Japan in English.

Collectanea or Japanese series

R103. Hamano, Tomosaburo. *Nihon sosho mokuroku* (Catalog of Japanese series) Tokyo, Rikugokan, Showa 2(1927) 256 p.

Some 700 series are entered, with the contents of some 18,000 titles arranged in order of their publication in the series. Index to series titles in Japanese syllabic order.

R104. Hirose, Toshi. *Nihon sosho sakuin,* zotei. (Index to Japanese series, revised edition) Tokyo, Kazama shobo, Showa 32(1957) 761 p.

Divided into two parts, the first consisting of an annotated list of some 700 series arranged by title in the Japanese syllabic order, and the second a listing of pre-1868 books in series, arranged by title also in the Japanese syllabic order, and stating author and collection in which the title may be located.

R105. Harvard University. Chinese-Japanese Library. *Japanese collected works and series in the Chinese-Japanese Library at Harvard University.* Cambridge, 1954. 96 p.

1,027 collectanea, with over 50,000 individual works, arranged by title in stroke order. Both *sosho* or collections of miscellaneous works, and *taikei* collections of monographs on specific subjects are included. Represents one of the strongest American collections of this type of material. Romanized title index.

Essay bibliography

R106. Ota, Tamesaburo. *Nihon zuihitsu sakuin* (Index to Japanese miscellanies) Tokyo, Iwanami shoten, Taisho 14-Showa 7(1925-32) 2 v.

392 collections of essays have been analyzed by subject, with the subjects arranged in Japanese syllabic order. The second volume supplements the first, including works omitted.

Western languages

R107. Cordier, Henri. *Bibliotheca japonica, dictionnaire bibliographique des ouvrages relatifs a l'empire japonais ranges par ordre chronologique jusqu'a 1870, suivi d'un appendice renfermant la liste alphabetique des principaux ouvrages paru de 1870 a 1912.* Paris, Leroux, 1912. 762 col. (Publications de l'Ecole des langues orientales vivantes, 5 serie, tome VIII.)

Includes some 7,000 books and periodical articles in a wide range of Western languages and Russian, but stressing English and French materials. Bibliographical information is detailed but there is no annotation. Chronological arrangement is not always the most meaningful. Especially useful for French influence and Catholic missions. Author index. Reprinted by George Olms Verlagsbuchhandlung, Hildesheim in 1969.

R108. Japaninstitut and Deutsches Forschungsinstitut. *Bibliographischer alt-Japan-Katalog,* 1542-1853. Kyoto, Deutsches Forchungsinstitut, 1940. 415 p.

1,624 books in Western languages are arranged by author, with full bibliographical citations. Indexed by year of publication. Valuable to supplement Henri Cordier *Bibliotheca japonica ...*

R109. Wenchstern, Friedrich von. *A bibliography of the Japanese Empire.* Leiden, E.J. Brill, Tokyo, Maruzen, 1895-1907. 2 v.

V.1 covers the period 1477 to 1893, and for the period to 1859 incorporates Leon Pages *Bibliographie japonais depuis le XV siecle jusqu'a 1859* and was published in Leiden. V.2 was published in Tokyo, and continues the bibliography to 1906. Contains 13,200 entries for books and periodical articles. Author index.

Continued by Oskar Nachod *Bibliography of the Japanese Empire,* 1906-1926. (London, Goldston,1928. 2 v.) with entries for books and periodical articles arranged by subject, and numbered 1-9,575. Korea and Taiwan are included. Author index.

Continued by Oskar Nachod *Bibliographie von Japan,* 1927-1929 (Leipzig, Hiersemann Verlag, 1931. 410 p.) entries are numbered 9,576 to 13,595, and include Korea and Taiwan. Author index.

Continued by Oskar Nachod *Bibliographie von Japan,* 1930-1932. (Leipzig, Hiersemann Verlag, 1935. 351 p.) entries are numbered 13,596 to 18,398, and include Korea and Taiwan. Author index.

Continued by Hans Praesent and Wolf Haenisch *Bibliographie von Japan,* 1933-1935 (Leipzig, Hiersemann Verlag, 1937. 452 p.) entries are numbered 18,399 to 25,376 and include Korea, Taiwan and Manchuria. Author index.

Continued by Hans Praesent and Wolf Haenisch *Bibliographie von Japan,* 1936-1937 (Leipzig, Hiersemann Verlag, 1940. 559 p.) entries are numbered 25,377 to 33,621, and include Korea, Taiwan and Manchuria. Author index.

These volumes constitute a comprehensive bibliographical foundation for the study of Japan through material in Western languages. A further *Bibliographie von Japan,* 1938-1943 was compiled by Hans Praesent and

Wolf Haenisch, but not published. A copy of the 3,500 cards, in German only, in bound form, in 3 volumes is held by the Library of Congress.

R110. Yabuki, Katsuji. *Japan bibliographic annual, 1956-1957.* Tokyo, Hokuseido Press, 1956-57. 2 v.

The first volume arranges 3,600 books and periodical articles by author. There is no annotation and some official publications are included. Not restricted to materials published in Japan. Indexes *Contemporary Japan* from 1946 to 1955, and *Japan Quarterly* from 1954 to 1955. Subject and title indexes. The second volume has entries arranged by subject, and has an author, title and subject index to both volumes. It contains 420 entries published in 1956 or before and not in the first volume, and 750 important articles from eleven major English language periodicals published since 1945.

R111. Silberman, Bernard S. *Japan and Korea, a critical bibliography.* Tucson, University of Arizona press, 1962. 120 p.

Similar to companion volumes for India and China, with 1,933 books and periodical articles mostly in English, and arranged under major subject headings. Each subject has a short introduction. A select and annotated work. Author, title and subject index.

R112. Kokuritsu kokkai toshokan, Tokyo (National Diet Library) *Catalog of materials on Japan in Western languages in the National Diet Library, April 1948-December 1962 (Preliminary edition)* Tokyo, 1963. 306 p.

2,300 books arranged in classified order and published for the most part from 1948 to 1962. Useful for locating Supreme Commander for the Allied Powers and official publications. Subject and author index.

R113. Kokusai Bunka Shinkokai, Tokyo (Society for International Cultural Relations) *A classified list of books in Western languages relating to Japan.* Tokyo, University of Tokyo Press, 1965. 316 p.

5,294 books published from the 17th century in the Kokusai Bunka Shinkokai library in 1962 are arranged under fifteen major headings. These are further subdivided. Subject approach through the table of contents. Index to authors and persons.

R114. Fukuda, Naomi. *Union catalog of books on Japan in Western languages.* Tokyo, International House Library, 1967. 543 p.

Approximately 9,800 entries arranged by author. Compilation is based on the printed catalogs, but owing to variations in cataloging practice at the International House of Japan, the Kokusai Bunka Shinkokai, the National Diet Library and the Toyo Bunko, entries may not correspond to those in the participating library, and there has been much subsequent checking. The most comprehensive catalog of its kind.

R114.1. Shulman, Frank J. *Japan and Korea, an annotated bibliography of doctoral dissertations in Western languages, 1877-1969.* Chicago, American Library Association, 1970. 340 p.

2,616 theses are arranged in a detailed subject order. Each entry is annotated, and has a note on related publications. An extremely thorough and comprehensive study. Institutional, biographical, and author indexes.

Russian language
R115. Lik'ianova, M. I., Kh. T. Eidus and A. Gluskina. *Bibliografiia iaponii.* Moskva, Izdaltelstvo Vostochnoi Literaturi, 1960. 328 p.

6,249 entries for Russian language books and periodical articles arranged under eighteen major subjects, and further subdivided by author, then by date. Reviews of major books are also included. Author index.

Subject bibliography

RELIGION AND THOUGHT
R116. Holzman, Donald. *Japanese religion and philosophy, a guide to Japanese reference and research materials.* Ann Arbor, Published for the Center for Japanese Studies, by the University of Michigan Press, 1959. 102 p. (University of Michigan. Center for Japanese Studies, Bibliographical series number 7)

992 books arranged in a classified order, emphasizing materials published since 1912, and the Japanese aspects of religion and philosophy from the East Asian mainland. Brief annotations. Author and editor index.

R117. Okura seishin bunka kenkyujo (Okura Institute for Spiritual Culture) *Nihon shisoshi bunken kaidai* (Annotated bibliography on the history of Japanese thought) Tokyo, Kadokawa shoten, Showa 40(1965) 432 p.

Some 2,000 printed books and manuscripts are arranged into three major periods to 1868, and then by title. Full bibliographical information is given, followed by an annotation. Ownership noted for manuscripts. Title index arranged by the Japanese syllabic system.

R117.1. Earhart, H. Byron. *The new religions of Japan, a bibliography of Western-language materials.* Tokyo, Sophia University, 1970. 96 p.

810 entries for books and articles on the new religions of Japan, divided into general, Shinto-derived, Buddhist-derived, Christian-derived, other and Utopian. Some annotation. Separate author and subject index.

Shinto
R118. Kato, Genchi. *Shinto shoseki mokuroku* A bibliography of Shinto, a collection of Shinto literature from the oldest times till Keio 4(1868) Tokyo, Dobunkan, Showa 13(1938) 646 p.

Some 14,000 books and manuscripts are arranged in three broad periods, with the third period given subject subdivision. Locations are noted. Alphabetical index of personal names and an index of titles in the Japanese syllabic order. The most comprehensive listing of Shinto materials for the period to 1868.

R119. Kato, Genchi. *Meiji, Taisho, Showa Shinto shoseki mokuroku, Meiji gannen yori Showa 15-nen ni itaru* A bibliography of Shinto literature from Meiji 1(1868) till Showa 15(1940) Tokyo, Meiji jingu shamusho, Showa 28(1953) 737 p.

Some 15,000 books are arranged in a detailed subject order, including Shinto classics, shrines, ceremonies, religious problems and sect Shinto. Alphabetical index to titles and an index to compilers and authors.

R120. Kato, Genchi, Wilhelm Schiffer and Karl Reitz. *Bibliography of Shinto in Western languages from the oldest times till 1952,* Tokyo, Meiji jingu shamusho, 1953. 58 p.

1,138 books and periodical articles arranged by author, with a subject index. Appendix lists another 79 books and articles published from 1941 to 1952. No annotation.

R121. Kokugakuin daigaku, Tokyo. Nihon bunka kenkyujo (Kokugakuin University. Research Institute on Japanese Culture) *Shinto rombun somokuroku* (Bibliography of articles on Shinto) Tokyo, Meiji jingu shamusho, Showa 38(1963) 755 p.

35,000 articles selected from some 300 periodicals arranged in a detailed classified order. There is a subject key to the classification. Library locations of articles noted.

Buddhism

R122. Ono, Gemmyo. *Bussho kaisetsu daijiten* (Annotated bibliography of Buddhist books) Tokyo, Daito shuppansha, Showa 8-11(1933-36) 12 v.

Approximately 50,000 entries for Buddhist works, with titles in characters, in Sanskrit and in romanized Japanese and Chinese, full bibliographical information, location of extant copies, if published in printed form, history of translation and size. The last volume is a history of the transmission of the Chinese translation of Buddhist materials and of the Tripitaka.

R123. Butten kenkyukai (Society for the study of Buddhist texts) *Bukkyo rombun somokuroku,* kaitei zoho (Catalog of articles on Buddhism, revised and enlarged edition) Tokyo, Taigando shobo, Showa 10 (1935) 729 p.

14,223 periodical articles, 1,559 more than in the 1931 edition, arranged in a detailed classified order, with a subject index. The articles selected from 113 periodicals.

R124. Ryukoku daigaku, Kyoto. Toshokan (Ryukoku University library) *Bukkyogaku kankei zasshi rombun bunrui mokuroku* (Classified catalog of periodical articles on Buddhism) Kyoto, Showa 6(1931) 495 p.

15,000 articles selected from 135 periodicals arranged in a detailed classified order with 280 headings. Author and subject indexes arranged in the Japanese syllabic order. A supplementary volume for the period Jan.1931 to Dec.1955, contains some 9,000 articles from 100 periodicals and collections of essays, published in Kyoto in 1961, 738 p. Subject index.

R125. Bando, Shojun. *A bibliography on Japanese Buddhism.* Tokyo, C.I.I.B. 1958. 180 p.

1,660 books and periodical articles in Western languages and arranged in a general section and under sections for each sect. No annotations. Locations in libraries in Japan stated. Index.

Christianity

R126. Laures, Johannes. *Kirishitan Bunko, a manual of books and documents on the early Christian Mission in Japan, with special reference to the principal libraries in Japan, and more particularly to the collection at*

Sophia University. Tokyo, Sophia University, 1957. 536 p. (Monumenta Nipponica monographs no. 5)

1,428 books and periodical articles arranged by year of publication, in Western languages, and located in 28 libraries in Japan. This is the third edition.

R127. Ebisawa, Arimichi. *Christianity in Japan, a bibliography of Japanese and Chinese sources, Part I,1543-1858.* Tokyo, International Christian University, 1960. 171 p.

3,648 books, manuscripts and other materials compiled from bibliographies and other sources and arranged by date of publication. Separate romanized author and title indexes.

R128. Kokusai kirisutokyo daigaku, Tokyo. Ajia bunka kenkyu iinkai. (International Christian University. Committee on Asian Cultural Studies) *Nihon Kirisutokyo bunken mokuroku, Meiji ki, Part II (1859-1912)* (A bibliography of Christianity in Japan, Meiji era, Part II, 1859-1912) Tokyo, 1965. 429 p.

Some 8,000 books in Japanese on Christianity and its influence. Arranged into four sections: books about Christian doctrine, books about Christian activities, books about Christianity and forthcoming books. Books are further subdivided by class. Information given includes locations. Title and author index.

R129. Ikada, Fujio and J. McGovern. *A bibliography of Christianity in Japan, Protestantism in English sources, 1859-1959.* Tokyo, International Christian University, 1966. 125 p.

Some 900 books and pamphlets and 286 periodical articles are arranged by author in two sections, with separate title, author and subject indexes. Most entries are in English, but a few are in other Western languages. The periodical article section is not regarded as complete.

SOCIAL SCIENCES

R130. U.S. Bureau of the Census. *Bibliography of social science periodicals and monograph series, Japan, 1950-1963.* Washington, U.S. Government Printing Office, 1965. 346 p. (Foreign social science bibliographies, series P-92,no.20)

1,030 periodicals and 1,082 serial monographs, all in the Library of Congress, have been arranged into 14 social science fields and bibliography. Entries are annotated. Separate indexes of titles, authors and subjects.

Statistics

R131. Japan. Sorifu. Tokeikyoku. Prime Minister's Office. Statistical Bureau) *Sorifu tokeikyoku toshokan zosho mokuroku, washo no bu* (Catalog of Japanese books in the Library of the Statistical Bureau of the Prime Minister's Office) Tokyo, Showa 30(1955) 568 p.

Some 9,000 periodicals are arranged in a detailed classification, with an alphabetical title index. Nearly all entries are concerned with Japan and this constitutes the most comprehensive listing of statistical materials for that country.

Anthropology and social anthropology

R132. Nihon minzokugaku kyokai, Tokyo (Japan anthropological society) *Minzokugaku kankei zasshi rombun somokuroku,1925-1959* (Bibliography of periodical articles on anthropology,1925-1959) Tokyo, Seibundo shinkosha, Showa 36(1961) 199 p.

6,000 articles from Japanese periodicals. One half of the listing is concerned with Japan, and materials on Japan are found under 34 general and area subject headings. No index.

Economics and economic history

R133. Honjo, Eijiro. *Nihon keizaishi daiichi bunken* (first collection of materials on Japanese economic history) Tokyo, Nihon hyoron shinsha, Showa 30(1955) 898 p.

A new edition of *Nihon keizaishi bunken* (1933, 703 p.) with coverage from the beginning of the Meiji period to 1931. Contains 2,800 entries for books and periodical articles.

Continued by *Nihon keizaishi daini bunken* (Second collection of materials on Japanese economic history) Tokyo, Nihon hyoron shinsha, Showa 30(1955) 709 p.

3,000 books and periodical articles compiled from the annual *Keizaishi nenkan* (Economic history yearbook) and covering publications from 1932 to 1940. First published in 1942 with title *Nihon keizaishi shinbunken* (New materials on Japanese economic history)

Continued by *Nihon keizaishi daisan bunken* (Third collection of materials on Japanese economic history) Tokyo, Nihon hyoron shinsha, Showa 28(1953) 612 p.

2,700 books and periodical articles covering publications from 1941 to 1950.

Continued by *Nihon keizaishi daiyon bunken* (Fourth collection of materials on Japanese economic history) Tokyo, Nihon hyoron shinsha, Showa 34(1959) 879 p.

5,600 books and periodical articles selected from publications issued from 1951 to 1957.

Continued by *Nihon keizaishi daigo bunken* (Fifth collection of materials on Japanese economic history) Tokyo, Mineruba shobo, Showa 40(1965) 853 p.

Some 5,400 books and articles selected from publications issued from 1958 to 1962.

An outstanding series compiled by one of Japan's leading economic historians, and including books and periodical articles by Japanese and Western authors, and not restricted to economic history alone, but including political and social materials also. Annotations are not only descriptive but also explanatory. Entries are arranged in a classified order, with a title index.

R134. Remer, Charles Frederick. *Japanese economics, a guide to Japanese reference and research materials.* Ann Arbor, University of Michigan Press, 1956. 91 p. (University of Michigan Center for Japanese Studies, Bibliographical series number 5)

1,191 books arranged in classified order, with headings for dictionaries, statistical information, periodicals, economic theory, economic history, finance, agriculture, industry, trade, labor and the corporation. Most entries briefly annotated. No index.

R135. Sumida, Shoji. *Kaiji kankei bunken somokuroku* (Bibliography of materials on maritime affairs) Tokyo, Nohon kaiji shinkokai, Showa 32(1957) 443 p.

Some 22,000 Japanese books and periodical articles on maritime transportation, shipping, maritime law, ships, routes and harbors, published from 1868 and arranged in classified order. Table of contents serves as a subject approach. No index and no annotation.

R136. Taeuber, Irene Barnes. *The population of Japan.* Princeton, Princeton University Press, 1958.

Bibliography of some 1,500 books, series and periodical articles on p.395-455. Materials are largely in Japanese or English and include the principal population and census series. Some items briefly annotated. No index.

R137. Nihon keizaishi kenkyujo(Japanese Economic History Institute) *Keizaishi bunken kaidai,* Showa 34 nemban- (Economic history bibliography, 1959-) Tokyo, Nihon hyoron shinsha, Showa 35- (1960-)

Books and periodical articles on economic history, but not restricted to Japan. Continues *Keizaishi bunken* (Materials on economic history) covering 1957 and 1958.

R138. Rosovsky, Henry. *Quantitative Japanese economic history, an annotated bibliography and a survey of U.S. holdings.* Berkeley, Center for Japanese Studies of the Institute for International Relations and the Institute of Business and Economic Research, University of California, 1961. 173 p.

476 monographs, annuals, series and serials, of which 79 are not available in the United States. Arranged in a classified order, with library locations, holdings and annotations given for most items. Separate author and title indexes.

Political science

R139. Kokuritsu kokkai toshokan, Tokyo (National Diet Library) *Gikai seiji bunken mokuroku, gikai kaisetsu shichijunen kinen* (Bibliography on parliamentary government, in commemoration of the 70th anniversary of its establishment) Tokyo, Showa 36(1961) 444 p.

In three sections, the first, which contains some 3,600 Japanese books and periodical articles on parliamentary government, is divided into four parts. There are no annotations. The second contains 2,200 books and periodical articles in Western languages, and has a similar arrangement to the first section, except that some entries have brief annotations. The third section contains papers and reports, all published before 1894, on the history of the opening of the Japanese Diet. Author index for Western language materials, and an author and title index for Japanese language materials.

R140. Hanabusa, Nagamichi. *Nihon gaikoshi kankei bunken mokuroku* (Catalog of materials on Japanese diplomatic history) Tokyo, Keio gijuku daigaku hogaku kenkyukai, Showa 36(1961) 485 p. (Keio gijuku daigaku hogaku kenkyukai sosho 9)

Some 14,000 books and periodical articles on the history of Japanese foreign relations and related fields of politics and economics are divided into four sections by language. The first section contains some 5,000 entries for books in Japanese, is arranged by title, and has an author and translator index. The second has some 6,000 periodical articles arranged by year of publication, the third some 700 books in Chinese, arranged by the Japanese readings of their titles, and the fourth some 2,500 books in English, French and German arranged by author. No annotations.

R141. Ward, Robert E., and Watanabe Hajime. *Japanese political science, a guide to Japanese reference and research materials,* revised edition. Ann Arbor, University of Michigan Press, 1961. 210 p. (University of Michigan Center for Japanese Studies, Bibliographical series number 1)

1,759 Japanese books, series, newspapers and periodicals are arranged in a classified order, with an author index. Concentration is less on the Meiji period and more on recent developments, but with its emphasis on events after 1868, complements the companion bibliography by John W. Hall *Japanese history, a guide to Japanese reference and research materials* (1954). Annotations are descriptive and evaluatory, and in common with other bibliographies in this series, there are introductions to each division of the subject field. Over two-thirds of the titles in this edition are not in the 1950 edition.

Socialism, Communism, the Labor movement

R142. Ohara shakai mondai kenkyujo (Ohara Social Problems Institute) *Nihon shakaishugi bunken* (Bibliography of Japanese socialism) Tokyo, Dojinsha, Showa 4(1929) 255 p.

396 Japanese books, periodicals and newspapers, pamphlets, and handbills, published from 1882 to 1914 on socialism and related fields are divided into two sections. The first contains 321 books and handbills arranged chronologically, and the second 75 newspapers and periodicals which have had at least one article on socialism. Index of authors and translators, and of newspapers and periodicals. No annotations.

R143. Oyama, Hiro. *Nihon rodo undo shakai undo kenkyushi, senzen, sengo no bunken kaisetsu* (Research history of the Japanese labor and social movement, prewar and postwar materials) Kyoto, Mitsuki shobo, Showa 32(1957) 296 p.

Over 2,000 Japanese books and periodical articles are arranged in three sections. The first contains 249 books and articles of a general nature, the second 1,220 books and articles of a more detailed nature, and the third 551 biographies, incidents and associated reference materials. Each section is arranged in chronological order and the entries are annotated. Coverage is from the Meiji period to 1956.

R144. Watanabe, Yoshimichi. *Nihon shakaishugi bunken kaisetsu, Meiji ishin kara Taiheiyo senso made* (Materials on Japanese socialism, from the Meiji Restoration to the Pacific War) Tokyo, Otsuki shoten, Showa 33(1958) 337 p.

538 books, newspaper and periodical articles are divided into five periods 1868-1911, 1912-1921, 1922-1926, 1927-1931, and 1932-1945. Entries are annotated. Chronological listing of publications on Japanese socialism appended. Author and title index.

R145. Uyehara, Cecil H. *Leftwing social movements in Japan, an annotated bibliography.* Rutland, Tuttle, 1959. 444p.

Some 1,800 books, periodicals and newspapers on the Japanese left wing from 1868 to 1956, with an emphasis on the period from World War I, arranged in a classified order, with some 200 divisions. Each section has a major explanatory introduction. Locations in American libraries given. Author and title index.

R146. Japan. Rodosho (Labour Ministry) *Sengo rodo kankei bunken mokuroku* (Bibliography of materials on postwar labor) Tokyo, Showa 39 (1964) 228 p.

6,050 books and series on labor published from 1946 to 1962, divided into nine parts for general works, employment, labor conditions, management and labor, labor management, living conditions, labor law, social security and culture. No annotations and no index.

Law

R147. Ikebe, Gisho. *Nihon hoseishi shomoku kaidai* (Bibliography of the history of the Japanese legal system) Tokyo, Daitokaku, Taisho 7(1918) 2 v.

Divided into three sections. The first contains 16 principal legal documents with commentaries, the second has 71 reference works for research on legal history, and an appendix with 18 Chinese legal documents known in Japan, and the third is an annotated list of 153 books arranged by subject. Entries in each section are arranged chronologically, and there is no index. Valuable for the study of Japanese law to 1868.

R148. *The Japan science review, law and politics,* no. 1- Tokyo, Nihon gakujutsu kaigi, 1950- annual.

Selected books and periodical articles arranged in classified order, and compiled to introduce current Japanese work on law to the outside world. Last issue noted for 1962, with some 1,000 entries.

R149. Japan. Homufu (Attorney-General's Office) *Horitsu kankei zasshi kiji sakuin* (Index to legal periodicals) Tokyo, Showa 27- (1952-)

Some 470 periodicals are surveyed to compile this major index arranged by a detailed subject classification. Substantial proportion concerned with Japanese law.

R150. Horitsu jiho henshubu. *Sengo hogaku bunken mokuroku* (Catalog of materials on postwar law) Tokyo, Nihon hyoron shinsha, Showa 29-41(1954-66) 3 v.

Over 50,000 books and articles from over 500 periodicals and collections arranged by a detailed classification. The first two volumes cover the whole field of law to 1954, the third private law only from 1954 to 1962.

R151. Japan. Saiko saibansho. Toshokan (Supreme Court Library) *Horitsu tosho mokuroku, washo no bu* (Catalog of law books, Japanese books) Tokyo, Showa 39-41(1964-66) 3 v.

Some 25,000 books on law, including a substantial number on Japanese law, arranged in a detailed classification. The most comprehensive bibliography of Japanese law books. Separate indexes for author and organization.

R152. Coleman, Rex. *An index to Japanese law,1867-1961, preliminary draft of all books, pamphlets, articles, essays, statutes, case and other legal materials concerning Japanese law in the English language.* Cambridge, Harvard Law School, 1964?181 p.

Some 1,200 entries are arranged in a detailed subject order. Over 76 periodicals, mostly in the field of law, are sources for the articles. No index.

Education

R153. Kokuritsu kyoiku kenkyujo(National Research Institute of Education) *Kyoiku bunken sogo mokuroku* Union list of educational books located in Japan. Tokyo, Showa 25-29(1950-54) 2 v.(in 3.)

The first volume, published in 1950, contains 14,417 Japanese books, periodicals and periodical articles on the problems of education in general, written from 1868 to 1949, and arranged under eight main headings, and a number of subdivisions. No annotation. The general index in volume 1 has two indexes, an author and subject index in the Japanese syllabic order, and a short foreign author index. Volume 2 is a catalog of local Japanese educational materials, with an author index.

R154. Ishikawa, Matsutaro. *Kyoikushi ni kansuru bunken mokuroku narabi ni kaidai* (Bibliography of materials on education history) Tokyo, Kodansha, Showa 28(1953) 242 p.

Some 2,000 titles are arranged in six parts, and cover the period from 1868 to 1950, but only the second part is directly concerned with Japanese education. Author and title index.

R155. Eells, Walter C. *The literature of Japanese education,1945-1954.* Hamden, Shoestring Press, 1955. 210 p.

Some 1,800 English books, reviews of books and periodical articles relating to Japanese education, arranged in dictionary style, with an index covering all major subjects, individuals, places and organizations named. Over half of the bibliography consists of periodical articles. Annotation is both critical and evaluative. Mr. Eells was an adviser on higher education to the Civil Information and Education Section of the Supreme Commander of the Allied Powers.

NATURAL AND APPLIED SCIENCES

R156. Bonn, George Schlegel. *Japanese journals in science and technology, an annotated checklist.* New York, The New York Public Library, 1960. 119 p.

660 Japanese scientific periodicals are arranged under subject headings, which are further subdivided by six kinds of issuing bodies. Periodicals issued by bodies other than commercial publishers are entered under the name of the issuing body, the remainder are issued under title. Well annotated, with a grading of the outstanding periodicals. Indexes cover subjects, titles, issuing bodies and evaluations.

R157. U.S. Library of Congress. Reference Department. Science and Technology Division. *Japanese scientific and technical serial publications in the collections of the Library of Congress.* Washington, 1962. 247 p.
The first part lists 354 serials in Western languages, and the second 1,136 in Japanese. Both parts are divided into major subject sections. Library of Congress holdings stated. Separate title indexes for Western language and Japanese serials.

R158. Schroeder, Peter Brett. *Japanese serial publications in the National Agricultural Library.* Washington, U.S. National Agricultural Library, 1962. 172 p. (Library list no.72)
1,112 serials are divided into two sections. The first, with multiple agricultural subjects, is divided by issuing agency, the second, with specific subjects, by the subject. Includes Japanese periodicals published in Taiwan. Holdings of the National Agricultural Library stated. Alphabetical title index.

R159. Kokuritsu kokkai toshokan, Tokyo(National Diet Library) *Directory of Japanese scientific periodicals,1967.* Tokyo, 1967. 670 p.
4,929 periodicals being currently published are arranged according to the Universal Decimal Classification. Under each subject division, periodical titles are arranged alphabetically, with information on issuing body and translation of title. Index to titles. Replaces the second volume of *Bibliographical list of Japanese learned journals, natural sciences, humanities, and social sciences* (1962)

Geology

R160. Fujimoto, Haruyoshi. *Nihon chishitsu bunken mokuroku, 1873-1955* (Bibliography of materials on Japanese geology,1873-1955) Tokyo, Chijin shokan, Showa 31(1956) 711 p.
Some 12,000 articles in two parts. The first,with coverage to February 1941, reproduces the entries of the 1941 edition. The second includes materials published largely between 1941 and 1955. Entries are arranged by regions, then by subject. No author or title index.

Biology

R161. Nihon gakujutsu kaigi, Tokyo (Science Council of Japan) *Japan science review, biological section,* 1- Tokyo, Gihodo, Showa 24- (1949-) annual.
The 1964 issue published in 1966, contained 2,284 entries for articles arranged by subject, and selected from Japanese periodicals. Those entries with an asterisk have abstracts.

Medicine

R162. Nihon gakujutsu kaigi, Tokyo (Science Council of Japan) *Japan science review, medical section,* 1- Tokyo, Gihodo, Showa 28- (1953-) annual.

Divided into two parts, bibliography and abstracts. Selected articles are arranged by the Universal Decimal Classification, and a number of the articles have abstracts also in the same issue. Pharmaceutical and dental periodicals are represented.

LANGUAGE AND LITERATURE

Language

R163. Tokyo daigaku (Tokyo University) *Kokugogaku shomoku kaidai* (Annotated bibliography on the Japanese language) Tokyo, Yoshikawa kobunkan, Meiji 35(1902) 606 p.

Some 650 books in printed and manuscript form written before 1868 are arranged in Japanese syllabic order. Author and subject index.

R164. Kokuritsu kokugo kenkyujo, Tokyo(National Language Research Institute) *Meiji iko kokugogaku kankei kanko shomoku* (Bibliography on the Japanese language after 1868) Tokyo, Shuei shuppan, Showa 30(1955) 301 p. (Kokuritsu kokugo kenkyujo shiryoshu 4)

3,027 books arranged under 17 subject headings covering aspects of the Japanese language, its history, dialects, education, dictionaries, mass communication and linguistics. Nearly all entries are written after 1926. Author index.

R165. Brower, Robert H. *A bibliography of Japanese dialects.* Ann Arbor, University of Michigan Press, 1950. 75 p. (University of Michigan Center for Japanese Studies, Bibliographical series number 2)

995 books and periodicals in Japanese arranged by prefectures, nearly all being briefly annotated. Most entries cited were not inspected by the compiler.

R166. Yamagiwa, Joseph Koshimi. *Japanese language studies in the Showa period, a guide to Japanese reference and research materials.* Ann Arbor, Published for the Center of Japanese Studies by the University of Michigan Press, 1961. 153 p. (University of Michigan Center for Japanese Studies, Bibliographical series number 9)

1,473 books, periodicals and periodical articles arranged under subject headings. Since modern linguistics in Japan may be said to have started in the early Showa period, the time division is appropriate; however some important pre-Showa works are noted.

R167. Yamagiwa, Joseph Koshimi. *Bibliography of Japanese encylopedias and dictionaries.* Ann Arbor, The Panel on Far Eastern Linguistics of the Committee on Institutional Cooperation, 1968. 139 p.

1,092 encyclopedias and dictionaries, mostly dictionaries, are arranged in a classified order, with annotations. No index. The most comprehensive listing of Japanese language dictionaries.

Literature

R168. Ishiyama, Tetsuro. *Nihon bungaku shoshi* (Bibliography of Japanese literature) Tokyo, Okura Kobundo, Showa 9(1934) 932 p.

Some 750 major classics are arranged by period and then by genre. Full annotation is followed by notes on editions and lists of commentaries and research works. Coverage to the mid-16th century.

R169. Aso, Isoji. *Kokubungaku kenkyu shomoku kaidai* (Annotated bibliography of studies in Japanese literature) Tokyo, Shibundo, Showa 32 (1957) 506 p.

Some 2,500 books are divided first by major period, then by genre or principal works. Principal works are followed by lists of commentaries and research studies. Title index in the Japanese syllabic order.

R170. Nihon Pen Kurabu(Japan P.E.N. Club) *Japanese literature in European languages, a bibliography,* second edition. Tokyo, 1961. 98 p.

Some 1,500 translations in book and article form are arranged under literature in general, classical literature, classical theater, modern literature, juvenile and folk literature sections and then by author. Author and title indexes. A *Supplement* (1964. 8 p.) lists an additional 250 items. The most comprehensive list of translations from Japanese.

R171. Murakami, Hamakichi. *Meiji bungaku shomoku* (Bibliography of Meiji literature) Tokyo, Murakami shobo, Showa 12(1937) 523 p.

A combined desiderata list and library catalog. The Murakami collection is now at the East Asiatic Library of the University of California, Berkeley. The main text lists some 6,000 titles. Other parts include catalogs of poetry and a catalog of collections. Title index.

R172. Okano, Takeo. *Meiji bungaku kenkyu bunken soran* (Bibliography of studies on Meiji literature) Tokyo, Fuzambo, Showa 19(1944) 810 p.

Some 2,000 original works and 3,000 critical works are arranged under broad headings for history, criticism, the original works, and periodicals. Chronology of important works. Title index.

R173. Bonneau, Georges. *Bibliographie de la litterature japonaise contemporaine.* Tokyo, Kokusai insatsu shuppansha, 1938. 102, 280 p. (Bulletin de la maison franco-japonaise,t.9.(annee 1937) no.1-4)

3,507 literary works published from the early Meiji period are arranged under 451 authors. Titles are given in romanization, characters and translation. Preceded by a study outline which introduces the works cited in the bibliography.

R174. Yamagiwa, Joseph Koshimi. *Japanese literature of the Showa period, a guide to Japanese reference and research materials.* Ann Arbor, Published for the Center for Japanese Studies by the University of Michigan Press, 1959. 212 p. (University of Michigan Center for Japanese Studies, Bibliographical series number 8)

1,248 books, periodicals and periodical articles arranged in a detailed classification for the period 1926 to 1959. The principal part of the bibliography is an annotated listing of Showa authors with their works. Author and editor index.

GEOGRAPHY

R175. Jimbun chiri gakkai(Association of Human Geographers) *Chirigaku bunken mokuroku* (Bibliography of materials on geography) Kyoto, Yanagihara shoten, Showa 28-38(1953-63) 3 v.

A bibliography of books, periodicals and periodical articles. The first volume has some 3,500 entries published from 1945 through 1951, the second some 10,500 from 1952 through 1956, and the third some 12,000 from 1957 through 1961. The volumes are divided into subject sections. The first has an author and a regional index. The second and third have more detailed subject breakdown, but lack indexes. On geography in general, but has a significant amount on Japanese geography.

R176. Hall, Robert Burnett. *Japanese geography, a guide to Japanese reference materials.* Ann Arbor, University of Michigan Press, 1956. 128 p. (University of Michigan Center for Japanese Studies, Bibliographical series number 6)

1,254 books and periodicals are arranged into sections. In the first by field of geography, and in the second by kind of material, as bibliography, encyclopedias, yearbooks and periodicals. Entries are annotated. No index.

ARCHEOLOGY

R177. Okamoto, Isamu and Aso Hitoshi. *Nihon sekki jidai sogo bunken mokuroku* (Bibliography of materials on the Japanese Stone Age) Tokyo, Yamaoka shoten, Showa 33(1958) 194 p.

3,870 books and periodical articles published from 1868 to 1955 are arranged chronologically. Author index and index by districts in Japan. No annotation.

HISTORY

R178. Kurita, Motoji. *Sogo kokushi kenkyu* (General guide to the study of Japanese history) Tokyo, Chubunkan, Showa 10-11(1935-6) 3 v.

Some 3,000 books, series, periodicals and historical materials published from 1868 to 1934 are arranged in three volumes. The first contains some 1,100 books and series for the earlier period of Japanese history, the second some 920 books and series for the modern period, and the third some 1,000 historical documents and a title and an author index, both arranged in Japanese syllabic order.

R179. Otsuka shigakkai (Otsuka Historical Society) *Sogo kokushi rombun yomoku* Important periodical literature on the history of Japan. Tokyo, Toko shoin, Showa 14(1939) 627 p.

22,000 articles published in 169 periodicals and symposia from 1868 to 1932 arranged under 29 subject headings, and then by author by the Japanese syllabic system. No annotation and no index.

R180. Hall, John Whitney. *Japanese history, a guide to Japanese reference and research materials.* Ann Arbor, University of Michigan Press, 1954. 165 p. (University of Michigan Center for Japanese Studies, Bibliographical series number 4)

1,551 Japanese books, periodicals and periodical articles are arranged in classified order, organized into five main sections: bibliographies, reference works, historical sources, periodicals and survey histories. Annotations are descriptive and frequently critical. No index to authors and titles, and this deficiency has been made up by *Index for Japanese history, a guide to Japanese reference and research materials*, by John W. Hall(Canberra,33 p.)

R181. *Sekai rekishi daijiten, dai 22-kan, shiryo-hen Nihon* (Dictionary of world history,volume 22, materials section, Japan) Tokyo, Heibonsha, Showa 30(1955) 601 p.

Arranged into 4 major periods: early, medieval, early modern and modern history, with each period divided into two parts, the first being concerned with discussion of the documentation and the second with selected documents.

R182. Endo, Motoo and Shimomura Fujio. *Kokushi bunken kaisetsu* (Bibliography on Japanese history materials) Tokyo, Asakura shoten, Showa 32-40(1957-65) 2 v.

The first volume has three sections, for books, for series and collected works and for materials in Chinese, Korean and Western languages. Each entry is fully annotated for contents, importance and for critical works. The second volume has a similar arrangement and supplements the first.

Local history

R183. Keio gijuku daiagku. Tokyo. Bunka chiri kenkyukai (Keio gijuku University, Tokyo. Cultural Geography Study Society) *Nihon kembetsu chishi mokuroku* (Catalog of local gazetteers arranged by prefecture) Tokyo, Kogakusha, Showa 30(1955) 244 p.

4,800 books are arranged by region and then by prefecture, and subarranged for city, township and topical aspects of local geography. Author, title, publisher and date of publication given. No index.

R184. Sakamaki, Shunzo. *Ryukyu, a bibliographical guide to Okinawan studies.* Honolulu, University of Hawaii Press, 1963. 353 p.

Some 1,000 primary sources, manuscripts, articles and books, almost entirely in Japanese, but with some works in Chinese and Korean, are arranged in a classified order. Annotated. Separate author and title indexes.

R185. Sakamaki, Shunzo. *Ryukyuan research resources at the University of Hawaii.* Honolulu, Social Science Research Institute, University of Hawaii, 1965. 454 p. (Ryukyu Research Center Research series no.1)

3,594 books and periodical articles, approximately one half being books, arranged by author. Including 400 entries for materials in Western languages, nearly all in English, and 603 microfilms of periodicals and documents mostly in Japanese. Title index to entries in Japanese, other than periodical articles. A key to the most comprehensive collection of Ryukyu materials.

R186. King, Norman D. *Ryukyu islands, a bibliography.* Washington, Department of the Army, 1967. 105 p. (Department of the Army pamphlet 550.4)

2,108 entries, a number of which are cross references, for books, reports and periodical articles, nearly all in English, arranged under broad subject headings, and with an author index. Some entries are annotated.

S.KOREA

The first king of Korea is reputed to have ascended the throne in 2333 B.C. and the Republic of Korea used this year as a base for its calendar until 1961, when standard Western dating was adopted. Korea was annexed by Japan in 1910, and Japanese rule lasted until 1945. The Republic of Korea was established in South Korea in 1948, and in the same year the Democratic People's Republic of Korea was established in North Korea.

REFERENCE WORKS

S 1. California. University. Institute of East Asiatic Studies. *Korean studies guide,* compiled for the Institute of East Asiatic Studies, University of California, by B.H.Hazard, Jr., and others, edited by Richard Marcus. Berkeley, University of California Press, 1954. 220 p.
Annotated guide to 491 selected reference works and sources in Japanese, Korean and Western languages on Korea, arranged by major topics. Each section has an introduction. The emphasis is on history. Eight maps show the historical development of Korea, and appendices contain chronological tables. The guide is now seriously dated by the large amount of new Korean reference works and sources which have appeared since 1954. A *Russian supplement to the Korean studies guide* (Berkeley, University of California, Institute of International Studies, 1958) 211 p. includes valuable Russian language material.
S 2. Henthorn, William. *A guide to reference and research materials on Korean history, an annotated bibliography.* Honolulu, East-West Center, Research Translations, 1968. 152 p. (Annotated bibliography series no.4) 612 entries for books and periodical articles, arranged in three major sections for bibliography, modern reference works, and selected source materials for traditional Korean history. Written in a style designed to be helpful to the student, with entries arranged to meet problems which will arise. Will help update the *Korean studies guide.*

ENCYCLOPEDIAS AND HANDBOOKS

S 3. Korea (Republic). Yunesuk'o Han'guk Wiwonhoe (National Commission for UNESCO) *UNESCO Korean survey.* Seoul, Dong-A Publishing Co., 1960. 936 p.
An encyclopedic survey of Korean culture, divided into 17 sections, each of which is further subdivided, with substantial signed articles by Korean scholars. Appendices contain texts of laws, lists of institutions of higher education, newpapers and periodicals, statistics, a chronology of Korean history. Well illustrated and fully indexed. Superior to *Korea, its land,*

people and culture of all ages (Seoul, Hagwonsa, 1963) a similar survey.
S 4. *Facts about Korea.* Pyongyang, Foreign Languages Publishing House,
1961. 240 p.
Description and history of Korea, with an emphasis on the postwar situation and on conditions in North Korea, stressing its economy and culture.
Section on conditions in South Korea. Some statistical information. Not
indexed. Not to be confused with a South Korean publication with the
same title.
S 5. Yi, Hong-Jik. *Kuksa tae sajon.* Encyclopedia of Korean history. Soul,
Chinumgak, 1965. 2085 p.
Historical dictionary of Korean history arranged according to the Korean
alphabet, and the most comprehensive volume of its kind. Has an extensive Korean history chronology from 2333 B.C. No character index. A
revision of the two-volume 1963 edition.
S 6. *Segye paekkwa tae sajon* World encyclopedia. Soul, Hagwonsa, 1966-67.
12 v.
A substantial and authoritative encyclopedia in Korean, with excellent
illustration. Approximately one-quarter concerned with Korea. Materials
arranged according to the Korean alphabet. Revision of *Taebaekkwa
sajon* (Korean encyclopedia) (Soul, Hagwonsa, 1958-65) 9 v.

YEARBOOKS

S 7. *Choson chungang yon'gam,* 1949- (Korean central yearbook, 1949-)
P'yongyang, Choson chungang t'ongshisa, 1949-
Surveys internal and international affairs relating to the People's Democratic Republic of Korea. Government and politics, culture, social affairs
and South Korea are covered. There is a chronology of events. No index
but a detailed table of contents. The 1959 issue was translated in *Information from 1959 North Korean central yearbook,* 1960. 541 p. JPRS
2691. The 1960 issue was also translated with a similar title, and published in 1962. 717 p. JPRS 16611, and the 1961 issue was translated as *The
1961 North Korean yearbook, Pyongyang, 1962,* 1963. 571 p. JPRS
17890. 1965 last issue noted.
S 8. *Han'guk yon'gam,* 1954- Korea handbook, 1954- Soul, Han'guk
yon'gamsa, Tan'gi 4286- (1953-)
Divided into four sections, the fourth and largest being concerned with
Korea, and discussing foreign relations, government, political parties, statistics, cultural activities, and the major provinces. Appendix lists important government officials. Indexed. A continuation of the *Kyongbuk
yon'gam* (Soul, Yongnam ilbosa)
S 9. *Korea annual,* 1964- Seoul, Hapdong newsagency, 1964-
Arranged by major subjects as chronology, government, foreign relations,
and the national economy. Appendices contain a who's who and statistical materials. Subject index. 1970 issue last noted. English edition of
Haptong yon'gam (United yearbook)

DICTIONARIES

S10. Kauh, Hwang-man. *A new English-Korean dictionary.* Seoul, Omungak Publishing Company, 1964. 2276 p.
Some 70,000 English words are given Korean equivalents. Usage with Korean translation also stated. The most comprehensive English-Korean dictionary.

S11. *Taejung chongchi yongo sajon* (Dictionary of popular political usage) P'yongyang, Choson nodongdang ch'ulp'ansa, 1964. 536 p.
Contains some 2,500 entries and is valuable for understanding contemporary usage in North Korea.

S12. Yang,Chu-dong. *Han-Han taejajon* (Chinese-Korean dictionary) Soul, Tong-A ch'ulp'ansa, 1964. 1544 p.
Some 4,000 characters are arranged in radical order, followed by their pronunciation in *hangul* (Korean alphabet) and by compounds. A standard *hanmun* (Chinese characters) dictionary. *Hangul* index.

S13. Martin, Samuel E., Yang Ha Lee and Sung-un Chang. *A Korean-English dictionary.* New Haven, Yale University Press, 1967. 1902 p.
With some 80,000 words in the Yale romanization of Korean, this new dictionary is reasonably comprehensive, but does not attempt to be exhaustive for *hanmun* compounds. Tables to assist with conversion of the Yale system to the standard McCune-Reischauer and to North Korean systems, but conversion is difficult for the non-specialist. The large format is easier to read than the many smaller print dictionaries previously in use.

BIOGRAPHICAL DICTIONARIES

S14. Korea (Government-general of Chosen,1910-1945) *Chosen jimmei jisho* (Korean biographical dictionary) Keijo, Chosen sotokufu, Showa 12(1937) 2012 p.
13,000 persons born in the 19th century and before are arranged by stroke order, with detailed information and sources stated. In addition, there are two lists. The first notes formal names of government offices, with their popular names, their date of establishment and jurisdiction. The second is a list of 15,000 successful candidates to the civil service examinations. Stroke order index to persons by their pseudonyms. A Japanese index arranged in Japanese syllabic order is appended as a separate volume (148 p.)

S15. Yi,Ka-won. *Yijo myongin yolchon* (Yi dynasty biographical dictionary) Soul, Uryu munhwasa, 1965. 932 p.
1,670 important persons who lived from the 14th century to the end of the dynasty in 1910, are arranged chronologically. Literary and artistic figures are included, and the *Chosen jimmei jisho* is supplemented in this respect.

S16. *Han'guk ui in'gansang* (Korean biographies) Soul, Sin'gu munhwasa, 1965. 6 v.

A very selective biographical dictionary with accounts of only some 200 persons. Each volume represents a group of similar persons. Valuable since it gives more extensive treatment for a select number of really important figures. Similar in content to *Inmul Han'guksa* (Biographical history of Korea) 5 v.

S17. *Han'guk inmyong taesajon* (Korean biographical dictionary) Soul, Sin'gu munhwasa, 1967. 1390 p.

Containing some 10,000 biographies, it is less extensive than the *Chosen jimmei jisho.* Includes prominent people of the 20th century, but no living persons. Some non-Koreans related to Korea have been listed, but this group is not complete. Since this dictionary was compiled in South Korea, prominent persons related to North Korea have not been included. Extensive chronological tables.

Contemporary biography

S18. Kasumigaseki-kai, Tokyo. *Gendai Chosenjin jimmei jiten,* 1962 nemban (Who's who in modern Korea, 1962) Tokyo, Sekai janarusha, Showa 37(1962) 356 p.

Some 1,600 South Korean and 800 North Korean persons are listed in two separate sections. Entries are arranged by the Japanese syllabary in each section. There are character and romanized indexes. For more up-to date information on North Korea, the September 1966 issue of *Sedae* has material on 192 North Koreans, and has been translated in JPRS no. 40,950(9 March 1967). For South Koreans a more up-to-date statement may be found in *Hyongdae Han'guk inmyong sajon,* 1967-

S19. *Hyongdae Han'guk inmyong sajon,* 1967- (Who's who of Korea,1967-) Seoul, Haptong yon'gamsa, 1967-

The 1967 edition, the first not to be included as a part of the *Haptong yon'gam,* contains 3,173 biographies of living Koreans, arranged by the Korean alphabet. The romanized form of the name is also given.

DIRECTORIES

S20. Kukhoe tosogwan,Seoul(National Assembly Library) *Kungnae haksul mit yon'gu tanch'e p'yonllam* (Research institutes in Korea) Seoul, 1966-67. 2 v.

Altogether some 400 institutes are arranged in the Korean alphabet in a separate sequence for each volume. The second volume which is in a larger format, has an index by place. For nearly all institutes a translated name is given in English, and objectives, staff, publications and library resources are stated. The emphasis is on science and technology.

ATLAS

S21. *Taehan min'guk chido* Standard atlas of Korea. Seoul, Saso ch'ulpansa, Tan'gi 4293(1960)1 v.

26 large colored maps showing physical features, communications, towns, villages, at the scale of 1 to 350,000. An index includes some 40,000 place and feature names, arranged by the Korean alphabet with Chinese characters also given. North Korea included.

GEOGRAPHICAL DICTIONARIES AND GAZETTEERS

S22. U.S. Office of Geography. *North Korea* ... Washington, U.S. Government Printing Office, 1963. 380 p. (Gazetteer no.75)
27,000 entries for place and feature names in North Korea, with their classification, and longitude and latitude.

S23. U.S. Office of Geography. *South Korea* ... Washington, U.S. Government Printing Office, 1965. 370 p. (Gazetteer no. 95)
26,500 entries for place and feature names in South Korea, with a classification and longitude and latitude for each.

CHRONOLOGICAL TABLES

S24. Chindan hakhoe. *Han'guksa, yonp'yo* (Korean history, chronology) Soul, Uryu munhwasa, Tan'gi 4292(1959) 373, 209 p.
The main text is a chronological table 195 B.C.-1945 A.D. It also gives the Tan'gi date, the sexagenary cycle date, reign titles, and regnal years for Korean kings, with similar information for China and Korea, and noting major events in Korea and outside Korea. The Western year date is given at the foot of the page. There are two appendices, the first giving a genealogy of the Yi dynasty, and the second a table for the period 918 to 1959 for conversion of Korean dates into Western.

CENSUS

S25. Korea (Republic). Naemubu. T'onggyeguk (Ministry of the Interior. Statistical Office) *Taehan min'guk kani ch'ongin'go chosa pogo* ... Report of the first general population census, Republic of Korea. Soul, Tan'gi 4292(1959) 181 p.
There was no decennial "complete" census for Korea in 1920, owing to internal disorder. Mid-decade simplified censuses were taken in 1925 and 1935, and a complete census in 1930. A summary census report is available for 1940, and a population survey report for 1944. The first postwar census was taken in 1949, but the information was destroyed in the war with North Korea. This report is based on the twelve interim reports of the "first" census of 1955. Field enumeration covered sex, date of birth, occupation, education and type of household, whether farm or non-farm. Title does not indicate that this is a summary report. In English and Korean.

S26. Korea (Republic). Kyongje kihoegwon. Chosa tonggye-guk (Economic Planning Board. Bureau of Research and Statistics) *Ilgu yukkong nyon in'gu chut'aek kukse chosa pogo* 1960 population and housing census of Korea. Soul, 1963-

The first volume is a complete tabulation for sex, age, marital activity, literacy, economic activity, occupation and industry. The first part is for the whole of South Korea, and the remaining ten parts are for each province and for Seoul. 2 volumes in 22 parts projected, of which volume 1 only seen.

OTHER STATISTICAL SOURCES

S27. Korea (Government-general of Chosen, 1910-1945) *Chosen sotokufu tokei nempo, Meiji 43-Showa 17 nen* (Annual statistical report of the Government-general of Korea, 1910-42) Keijo, Chosen sotokufu, Meiji 45-Showa 19(1912-44) 36 v.

Each volume covers area, population, agriculture, forestry, industry, trade, communications, monopolies, religion, education, police, health and finance. The 1942 volume contained 414 tables. Continues *Tokanfu tokei nenkan* (Statistical annual for the Resident-general of Korea) for 1906-9, and published 1907-11 in 3 v. Continued by Korea. South Korea Provisional Government *Choson t'onggye yon'gam,* Tan'gi 4276 yon (Sogi 1943 yon)

S28. Korea (Republic) Kyongje kihoegwon (Economic Planning Board) *Han'guk t'onggye yon'gam,* 4285 yon- Korea statistical yearbook, 1952- Soul, Tan'gi 4286- (1953-)

First published with title *Taehan min'guk t'onggye yongam.* From 1961 published by the Kyongje kihoegwon with title and added title noted above. Gives statistical information for population, economy, social affairs, and culture. In Korean and English. Economic statistics for the period 1944-45 for all Korea, and for 1946-48 for South Korea only are found in *Choson kyongje yon'be* Annual economic review of Korea, 1948- (Soul, Choson unhaeng, chosabu, 1948-) which suspended publication from 1950-55.

S29. Korea (Democratic People's Republic) Kukka kyehoek wiwonhoe. Chungang t'onggyeguk (State Planning Commission. Central Statistical Board) *Statistical returns of national economy of the Democratic People's Republic of Korea, 1946-60.* Pyong-yang, Foreign Languages Publishing House, 1961. 189 p.

174 statistical tables and charts illustrate the industrial, agricultural, transportation and communication, capital construction, labor, commodity turnover, foreign trade, educational, cultural and public health development of North Korea.

BIBLIOGRAPHY

Korean books published to 1910

S30. Courant, Maurice. *Bibliographie coreene.* Paris, E. Leroux, 1894-96. 3 v.
(Publications de l'Ecole des langues orientales vivantes. 3 ser., v.18-20.)
Some 3,000 books in Korean published to 1890, are arranged in subject
order, with descriptive and analytical annotation. Author and title index.
A major Western contribution to traditional Korean bibliography. Sup-
plemented by *Supplement a la Bibliographie coreene(jusqu'en 1899)*
Paris, Imprimerie national, Leroux, 1901. 122 p. (Publications de
l'Ecole des langues orientales vivantes. 3 ser., v.21.) Reprinted by Burt
Franklin, New York.

S31. Korea(Government-general of Chosen,1910-1945) *Chosen tosho kaidai*
(Annotated bibliography of Korean books) Keijo, Chosen sotokufu,
Showa 7 (1932) 578 p.
A select list of some 2,500 early Korean books, with annotations, arranged
in the traditional Chinese bibliographical order. Indexes list titles in
the traditional order and also in the Japanese syllabic order. There are
also indexes of authors and titles arranged in stroke order.

S32. Toyo bunko, Tokyo(Oriental Library) *Toyo bunko Chosen-bon bunrui
mokuroku, fu Annam-hon mokuroku* (Classified catalog of Korean books
in the Oriental Library, with an appended catalog of Annamese books)
Tokyo, Showa 24(1939) 100 p.
Some 1,000 Korean books arranged in traditional Chinese bibliographical
order. Information on modern editions of early Korean books given.

S33. Maema, Kyosaku. *Kosen sappu* (Record of early Korean books) Tokyo,
Toyo bunko, Showa 19-32(1944-57) 3 v. (Toyo bunko sokan 11)
Some 8,000 books arranged by title in the Japanese syllabic order. Nearly
all entries are annotated with an indication of location. No index to
authors or to titles by stroke.

S34. Harvard University. Harvard-Yenching Institute. Library. *A classified
catalogue of Korean books in the Harvard-Yenching Institute Library at
Harvard University.* Cambridge, 1962-66. 2 v.
The first volume contains 3,160 books and periodicals, and the second
3,400. Both volumes are arranged in a classified order, and the second
volume has an author and title index to both volumes arranged by the
Korean alphabet. The Harvard collection is strong on traditional Korea,
and individual writings, genealogical records and rosters of examination
passes are well represented. The number of modern works is second only
in size to the collection of the Library of Congress. An author and title
index in Korean alphabetical order to both volumes in volume 2. Since
the cut-off date for the catalogue was 1964, there are now an additional
3,000 titles in the collection which are not listed.

S35. Soul taehakkyo. Tosogwan(Seoul National University Library) *Kyujang-
gak toso mongnok Han'gukpon ch'ong mongnok* Catalogue of Korean
books and manuscripts in the Kyujang-gak collection, Seoul National
University Library. Soul, 1965. 691 p.

The Kyujanggak or the Yi dynasty Royal Library was founded in 1776. Under the Japanese occupation of Korea it was transferred to the Keijo Imperial University, the present Seoul National University in 1931. Over three-quarters of the 8,000 entries were published after 1850. The remainder are fairly well representative of all periods since 1700. The books are arranged in the traditional Chinese bibliographical order, with a title index in the Korean alphabet and a character key. Some selected titles are annotated. An important bibliographical tool, since it is now possible to order books listed on microfilm. An earlier edition, commenced publication in 1964. This was issued in a number of volumes.

Korean books published 1910-1945

S36. Kungnip chungang tosogwan, Seoul(National Central Library) *Changso pullyu mongnok* (Classified catalog of books in the collections) Soul, 1961-62. 5 v.

The books listed are published almost entirely in Japan, but some publications in Japanese and Korean published in Korea are included. Books on Korea are arranged in a separate sequence in the last volume, with a similar classification to that in the main text. A revised and enlarged edition of Korea(Government-general of Chosen,1910-1945) *Shinshobu bunrui mokuroku* (Classified catalog of new books) Keijo, Showa 12-13(1937-38) 3 v.

Korean books published 1945-

S37. Yang, Key Paik. *Reference guide to Korean materials, 1945-1959.* Washington, 1960. 131 p.

A master's dissertation at Catholic University of America, and based on materials selected from the Korean collection of the Library of Congress. 800 items are arranged in a classified order, and most items have short annotations. The selection stresses reference works. Separate author and title indexes.

S38. Koryo taehakkyo, Seoul. Asae munje yonguso(Korea University. Asiatic Research Center). *Bibliography of Korean studies, a bibliographical guide to Korean publications on Korean studies appearing from 1945 to 1962.* Seoul, 1961-65. 2 v.

The first volume lists 863 books and periodical articles, and arranges these in subject order. Each entry is fully annotated, and the period covered is from 1945 to 1958. The subject index gives greater subdivision than the main text. Index to authors. Volume 2 has a similar arrangement, but covers the years 1959 to 1962, again with 863 entries.

TRADE BIBLIOGRAPHY

S39. *Ch'ulp'an taegam* (Register of publications) Soul, Choson ch'ulp'an munhwa hyophoe, 1949. 108 p.

Lists 1,400 publications issued from 1945 through 1948, arranged in major subject groups. Supplement to *Ch'ulp'an munhwa* (Publishing culture) no.7(April 1949)

S40. *Han'guk ch'ulp'an yon'gam,* 4290- Korean publications yearbook, 1957-

Soul, Taehan ch'ulp'an munhwa hyophoe, Tangi 4290 (1957-)
More of an in-print catalog than a record of books published in the
previous period. The 1968 issue, the latest noted, lists books published
from 1955. Entries are arranged in Korean Decimal Classification order.
Issues also noted for 1963,1964 and 1966. The 1957 issue has title
Ch'ulp'an yon'gam (Publications yearbook)

S41. *Choson toso* Korean books. Pyongyang, Kukze sedom, 195 ?-
Issued on an irregular basis, and listing books for overseas distribution.
Entries translated into Russian, Japanese, English and Chinese. In the
absence of an available North Korean bibliographical record, this is the
best listing we have. Only a small proportion of the total number of
periodicals and books published in North Korea are listed. For 1964 and
1965 Choson ch'ulp'anmul such'urip sangsa, Pyongyang (Korean Publication Export and Import Corporation) *Choson toso ch'ongmongnok* General catalog of Korean books(Pyongyang) was issued aiming at the foreign
market for Korean books.

NATIONAL BIBLIOGRAPHY

S42. Kungnip chungang tosogwan, Seoul (National Central Library) *Han'guk
somok* Korean national bibliography,1945-1962. Soul, 1964. 722 p.
Lists 21,660 books, periodicals, dissertations, music scores, maps, and
principal official publications published from 1945 through 1962. Entries
are arranged by the Korean Decimal Classification. There are two indexes
arranged by the Korean alphabet. The first is for books, the second for
dissertations. No author index.
The National Central Library was formerly the National Library, and
from 1923 to 1945 it was the Library of the Government-general of
Korea. Continued by the *Taehan min'guk ch'ulp'anmul ch'ongmongnok,
1963-64* Korean national bibliography,1963-1964 (Soul,1965) the first
part of which contains some 4,000 books and year books including government publications and arranged by the Korean Decimal Classification,
and the second 580 periodicals and newspapers arranged by frequency of
publications. Index to authors and titles. Annual volumes for 1965 and
1966 published in 1966 and 1967.

Chinese and Japanese books

S43. Sakurai, Yoshiyuki. *Meiji nenkan Chosen kenkyu bunkenshi* (Bibliographic record of Korean studies in the Meiji period) Keijo, Shomotsu doko-
kai, Showa 16(1941) 421 p.
Some 600 books in Japanese on Korea, and published from 1868 to
1912, are arranged in eight sections. Annotations are full and there is an
author index and a title index, arranged by the Japanese syllabary.

S44. Beal, Edwin G., and Robin L. Winkler. *Korea, an annotated bibliography
of publications in Far Eastern languages.* Washington, Library of Congress, 1950. 167 p.
528 books, periodicals and periodical articles arranged in subject order,
with a combined author and select subject index. Stresses the modern

period and does not include some 1,687 older Korean books in the Library of Congress at the time of publication.

S45. Kondo, Kenichi. *Chosen kankei bunken shiryo somokuroku* (Catalog of materials on Korea) Tokyo, Chosen shiryo kenkyukai, Showa 36(1961) 180 p.
4,333 books in Japanese, emphasizing history, social sciences, technology and industry, are arranged by the Nihon Decimal Classification. No index.

Western languages

S46. Gompertz, G. St.G.M. *Bibliography of Western literature on Korea from the earliest times until 1950.* Seoul, Dong-A Publishing, 1963. 263 p. (Transactions of the Korea Branch Royal Asiatic Society of Great Britain and Ireland no.40)
2,276 books and periodical articles arranged in a detailed subject order. No index. A revision of H.H.Underwood "A partial bibliography of Occidental literature on Korea from early times to 1930." *Transactions of the Korea Branch Royal Asiatic Society,* v.20, 1931 and first supplement *Transactions...,* v.24,1935.

S47. Kukhoe tosogwan, Seoul(National Assembly Library) *Soyangbon Han'guk munhon mongnok, 1800-1963 (nosabon p'oham)* Bibliography of Korea, publications in the Western language, 1800-1963(in the Russian language) Soul, 1967. 227 p.
This publication reprints: Helen Dudenbostel Jones and Robin L. Winkler. *Korea, an annotated bibliography of publications in Western languages.* (Washington, Library of Congress, 1950. 155 p.) which has 632 books, periodicals, and official documents, mostly in English, published between 1886 and 1951, but emphasizing those issued after 1930. Indexed; Yi Sun-hi(Soon Hi Lee) *Korea, a selected bibliography in Western languages, 1950-1958.* (Washington, 1959, 55 p.) a master's dissertation at Catholic University of America, with 500 entries for books arranged in subject order, and almost entirely in English. This may be regarded as a continuation of the preceding bibliography. Indexed; Yong-Sun Chung *Publications on Korea in the era of political revolutions* (Kalamazoo, Korean Research and Publication, Inc. 1965. 117 p.) with 967 entiries suplementing the two bibliographies above, but including Far Eastern langauge material also. Indexed; and U.S. Library of Congress. Bibliography Division. *Korea, an annotated bibliography of publications in the Russian language* (Washington, Library of Congress, 1950, 84 p.) noting 436 books and periodical articles. Combined author, title and subject index.

Official publications

S48. Korea(Government-general of Chosen,1910-1945) *Chosen sotokufu oyobi shozoku kansho shuyo kanko tosho mokuroku* (Catalog of the chief publications of the Government-general of Korea and its agencies and offices) Keijo, Chosen sotokufu, Showa 5- (1930-)
Publications are arranged under 28 subject divisions with no index. Issues

for 1930,1932-34,1936 and 1938 have been noted. Korean official publications are also noted in Japan. Naikaku insatsukyoku(Cabinet Printing Office) *Kancho kanko tosho mokuroku,* Showa 2-12(Catalog of government publications,1927-37) and its continuation *Kanko kancho tosho geppo, Showa 13-18* (Government publications monthly,1938-43)

S49. Kukhoe tosogwan, Seoul(National Assembly Library) *Chongbu kanhaengmul mongnok.*
Government publications in Korea, 1948-1965. Seoul, 1966. 58 p. Some 2,000 books and serials are arranged by issuing agency. No index.

Periodicals and newspapers

KOREAN LANGUAGE
S50. Yang, Key Paik. *Han'guk sinmun chapchi ch'ong mongnok* Catalogue of Korean periodicals,1883-1945. Soul, Taehan min'guk kukhoe tosogwan, 1966. 230 p.
799 entries for periodicals published in Korea, 234 for periodicals published outside Korea, and 105 for newspapers published in or outside Korea. However some entries are cross references. The titles are arranged alphabetically in each section. Characters and dates of issue are given. The fourth section is a chronological list arranged by date of first issue from 1892 to 1944. Index of titles arranged by the Korean alphabet.

S51. Yi, Pyong-mok. *Han'guk ui taehak chonggi kanhaengmul* Bibliography of university periodicals in Korea,1945-1964. Soul, Yonse taehakkyo tosogwan hakkwa, 1964. 265 p. (Library science series of Yonsei University, no.15)
724 titles, including 147 university newspapers, and 85 catalogs and bulletins, are arranged by title in Korean alphabet order. Classified index to titles. Also contains a directory of institutions of higher education, listing 1537 departments in 164 institutions, with an index to disciplines. This is intended to be an aid to library exchange.

S52. U.S. Library of Congress. *Union card file of Oriental vernacular serials, Chinese, Japanese and Korean. Korean file.* Washington, 1966. 2 reels.
Contains 3,037 holdings cards from leading American academic institutions for Korean language periodicals. Available from the Library of Congress on microfilm or on electrostatic reproduction in card size.

S53. Korea(Republic). Kongbobu(Ministry of Information) *Chonggi kanhaengmul sil t'ae illam, 4294.* (Directory of Korean periodicals and newspapers, 1961) Soul, 1962? 1053 p.
Divided into five sections. The first contains 38 newspapers arranged by place, the second lists six newspaper agencies, the third 30 weekly periodicals, the fourth 158 monthlies, and the fifth is a miscellaneous section with 61 entries. Information given on date of first issue, numbers of copies published, and lists editorial staff. Lacks comprehensive index.

INDEXES TO KOREAN LANGUAGE PERIODICALS

S54. Kukhoe tosogwan, Seoul(National Assembly Library) *Hanmal Han'guk chapchi mokch'a ch'ongnok* Catalogue of contents of Korean periodicals published in the end of Yi dynasty, 1896-1910. Soul, 1967. 138 p.
Contents of 29 periodicals are listed, but some issues are lacking.

S55. *Kungnae kanhaengmul kisa saegin,* 1960- Korean periodical index, 1960- Soul, Taehan min'guk kukhoe tosogwan, 1964-
An index to 155 scholarly and official periodicals, arranged by subjects. Newspapers, statistical and recreational periodicals are excluded. Each issue contains some 3,500 entries. Lists of periodicals indexed, and index to authors appear in the last issue for each year. The 1960 issue duplicates the *Haksul chapchi saegin,* 2960(Index to Korean learned periodicals,1960) no issue was published for 1961-62, but there is an issue of the *Haksul chapchi saegin,* 1961/62. 1963 and 1964 are annual volumes. Quarterly from 1965. This series now includes coverage from 1945.

INDEXES TO PERIODICALS AND NEWSPAPERS IN ENGLISH

S56. Elrod, Jefferson Mcree. *An index to English language periodicals in Korea,1890-1940.* Seoul, Yonsei University, 1960. 214 p.
A master's dissertation for George Peabody College for Teachers. 2,970 entries from a group of 10 periodicals published in Korea and mostly edited by missionaries, but including the important *Transactions of the Korean Branch of the Royal Asiatic Society.* Also published by the National Assembly Library in 1965.

S57. Elrod, Jefferson Mcree. *An index to English language newspapers published in Korea, 1896-1931.* Seoul, National Assembly Library, 1966. 66 p.
1,250 entries are indexed from the *Independent,* 1896-1899, *Korea Daily News,* 1904-5,1909, *Korea repository,* local edition 1899 (weekly), *Seoul Press,* 1907-1910,1927-1937, and *Seoul Press weekly,* 1905.

S58. Kang, Sang-un. *Han'guk kwangye oeguk nomun kisa ch'ong mongnok* A list of articles on Korea in the Western languages, 1800-1964. Soul, Tamgu dang, 1967. 192 p.
Title is misleading since it commences with articles published in 1890. Based on a review of the more general American periodicals, indexed in the *Readers' guide to periodical literature.* Arrangement is by chronological periods, and then by subject. Altogether there are some 5,700 entries, of which approximately 900 were published before 1945.

S59. Chon, Munam. *An index to English periodical literature published in Korea, 1945-1966.* Seoul, Korean Research Center, 1967. 153 p.
Covers eight English periodicals published since 1945, and contains some 2,200 subject and author entries, arranged in alphabetical order.

Subject bibliography

SOCIAL SCIENCES

S60. Yonse taehakkyo, Seoul. Sanop kyongje yonguso(Yonsei University. Industrial Economics Institute) *Sanop kyongje munhon mongnok...* (Catalog of materials on industrial economics) Soul, Yonse taehakkyo ch'ulp'anbu, 1961-65. 2 v.

Lists over 11,000 books and periodical articles published in the fields of business and economics, with over 5,000 from 1945 to 1960 in volume 1, and over 6,000 from 1961 to 1964 in volume 2. Each volume is divided into major subject fields, which are further subdivided. Lists of periodicals, annuals, and dictionaries in economics and business are appended.

S61. U.S. Bureau of the Census. *Bibliography of social science periodicals and monograph series, North Korea, 1945-1961.* Washington, U.S. Government Printing Office, 1962. 12 p. (Foreign social science bibliographies, Series P-92,no.8)

Lists 38 periodicals and 3 monograph series, giving considerable bibliographical and other information for each entry. Materials cited are to be found at the Library of Congress. Separate subject and title indexes.

S62. U.S. Bureau of the Census. *Bibliography of social science periodicals and monograph series, Republic of Korea, 1945-1961.* Washington, U.S. Government Printing Office, 1962. 48 p. (Foreign social science bibliographies, Series P92,no.9)

127 periodicals and 134 monograph series in the Library of Congress are arranged under 14 social science fields and bibliography. Each entry is annotated. Separate subject, title and author indexes.

S63. Bark, Dong-suh and Jai-poong Yoon. *Bibliography of Korean public administration, September 1945- April 1966.* Seoul, United States Operations Mission to Korea, 1966. 174 p.

A short list of 99 Korean books and government publications, arranged chronologically, is followed by 1,355 articles on Korea divided into 17 main divisions and then chronologically, and by 513 master's theses, also arranged by major subjects. Valuable for the non-Korean speaker to learn what is being published in the public administration field in Korea. No index.

NATURAL AND APPLIED SCIENCES

S64. Miki, Sakae. *Chosen isho shi* Bibliography of Korean medicine, ancient and medieval . Sakai, Showa 31(1956) 477 p.

Lists over 400 medical books arranged into six groups: early Korean medical books, Chinese medical books published in Korea, Korean books on materia medica, Korean medical books published in China and in Japan, and catalogs of Korean medical books. Index to titles by stroke.

S65. Schroeder, Peter Brett. *Korean publications in the National Agricultural Library.* Washington, National Agricultural Library, U.S. Department of Agriculture, 1963. 25 p. (Library list no.79)

Includes 79 periodicals and 110 monographs in English or Korean and mostly published in South Korea. The holdings of the National Agricultural Library are noted. Author index, list of titles in English and list of publishers appended.

HISTORY

S66. Kukhoe tosogwan, Seoul(National Assembly Library) *Han'guksa yongu nonmun ch'ong mongnok, 1900-1966.* Catalogue of articles on Korean studies, 1900-1966. Soul,1967. 191 p.

6,800 periodical articles in Japanese and Korean, and arranged for the most part into sections for the early, Koryo and Yi dynasty periods, then subdivided by broad topics. There are in addition a number of general sections on archeology, art history, epigraphy, folklore, linguistics and ethnography. Author index.

S67. Lew, Young Ick. *Korea on the eve of Japanese annexation.* Seoul, 1967. 194 p.

1,938 books, periodical articles, theses and archive sources in Chinese, Japanese, Korean and English covering the period 1904-10 arranged under 59 subject groups. Library locations in the United States, Japan and Korea are stated. No index.

S68. Blanchard, Carroll Henry. *Korean war bibliography and maps of Korea.* New Albany, Korean Conflict Research Foundation, 1964. 181 p.

An extensive unannotated bibliography on the Korean war. In the first part some 900 books are listed by subject; in the second some 200 books from foreign publishers, including materials from Communist countries; in the third some 360 periodicals which have had articles concerning the war; and in the fourth some 5,330 articles from these periodicals arranged by subject. The fifth part has 25 black and white maps. Comprehensive, but no table of contents or index.

T.MONGOLIA

Outer Mongolia, or the present Mongolian People's Republic (MPR) proclaimed its independence from China in 1911. However, more Mongols still live in the People's Republic of China than in the MPR, and there they are concentrated in Inner Mongolia, which has been extended to include a large part of the former Western Manchuria. The MPR was formally established in 1924. Extensive references to the Mongols and to Mongolia may also be found in the section on China.

DICTIONARIES

T 1. Boberg, Folke. *Mongolian-English dictionary*. Copenhagen, Munksgaard, 1954-55 3 v.
A Mongolian-English dictionary comprises the first two volumes, and contains over 18,000 Mongol words and expressions. The third volume is an English- Mongolian dictionary keyed to the Mongolian words in the first two volumes.

T 2. Lessing, Ferdinand D. *Mongolian-English dictionary*. Berkeley, University of California Press, 1960. 1217 p.
The emphasis of this dictionary is on modern Mongolian. The strictly archaic language is avoided, and technical Buddhist phrases and words are in an appendix. Entries are arranged alphabetically and English meanings, Mongol and Cyrillic transcriptions are given. Cyrillic index.

BIBLIOGRAPHY

T 3. Iakovlena, E.N. *Bibliografiia Mongol'skoi Narodnoi Respubliki*. Moskva, Izd. Nauchno issledovatel'skoi assotsiatsii po izuchenuiiu natsional'nykh i kolonial'nykh promlem, 1935. 230 p.
A bibliography by one of the leading Soviet Mongolists includes 2,422 entries for books and periodical articles on the Mongolian People's Republic and on the Mongols and Mongolia in the Russian language. Materials published from the beginning of the 18th century to 1934 have been included. The arrangement is first by topic, then by year. Entries for books are annotated. The index lists authors, translators, editors and titles of works by anonymous authors. For a selection of the more recent Russian literature on Mongolia refer to Robert A. Rupen *Mongols of the twentieth century*.

T4. Iwamura, Shinobu and Fujieda Akira. *Moko kenkyu bunken mokuroku, 1900-1950*. Bibliography of Mongolia for 1900-1950. Kyoto, Kyoto daigaku jimbun kagaku kenkyujo, Showa 28(1953) 46 p. (Toyoshi kenkyu bunken bessatsu dai 1)

Contains approximately 1,500 entries of books and periodical articles in Japanese, and is arranged by author, considered by the compilers to be the most useful approach. Articles far outnumber books. No annotation and no subject index.

T 5. Washington(State) University. Far Eastern and Russian Institute. *Bibliography of the Mongolian People's Republic.* New Haven, Human Relations Area Files, 1956. 101 p. (Behavior Science bibliographies)

Major sections on general materials, economics, linguistics and materials in Japanese. The first and last sections have further subdivision. There are approximately 1,200 entries, and nearly all are annotated. One half of the entries are in Japanese, and the remainder are in Western languages, except for the section on economics which is almost entirely in Russian. No index.

T 6. Chang, Hsing-t'ang. *Meng-ku ts'an kao shu mu* (Reference catalogue on Mongolia) T'ai-pei, Chung hua ts'ung shu wei yuan hui, Min kuo 47(1958) 278 p. (Chung hua ts'ung shu)

Divided into broad subject divisions further subdivided by language. There are 1,831 entries, of which 1,123 are in Chinese, 376 in Japanese and 28 in Mongol. 304 entries are in Western languages, of which nearly two-thirds are in English. Both books and articles are included. Sources from which the bibliography was compiled are stated. No annotations and no index.

T 7. Rupen, Robert A. *Mongols of the twentieth century.* Bloomington, Indiana University and the Hague, Mouton and Co., 1964. 2 v. (Indiana University publications, Uralic and Altaic series, v.37)

The first volume is a major survey of modern Mongol history, and the second is an unannotated bibliography of over 3,000 books, periodicals, and periodical articles, principally in Russian and English, with nearly four fifths in an alphabetical listing by author. The key to this bibliography is provided by a short subject index. Easily the most extensive bibliography on Mongolia. This is not a publication of Indiana University Press.

INDEX

CHINESE, JAPANESE AND KOREAN CHARACTERS FOR TITLES

A27 東洋學研究文獻目錄

A28 東洋古美術文獻目錄

A32 日本における東洋史論文目錄

Q3 古今圖書集成

Q9 佛學辭典

Q17 支那年鑑

Q18 中國年鑑

Q19 新中國年鑑

Q20 申報年鑑

Q21 人民手冊

Q22 中華民國年鑑

Q25 國語字典

Q26 中文大字典

Q27 辭海

Q30 中華成語辭典

Q33 中國人名大辭典

Q34 中外人名字典

Q35 中國文學家大字典

Q38 中華民國人實錄

Q42 現代中國人名事典

Q43 中共人名錄

Q49 中國工業工場總覽

Q54 共匪竊據下的中國大陸分省地圖

Q56 中國地名大辭典

Q57 中國古今地名大辭典

Q106 人文月刊

Q107 期刊索引

Q108 中文期刊論文分類索引

Q109 全國主要報刊資料索引

Q114 日報索引

Q115 人民日報索引

Q117 中文報紙論文分類索引

Q118 中國叢書綜錄

Q120 中國隨筆雜著索引

Q137 中國合作文獻目錄

Q144 科學技術參考書提要

Q146 中國醫籍考

Q147 中國醫學書目

Q148 中國農學書錄

Q153 中國礦業期刊論文索引

Q159 中國通俗小說書目

Q161 曲海綜目提要

Q162 元代雜劇全目

Q163 明代雜劇全目

Q164 明代傳奇全目

Q166 中國音樂書譜目錄

Q167 中國古代音樂書目

Q168 中國地學論文索引

Q171 中國史學論文索引

Q172 中國古代中世紀報刊論文資料索引

R29 日本紳士錄
R30 人事興信錄
R33 文化人名錄
R38 職員錄
R40 日本職員錄
R47 全國學協會要覽
R48 全國研究機關總覽
R49 日本經濟地圖
R50 日本歷史地圖
R52 日本列島の地域構造
R55 日本地名事典
R56 全國市町村要覽
R57 國史大年表
R58 索引政治經濟大年表
R60 新日本史年表
R61 國勢調查報告
R64 日本帝國統計年鑑
R65 日本統計年鑑
R66 本邦書誌の書誌
R67 國書解題
R68 明治文獻目錄
R69 國書總目錄
R70 東京書籍商組合圖書總目錄
R71 出版年鑑
R72 書籍年鑑

S18 現代朝鮮人名辭典

S19 現代韓國人名辭典

S20 國內學術및硏究團體便覽

S21 大韓民國地圖

S24 韓國史年表

S26 1960年人口住宅國勢調查報告

S27 朝鮮總督府統計年報

S28 韓國統計年鑑

S31 朝鮮圖書解題

S32 東洋文庫朝鮮本分類目錄

S33 古鮮冊譜

S35 奎章閣圖書目錄,韓國本總目錄

S36 新書部分目錄

S39 出版大鑑

S40 韓國出版年鑑

S41 조선도서

S42 韓國書目

S43 明治年間朝鮮硏究文獻誌

S45 朝鮮關係文獻資料總目錄

S47 西洋本韓國文獻目錄

S48 朝鮮總督府及所屬官署主要刊行圖書目錄

S49 政府刊行物目錄

S50 韓國新聞雜誌總目錄

S51 韓國의大學定期刊行物

S53 定期刊行物實態一覽